Cyclecraft

The complete guide to safe and
enjoyable cycling for adults and children

Recommended reading for Bikeability,
the National Cycle Training Standard

John Franklin

Fifth Edition 2014

information & publishing solutions

Published by TSO (The Stationery Office) and available from:

Online
www.tsoshop.co.uk

Mail, Telephone, Fax & E-mail
TSO
PO Box 29, Norwich, NR3 1GN
Telephone orders/General enquiries: 0870 600 5522
Fax orders: 0870 600 5533
E-mail: customer.services@tso.co.uk
Textphone 0870 240 3701

TSO@Blackwell and other Accredited Agents

An earlier edition of this book was published by Unwin Paperbacks in 1988

First TSO Edition published 1997
Second TSO Edition published 2007
Third TSO Edition published 2014

ISBN 978 0 11 708243 4

The information contained in this publication is believed to be correct at the time of manufacture. Whilst care has been taken to ensure that the information is accurate, the publisher can accept no responsibility for any errors or omissions or for changes to the details given.

Printed in Malta for The Stationery Office

J002861373 c50 06/14

About the author

John Franklin has been closely involved in cycle planning and safety activities for more than 35 years. In his capacity as a consultant and a registered expert witness to the courts on cycling skills and safety, he is often called upon to advise on a wide range of matters concerning cycling.

As a member of a government/CTC* reference group on cycle training, he was involved with the establishment of the National Cycle Training Standard, now promoted as Bikeability. The syllabus for the national standard is based on *Cyclecraft*, which is required reading for instructors accredited to teach to the standard, and is recommended reading for trainees. John is himself an accredited instructor.

Encouraging more people to enjoy the pleasures of cycling is a passion of the author, who has been involved in many initiatives to help bring this about. John remains actively involved in cycling activities from international to local level.

A cyclist of wide experience who uses his bike both as his primary means of transport and for leisure, John has cycled extensively under all kinds of conditions throughout the UK and in more than 25 other countries.

* *CTC, the Cyclists' Touring Club, is the national cycling charity.*

Acknowledgements

I am grateful to everyone who has contributed to this revised edition of *Cyclecraft*, especially those who have provided feedback from the implementation of modern cycle training in Britain. The National Cycle Training Standard is now a mature product and a UK success story, enabling thousands of children and adults to realise safe, enjoyable cycling each year. *Cyclecraft* continues to support the development of the national standard.

Special thanks are due to John Mallows, who took most of the photographs in this edition, and to LifeCycle UK, for their enthusiastic cooperation in providing accredited cycle trainers to demonstrate the various manoeuvres. Individual thanks are due to Jacks Jarrett, Frances and Elinor McMillan, Veronica Pollard, Trudi Righton, Mark Spure, Polly Stubley and Jacqui Wilcox, whose professional approach and knowledge of skilled cycling made it all the easier to obtain good images.

Other photographs are courtesy of Anthony Bearon (with Naomi and Ben), Keith Cadwallander, CTC/Chris Juden and Roland Werk GmbH. The kind assistance of SJS Cycles, Graham and Helen Ricketts, and Mark Wilcox is also acknowledged.

With regard to the text, I remain grateful to Chris Juden, CTC's Technical Officer, for giving me the benefit of his extensive knowledge about the 'hardware' and science of cycling, particularly with regard to developments in cycle and component design.

My thanks to all concerned.

John Franklin

Contents

Chapter 8: Everyday movements

Introduction >

Cycling for health, enjoyment and you

Cycling is a wonderful activity. It is the most efficient means of travelling known to man, a pleasurable pastime that can be enjoyed by young and old alike, one of the best ways to maximise health and well-being, an elixir of life, and a completely sustainable mode of transport. Almost everyone is able to cycle and, for a child, learning to ride a bike is an important landmark in their development as an independent person.

Many people would like to cycle or to cycle more. However, the traditional myths that cycling is hard work and slow have been augmented in recent years by the perception that cycling is also inevitably unsafe. Many people fear riding in today's traffic, on roads too often designed primarily for motor vehicles, and feel that there is little cyclists can do to protect themselves from the hazards present.

Experienced cyclists know otherwise. They know that by controlling their machine correctly and using appropriate riding techniques, cycling can not only be safe but also fun. Learning to ride efficiently means that cycling is seldom strenuous and is frequently a very speedy means of getting about, particularly in towns. One of the key challenges for someone learning to cycle is to overcome the prejudices and misconceptions which have become part of cycling folklore.

In fact, far from cycling being an unsafe activity, research shows that cycling regularly is the single most effective action you can take to increase your life span. Cyclists, on average, live longer than non-cyclists and experience much less ill health. They are twelve times less likely to die of heart disease. Whatever the negative effects of sharing the roads with heavy traffic, it is evident that, on balance, cycling leads to longer and healthier lives. Moreover, when you choose to cycle rather than to travel by car, everyone benefits from reductions in pollution and congestion.

If you learn to cycle skilfully you will enhance your ability to use the roads in safety. Although you will encounter much bad driving, most of it can be anticipated and its effects avoided. Surveys suggest that competent cyclists are much less likely to be involved in a conflict, and vulnerability generally decreases as a rider's skill and experience increase.

How *Cyclecraft* can help you to cycle well

Cyclecraft teaches cycling technique in a similar way to teaching someone to drive a car – how to acquire the skills and confidence to ride with traffic, not fear it. The general aims are to maximise your safety and riding efficiency, while minimising inconvenience to others and wear to your machine.

Advice is given on how to deal with all common road situations, recognising how impractical it often is to avoid the more difficult ones. It follows the supposition, well endorsed by skilled riders, that the only way to be safe is to learn to control a cycle as a vehicle and to read and respond to what is going on around you. For this reason the cyclist is frequently referred to as a vehicle driver, for that is what you must be. *Cyclecraft* also outlines the problems experienced by other road users; by taking these into account, you can react in the ways most likely to benefit your journey.

This guide makes no attempt to excuse the bad behaviour which is sometimes evident on today's roads; nor does it excuse those road designs which can be particularly difficult for more vulnerable road users. Priorities are changing and conditions for cycling should improve, but in the meantime it is necessary for anyone wishing to cycle to come to terms with present circumstances. There is also little doubt that most cyclists could do more to make themselves safer, for they often make conditions more difficult than they need be. Although motorists are most often primarily at fault in crashes with adult cyclists, very often conflicts could be avoided altogether by the cyclist riding more diligently. Children, too, can achieve similar levels of safety by cycling skilfully. *Cyclecraft* is therefore all about how to deal with the existing and imperfect state of affairs, rather than lamenting the fact that conditions could be better.

Cyclecraft is not concerned with setting examples to others. Although a skilled rider will often do this as a matter of course, a cyclist is too vulnerable to follow rigid rules irrespective of the risk. *Cyclecraft* shows how to respond to actual conditions rather than acting as a strict rule book.

Vehicular cycling

The style of cycling taught in *Cyclecraft* is sometimes referred to as vehicular cycling. This is cycling in accordance with the rules of the road as an integral part of traffic. Vehicular cyclists seek to cooperate with other drivers, to mutual benefit, while always being prepared for situations that might otherwise make them vulnerable. This way of cycling is quite different from acting as a pedestrian, when it is more difficult to influence traffic and therefore requires much more deference.

Vehicular cycling is an American term, but describes the traditional way of cycling in the UK, as practised over many generations. With only a few exceptions (highlighted in this publication), it is achievable by most people and does not depend upon the physique of the cyclist.

Although vehicular cycling is most often referred to in the context of cycling on the roads, its principles also define the safest way to cycle anywhere, including cycle paths and other special infrastructure. However, special account may need to be taken of the limitations of some cycle facilities, as described in Chapter 13.

Bikeability: The National Cycle Training Standard

The content of *Cyclecraft* is closely associated with Bikeability, the National Cycle Training Standard, for which it is the principal reference and required reading for accredited instructors. Each new edition of *Cyclecraft* benefits from feedback obtained as a result of implementation of the national standard.

For whom *Cyclecraft* is intended

Cyclecraft is intended to be read by anyone who cannot cycle, by cyclists of any level of ability who would like to confirm and improve their skills, and by the parents of children who are to be taught to cycle. Chapter 2 includes specific advice to guide parents.

The content could also be useful to other road users and those involved professionally with road safety, driving instruction and the design and use of the highway network, in order to understand the principles of good cycling and the difficulties that cyclists sometimes face.

Most people of reasonable fitness should be capable of acquiring the skills that are taught. However, a key consideration is that you should become competent at each stage before progressing further, taking care not to proceed too quickly, nor beyond your capabilities at any time. Gradual acclimatisation to cycling in traffic is the best approach, getting used to more demanding traffic situations one by one. People who are particularly slow, timid or nervous may need patience and perseverance to attain the more advanced skills, but they are encouraged to try, and to seek the help of a national-standard cycle training instructor if necessary.

The advice given in *Cyclecraft* applies to all types of cycle in common use, although the limitations of some may militate against tackling some of the more advanced manoeuvres. Chapter 3 compares the characteristics of various types of machine, and other chapters refer to significant differences in riding technique as necessary. For most of this guide, however, the use of a large-wheel multi-geared hybrid, road or touring bicycle is assumed, as these types are the most versatile for cycling in traffic.

Part I
Before
you ride

〉

Chapter 1

Getting started

This chapter should help you to:

- ❍ consider borrowing a bike before you buy one
- ❍ understand the National Cycle Training Standard and how this relates to where you should cycle while you learn
- ❍ appreciate the need for a structured approach to your learning.

Borrowing a bike

If you've not cycled before, you may be reluctant to buy a bike straight away. Even if the financial outlay is no obstacle, it can still be best to delay purchasing a new machine until you know more about the different types of cycle that are available and which would be best for the kind of cycling you want to do. It is not uncommon for people's horizons to widen as they experience the pleasures of cycling for themselves, and the desire for a more versatile machine can follow.

It can be useful to borrow a bicycle from a friend or relation, or to hire one from a cycle shop or hire company. If you are going to take a course of cycle training (see below), your instructor may be able to provide one for you to use. In all cases, it is essential that the bike you use is in good condition, of the correct size for you and properly set up. If possible, it should be of the type that best matches your current aspirations for cycling. Further information about types of bicycle and the requirements for a safe bike are given in Chapter 3.

Cycle training courses and the national standard

Cyclecraft provides comprehensive coverage of what you need to know to cycle well. Nevertheless, it can be very useful to have the personal guidance of a cycle training instructor to help you acquire at least the basic skills of cycling. A qualified instructor will be quick to alert you to shortcomings, and will be able to suggest practical ways to correct these.

Finding a cycle training instructor

A list of accredited cycle training instructors can be found at www.ctc-maps.org.uk/training

---

Cycle training courses are available for both adults and children, and are provided by specialist cycle training companies, independent cycle training instructors, and local authorities. Group courses are also available, especially for children. Be sure that the instructor you select is an experienced cyclist accredited to train to the National Cycle Training Standard (see box above).

The national standard defines three levels of cycle training:

▶ Level 1: for people who cannot cycle at all and those who lack the basic skills of starting and stopping, balancing and steering, looking behind, signalling, use of gears and obstacle avoidance.

▶ Level 2: for people who have the basic skills but who are not confident at cycling in traffic or undertaking common manoeuvres.

▶ Level 3: for regular cyclists who are competent in moderate traffic and who would like to learn the more advanced skills necessary for cycling on faster and busier roads.

Everyone should regard Level 2 as the minimum standard they should seek to achieve. After this, some months' practical experience should be acquired before considering Level 3.

Cycle training with an accredited instructor is a great way to boost skills and confidence

Where to ride

Training to Level 1 will usually take place in a traffic-free environment, while all training to Levels 2 and 3 must occur on-road in real traffic conditions. If you are teaching yourself, or your children, without taking a course, you should follow the same practice.

The best place to learn Level 1 skills is a large flat area such as a quiet car park or a school playground. This is particularly beneficial in the earliest stages so that you are not made anxious by a fear of colliding with anything while you practise bike control. A good, firm and even surface is important, without potholes, and a level or slightly sloping gradient.

Off-road cycle paths are not good places to learn the basic skills of cycling as they are too narrow and may not have adequate surfaces or visibility. Other users can also be a problem. When you have mastered the basic skills, off-road paths can provide a useful resource to gain practice in bike control before you move on to the on-road environment for Level 2.

If you don't have access to a suitable off-road area, you should seek out a quiet, wide road with little traffic and a minimum of kerbside parking. Roads in an industrial area at weekends can sometimes be a good choice, or perhaps a cul-de-sac.

Level 2 cycling should start on quiet roads with little traffic and then progress, as competence increases, onto busier roads with junctions of increasing complexity. A typical residential area is ideal. As your skills permit, you should include the roads that you will need to use for the journeys that you wish to make.

Level 3 cycling progresses from the roads used for Level 2, according to local circumstances and what you wish to achieve.

A structured approach

Cyclecraft follows a structured approach, as do training courses to the national standard. Starting by ensuring that the bicycle is suitable and correctly adjusted for its user, this guide then gives a thorough grounding in basic cycling skills before dealing with on-road situations of increasing complexity.

It is strongly recommended that you follow the guide systematically as complete competence in the earlier skills is essential before more complicated manoeuvres can be carried out successfully. At all times your progress should be determined by the outcomes of what has gone before; don't let your enthusiasm to get cycling lead you to taking shortcuts or becoming complacent.

In special circumstances, you may need to bring forward the learning of some more advanced skills. For example, if you live in an area where roundabouts are common, it may be necessary to learn how to negotiate these before it is practical to acquire good practice in other skills. In doing this you should check that you do not omit essential preparatory tasks and that you appreciate your limitations.

Check your understanding:

☐ What should you consider when borrowing a bike?

☐ What are your aspirations in achieving the National Cycle Training Standard?

☐ Where should you ride when learning to cycle?

Chapter 2
Advice to parents

This chapter should help you to understand:

- ● the importance of being positive about your children cycling
- ● why children should be introduced to cycling on the roads as early as possible
- ● how to ride with your children to develop their skills while affording a sensible level of protection.

Most children want to cycle, and get great pleasure from doing so. Learning to cycle is a principal means by which children can achieve independent mobility, so that they are no longer dependent upon lifts from parents or other adults. This is something that is essential for their proper physical, psychological and social development. Cycling is also a key contributor to health and fitness, and can positively influence subsequent lifestyle choices that will maintain well-being in later life.

As a parent, you should do all you can to encourage your children to cycle, and be as positive and supportive as you can about the activity.

Cycling among children has declined dramatically in Western countries over recent decades. In most countries, cycling was previously the most common physical activity undertaken by children out of school. The loss of such a key activity has most likely been a principal cause of the dramatic rise in childhood obesity, which is probably the greatest threat to the future health and well-being of the younger generation. Very few children who cycle regularly become obese.

One reason for the decline in children cycling has been a much less positive attitude towards cycling amongst parents, who have limited their children's independence in response to fears generated by increased traffic, road safety campaigns and the media. But the risk in cycling has been greatly exaggerated and does not justify such a response. Children, like adults, are much more likely to extend their life span through cycling than to reduce it, and to experience much healthier lives. It is important that parents keep the limited risks of cycling in perspective, and address them through the encouragement of safe cycling practices as described in *Cyclecraft*.

Experience gained through implementation of the National Cycle Training Standard has shown clearly that there is no justification for distinguishing between cyclists based solely on age. Young teenagers can be better and safer cyclists than many adults, especially if they come from families who cycle. The most important factor is that cycling by anyone, child or adult, should be guided by their actual ability and maturity at the current time. Children can sometimes be over-confident and want to attain the higher skills too quickly. So keep track of your children's progress and ensure that they move through the syllabus described in *Cyclecraft* systematically and only as their competence justifies.

Parents should encourage their children to respect cycling as a 'grown-up' activity, in which they should take pride in doing well, rather than as a play activity. That's not to say that children should be discouraged from having fun on their bikes. But they need to appreciate that for good reason there are rules to follow when cycling and best ways to ride. Tell them they will have more fun on their bikes, and be able to ride more widely, if they first learn to ride skilfully. Children are more likely to take notice if it is explained to them why something should be done in a particular way, and you should try to ensure that they get the full picture.

It is particularly important that children are equipped, through training, to cycle on-road as soon as possible and that pavement cycling is thenceforth discouraged. Pavements are seldom safe places to cycle except by riding submissively at very low speeds, even if signed for sharing by cyclists. Children are rarely inclined to ride this way and pavement cycling is a common cause of avoidable injury to them. Children are safer on the roads once they have acquired the basic skills to ride there. A key skill is positioning, where children should follow the same guidance set out later in this guide as for adults. The additional risks associated with poor positioning affect them like everyone else and the solutions are the same.

Ensure, too, that your children understand the principles behind the guidance, and that it is not introduced to them simply as a set of rules to follow. Most children will be keen to know more and if they appreciate the underlying reasoning, they are more likely to act to their best advantage even at times when circumstances are unusual.

The early years

Almost from birth, young children can be carried on a parent's bicycle, where they will already be learning a lot about cycling, and the options for doing this are described in Chapter 15. From about the age of four, children can ride as active tandem partners (see Chapter 16) and this is an excellent way for them to become familiar with the skills needed for cycling in traffic. Children can also ride their own bicycle from about the same age.

Some children start their independent cycling with a tricycle or by using stabiliser wheels on a bicycle. This is not such a good idea as these children will usually take longer to balance a bicycle than those who start on two wheels. As will be explained in Chapter 16, the skills needed to balance a bicycle are quite different from those needed to ride a more stable machine, and the child's skill set will have to be renewed. Young children can be assisted to balance a bicycle without stabilisers using the same procedure to be described in Chapter 5 for beginners of all ages, and will usually succeed very quickly.

Riding with your children

The best encouragement that parents can give to their children is by setting an example for them to follow. Children who cycle with their parents from an early age pick up most of what they need to know about cycling without any formal tuition. Of course, parents should set a good example. Read through *Cyclecraft* and make sure that you, too, follow the best practice that is described.

Most children yearn to cycle, and the best help a parent can give is to ride with them

If you do not, at present, cycle, you should give serious thought to doing so. There is much enjoyment to be gained from families cycling together and you will achieve a much better understanding of your children's experience and how they should ride.

At as early an age as possible, you should introduce children to cycling on roads. This is crucial to them gaining the confidence necessary to cycle well. Like the use of stabilisers, encouraging children to cycle only off-road gives false messages about the skills and behaviour that are needed and will make the transition to riding safely on the road later on more difficult.

Start on quiet, local roads and then, as their confidence and skill increase, take them onto roads with more traffic. Increase the difficulty of the route in stages. For example, the first trip onto a busy road should involve only left turns on and off. Subsequently, go straight through a few minor junctions, then cross a more complicated junction at a time when traffic is relatively light. As long as the parents know how to shepherd their children well (described below), young children can ride accompanied safely on most roads, and their skills will benefit accordingly.

When only one adult rides on a road with children, they should ride close behind and slightly to the right. In this way you can see exactly what the children are doing, instruct them as necessary and encourage other road users, through your position, to afford good clearance. If it becomes necessary, you can quickly come alongside to protect or assist. As a child becomes more accomplished, move further left away from hazards so that you don't obstruct the child's view when they are looking behind.

Until a child has demonstrated sufficient skill to deal with the traffic situations you meet, you should instruct them to pull in and stop before busy junctions and whenever else you specify. You should then explain to the child the nature of what lies ahead, how you intend to proceed and what others might be expected to do. It's important that there should be no surprises. At very busy locations it may be best that you all dismount and follow a pedestrian route, but continue by riding if the risks are manageable. Try to choose your routes so that walking is not necessary, as this can create a negative association between cycling and traffic, which will be unhelpful to your child's progress. To pass through junctions, you should ride alongside a child, usually on the right, to give protection and reassurance, and to ensure that you are both clearly visible to other road users.

If both parents cycle with their children, one parent should lead the group and the other should ride at the back. The front rider should cycle exactly where the children are expected to ride, and take care to keep the group close together so that no one else can come in between. The rear rider should ride a little further out to deflect following traffic, as described previously. When riding through busy junctions with more than one child, both parents should ride alongside their children. Don't be hurried – other drivers will usually be patient with a family group.

More advice about riding with a group of children will be found in Chapter 17.

Growing up

As your children become older, they should be encouraged to ride to school and for as many of their day-to-day journeys as possible. Make it difficult for them to get a lift by car! Maintaining cycling through the older teenage years may require tact and some cunning, but is important if they are to reap the benefits into adulthood.

Keeping it 'cool'

Peer perception is important to children, especially as teenagers. You may want to buy them the bike best suited to the journeys they will make, but they may have their minds set on something different – most likely a BMX or a mountain bike with full suspension and every conceivable add-on! They may refuse to cycle rather than ride anything else.

Prudence is needed, for the most important thing is that they cycle, and then that they learn to cycle well. For the kind of distances that most teenagers will ride, the 'wrong' type of bike is unlikely to do much harm, as long as it is the right size and they ride it properly.

As young people get older or cycle more, having the right bike becomes more important. Maturing teenagers will often come to recognise this and opt for something different for the next purchase. Some parents pacify younger rebels by buying two bikes: one for longer journeys and more serious cycling; another to ride with friends.

Check your understanding:

☐ Why is it good for children to cycle?

☐ How can you best help your children to cycle well and safely?

☐ Why is it important that children are taught to cycle on the roads as soon as possible?

☐ How should you ride when accompanying your children?

☐ What should you consider when choosing routes for family rides?

Chapter 3

A safe and efficient bike

This chapter should help you to:

- ➔ choose the best type of bike for your needs
- ➔ understand how the main bicycle components work and what options there are
- ➔ ensure that your bike is maintained in good condition.

For safe, efficient and enjoyable cycling, your bicycle should be suited to the uses you will make of it. There must be a good fit between it and its rider, and the cycle needs to be adjusted to perform properly. A good bike, well suited to its rider and regularly maintained, will give many years of satisfying service, allowing cycle and cyclist to operate as one, the machine almost being an extension of the limbs of its rider.

However, a bad match or poor adjustment will at best lead to disappointment and disillusionment with cycling; at worst it could result in a spill in traffic. Bear in mind that even a multiplicity of approval marks does not signify a safe bike if the size is wrong or if it has not been set up correctly.

This chapter discusses the various types of cycle that are available, explains the parts which are important for safety and efficiency, and gives brief notes on adjustments for optimum performance. However, it cannot tell you in detail how to adjust your particular machine, as individual components and their adjustment vary so much. For more information on your specific model, read a detailed repair manual or get help from an experienced cyclist or a cycle shop.

Which type of bike?

Just as there are many types of cyclists and many reasons why people cycle, so there are many types of cycle, each best suited to particular circumstances.

The traditional **roadster** bicycle with a curved handlebar is still in use, though it is now much less common in Britain than in many other countries. It is robust and reliable, but also heavy, which restricts its ability to keep pace with traffic even over short distances.

Small-wheel bicycles are popular with many people. They can be very manoeuvrable and stable, and have the special advantage of being readily adaptable in size to a number of users. Some can be folded, which is particularly useful for commuting by public transport. Some up-market models have many of the attributes of a sports cycle, but most others are inefficient and suited only to cycling short distances.

The **mountain** or **all-terrain bike** has broad wheels, an almost straight handlebar, lots of gears and good brakes. Suspension systems are common, but make riding harder work. Originally developed for use off-road, where it has particular advantages in terms of grip, robustness and comfort on rough tracks, this type of bike has also become popular for general use in both town and country. On-road its main attribute is a greater resilience where surfaces are worn or potholed; on the other hand, these cycles are sluggish and poorly suited to manoeuvring in traffic. Mountain bikes are not the best choice for most people's cycling needs, but may be improved for road use by fitting narrower tyres.

The **road, sports** or **touring** styles of bicycle are often, mistakenly, referred to as racing bikes. However, there are wide differences in specification and most models are not intended for competition. This type of cycle – characterised by large wheels and dropped handlebars – is becoming more popular again; it is the best choice for longer-distance touring and is good for commuter cycling too. Excellent manoeuvrability and efficiency make it ideal for integrating with traffic. High-pressure tyres increase efficiency, a benefit over longer distances, but are much less tolerant of poor surfaces and conditions off-road.

The **hybrid bike** is a cross between a mountain bike and a road bike. Like the latter, it has large wheels with low-profile tyres, but these are wider for greater comfort and better grip off-road. Gear systems and brakes are similar to those fitted on mountain bikes, and controls next to the brakes make gear changing very easy. Suspension systems are omitted. There is a choice of handlebar designs and better hybrids have handlebar stems that are fully adjustable for reach and height, which makes it easier to achieve a good fit to the rider who adopts an upright riding position. Full mudguards and pannier racks make hybrids ideal for everyday journeys. Hybrids can be lightweight and are the best all-round type of bicycle, equally suitable for town roads and the kind of off-road use and short-distance touring undertaken by most people. In most cases, this is the type of bike for people to choose if they are new to cycling.

City bikes are another compromise between a mountain bike and a road bike. Here, however, the emphasis is on road cycling for relatively short trips; these bikes are not designed for use off-road. With an angled handlebar, upright riding position and slim, efficient, tyres, many city bikes come with hub gears to create a durable and reliable, if a little weighty, workhorse for everyday transport.

Cyclocross bikes have fatter tyres than normal road bikes, beefed-up frames and more powerful brakes. They can be good for commuting on pothole-strewn urban streets as well as in competitive events off-road.

Electrically assisted cycles can be useful for older people and those with disabilities, especially if they live in a hilly area. With some models the rider must pedal most of the time as if riding an ordinary cycle, but this is assisted by a small electric motor when the energy demand increases. Other models provide assistance for a greater part of the time. Riding these machines is similar in most respects to riding an ordinary cycle, except that they are much heavier and therefore less responsive. You must be prepared to carry out many manoeuvres more cautiously.

Still unusual but growing in popularity are **recumbent** cycles, which come in a wide variety of designs. Recumbent bicycles require more skill to balance, paradoxically due to their low centre of gravity. This factor is turned to advantage, however, in a recumbent tricycle, which can be most stable and comfortable, albeit slow uphill. The 'laid back' position of the rider may be of benefit to people with back or neck problems, while there are safety advantages in riding feet, rather than head, first that may compensate for their reduced conspicuity due to their low height.

Tricycles are becoming more popular as utility machines and provide a solution for people who cannot balance well on a bicycle. They are useful for carrying shopping and children. Riding a tricycle requires different skills from riding a bicycle, especially when turning. Their stability is an advantage in traffic, but they are less manoeuvrable where roads are congested.

Tandems and **tandem tricycles** are a great way for two people to travel together, particularly if one rider is stronger than the other. Children and visually impaired people may be tandem partners with adults or those with normal sight. Touring, all-terrain and recumbent tandems are available. **Triplets**, suitable for three family members, can also be purchased.

Cycles with a lower top tube

Many cycles are available with a lower top tube. These make it easier to cycle when wearing a skirt or dress. The downside is that these frames are less efficient structurally, so they must either be heavier or less rigid and less strong. Usually they have a bit of all three disadvantages, so for touring or other more serious cycling, many women prefer to ride the more conventional diamond-shaped frame or 'man's' bike.

The skirt-specific advantage of a dropped top tube is that it lets the rider get astride the bike by lifting one foot rather than throwing a leg over the saddle. This step-through facility is also beneficial to people with restricted hip movement and certain other disabilities. Super-low-step frames, some with a single tube no higher than the pedals, are also available.

Cycles for children

An important consideration when buying a bike for a child is that the cycle should accommodate the child's normal growth for as many years as possible. However, you should never buy a bike that is too large for a child at the time of first riding with the expectation that the child will 'grow into it'.

It is unsafe to ride a bicycle that is too large as it will not be possible to exert proper control over it.

As your child grows, check the height of the saddle and handlebar every few months and adjust when necessary to ensure that it remains a good fit. Always look out for the warning marks on the saddle and handlebar stems that indicate that these components must be extended no further.

The people who cycle, their bikes and suitable clothing are many and varied. From left to right are shown a road bike, a small-wheeler and two hybrid models.

Cheap bikes are sometimes very heavy bikes. If you want your children to enjoy cycling as an ongoing activity, it is worth paying more if you can.

The parts of a cycle

Figure 3.1 illustrates the location of the parts of a cycle, using a hybrid bicycle as an example.

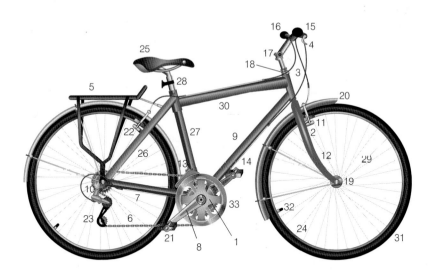

Figure 3.1 *The parts of a hybrid bicycle*

1 Bottom bracket	13 Front gear	24 Wheel rim
2 Brake block in shoe	14 Gear cables	25 Saddle
3 Brake cables	15 Gear levers	26 Seat stays
4 Brake levers	16 Handlebar	27 Seat tube
5 Carrier	17 Handlebar stem	28 Seatpin
6 Chain	18 Headset	29 Spokes
7 Chain stays	19 Hub	30 Top tube
8 Crank	20 Mudguard	31 Tyre
9 Down tube	21 Pedal	32 Valve (part of
10 Freewheel	22 Rear brake	inner tube)
11 Front brake	23 Rear gear	33 Chainwheel(s)
12 Front forks	(derailleur)	

Frame

The most fundamental specification of a bicycle is its **frame size**, which determines all the basic dimensions of the machine. If this is wrong, there is really nothing that can be done except to buy a new bike. The frame should be large enough so that the handlebar can be raised as high as needed relative to the saddle and small enough to permit you to straddle the topmost tube safely, with both feet flat on the ground when stopped. The handlebar stem and seatpin must not protrude from the frame beyond their safety markings. The horizontal distance between the saddle and handlebar, which also varies with frame size, should enable a comfortable riding position which neither cramps the body nor makes it difficult to operate the brakes.

Given the great diversity of cycle designs on the market today, there is no longer any straightforward relationship between frame size and the build of the rider. Indeed, some manufacturers have dispensed with using dimensions and now label their bikes like clothing: S, M and L. You should pay attention to each manufacturer's specific sizing advice for the type of bike you want to buy.

Sometimes you'll be on the borderline between two sizes and, in any case, the relative sizes of the parts of a frame can vary for a given frame size. You should try riding a few cycles that claim to be made for someone of about your height – with saddle and handlebar adjusted as described below – until you find the best fit. Good cycle dealers will be happy for you to do this; on the other hand these important checks will not be possible if you buy by mail-order or from most chain stores.

A very important point for safety is to check that your foot on the pedals cannot hit the front wheel or its mudguard as you turn the handlebar.

Saddle and handlebar

There are three adjustments to be made to the saddle: height, horizontal position and tilt. The ease and precision with which these adjustments may be made varies according to the type of seatpin, and all three interact.

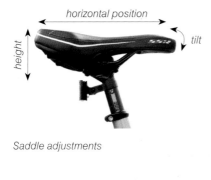

Saddle adjustments

The **saddle height** should be set with reference to the pedals, to make best use of your leg muscles. The usual rule for adjustment is to set the saddle height so that the heel of your foot can just rest on the pedal with your leg fully stretched. This is not how you will ride, but allows for the flexing of your knee when you pedal correctly with the ball of your foot.

As a general rule, your knee should be straight with your heel on the pedal when it is in line with the seat tube, but see text for exceptions

If you are new to cycling, a saddle set slightly lower than this may give you more confidence, but don't forget to raise it later. As well as being inefficient, low saddles stress the knees and can lead to injury.

Some designs of bike (especially mountain bikes) have their pedals so far above the ground that it is not possible to position the saddle high enough for efficient pedalling and also put a foot down when stopping. In that case you may need to ride with a low saddle until off-the-saddle starts and stops become automatic.

The **saddle horizontal position** is set to give the most comfortable position for pedalling. Start with the nose of the saddle about 5 cm (2 inches) behind a line passing vertically through the bottom bracket (1 in Figure 3.1), but slight adjustments can make a lot of difference to comfort.

Saddle tilt also has an important effect on comfort, particularly when riding longer distances. Men often prefer the nose slightly higher than the back, but for women the reverse is usually true, with the saddle tilted slightly downwards. Adjust the tilt so that you feel comfortable without sliding forwards or backwards as you ride.

Next set the **handlebar height** (Figure 3.2), starting at about the same height as the top of the saddle. Slower or less supple riders may prefer the handlebar slightly higher than this, while a lower position can aid sprinting. If an older quill stem is fitted, fine adjustments are easy to make. With a newer threadless stem, however, adjustment is less straightforward. Check with a bike shop if you're unsure about how to adjust your handlebar.

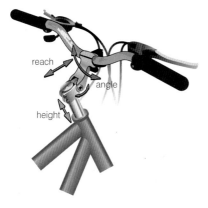

Figure 3.2 *Handlebar adjustments*

When adjusting the saddle height or handlebar height, if less than 10 cm (4 inches) of the seatpin or handlebar stem is left in the frame (there is usually a warning mark), the frame size is too small. Such a position is not safe.

The **handlebar angle** is also important. A straight handlebar should be flat or sloping downwards a little towards the rider, and bar ends on mountain and hybrid bikes should be inclined a little more. Dropped handlebars should be set so that the top of the handlebar is horizontal.

The **handlebar reach** (a property of the stem extension), in conjunction with the frame **top tube length** (30 in Figure 3.1), also affects riding comfort by determining how easily you can hold the handlebar. Optimum reach depends upon many factors, such as arm length, flexibility of your spine and how hard you want to pedal. It also depends upon the shape of the handlebar and what part of it you normally hold. If it feels to you that the handlebar needs to be further, closer, higher or lower, it almost certainly does.

Adjustable stems are supplied with some bikes; otherwise, changing handlebar reach requires replacement of the handlebar stem. With modern 'front opening' stems, this is very easy and stems are available in a great variety of lengths and heights. Women and very short or very tall men may nevertheless find it difficult to achieve a comfortable saddle-to-handlebar distance on some cycles, even though the frames are nominally the correct size; in this case you should pay particular attention to choosing a frame with a top tube of suitable length. You should experiment with all the variables for the saddle and handlebar positions until you achieve the most comfortable ride.

Brakes

Most modern bikes are fitted with 'V' – or direct-pull – brakes, which are very efficient and provide excellent stopping power. Indeed, if you're used to older brake types, you may need to take care at first not to pull on the levers too sharply when you ride a bike with V-brakes.

V-brakes gain their efficiency by requiring a long pull of the cable to operate them and this requires appropriate brake levers, which are most often designed for straight handlebars. If your bike has a dropped handlebar, then dual-pivot side-pull brakes are the best type available, but if you need more tyre clearance than these allow, choose cantilever brakes.

The adjustments so far have been, within reasonable limits, primarily concerned with comfort and efficiency. The ability to operate the brakes, however, is essential to safety. The correct positioning of the handlebar is an important factor in this, but the **brake levers** can also be moved along the handlebar and rotated around it. In some cases the **lever reach** (the distance from the handlebar to the lever) can also be adjusted.

Determining the best position for the brake levers is easiest with straight handlebars. There is usually only one hand position on the bars and the brake levers should be adjacent to this, angled so that they are within comfortable reach of the fingers when extended naturally. Keep brake levers as far as is practical towards the end of the handlebar, to maximise stability when braking.

With dropped handlebars, the situation is a little more complicated as there are several ways to hold the bars. The levers should be placed so that they can be operated from either below, on the drops, or above, from the top of the bars. Chapter 5 will explain more about the correct ways to operate these levers. Because most people make little use of the drops, the placing of the levers should normally favour the position which permits the easiest operation from above. You should be able to slide your hands smoothly and quickly forward from the top of the bars onto the brake levers, the tops of which should be at a similar height to the bars. A common error is to place the levers too low. As with other handlebars, the angle of the levers on dropped handlebars should be set so that these can be operated comfortably. They are often turned outwards slightly.

Whatever type of handlebar you have, it is customary in left-hand-drive countries for the left lever to operate the rear brake and the right lever to operate the front brake, since this allows safe control of the speed of the bike, with the rear brake, while signalling to cross traffic (such as when turning right), which is usually the most important turn to signal. In other countries, cycles have their levers the other way around. Always check the brake arrangement on an unfamiliar bike, as it is essential for the development of instinctive braking skills that the levers behave as expected. Check, too, that plugs are fitted to the ends of the handlebar to protect you from injury if you fall against them.

Cable clamp

Blocks

Clamp nut and bolt

V-brakes

The **brakes** themselves need regular attention, as the blocks wear and the cables stretch. The **brake blocks** should be set so that, although they normally clear the wheel rims, they come into operation with only a small movement of the levers and the ends of the levers do not touch the handlebar, even when braking hard.

A released clearance of 2 mm (0.08 inch) between each block and the rim is about right. With new blocks, this clearance should be set by adjustment at the brake mechanism itself. A 'third hand' tool is useful for keeping the brakes applied while you do this. Thereafter an in-line cable adjuster, if provided on the brake levers or brake mechanism, can be used to compensate for wear. If either wheel will not spin freely with close block adjustment and if this cannot be corrected by slightly turning the whole brake mechanism, either the hub cones are loose or the wheel is out of true.

Always ensure that the brake blocks are set over the rims to give the greatest area of contact without touching the tyre wall at either end. If the shoe holding any block is open-ended, check that this points towards the back of the bike or the block may come out during use. Sometimes, brake blocks squeal in use, which is not only embarrassing but also results in decreased stopping power. Toeing the blocks in a little towards the front of the bike can help to overcome this. New blocks are best worn in by being used on a wet day. Make sure that you use the correct type of block for your rims.

The **brake cables** bear considerable strain and must be inspected frequently, particularly the end-nipples, which are hidden inside the brake levers. This is where most cables fray and then break. A little grease here can prolong life, while greasing the cable wire inside the outer sleeve also reduces friction and wear. If you ever brake hard in an emergency, or feel a lever moving more than normal, examine the cable for damage straight away.

Gears

Good gears are one of the most important assets a cycle can have if your cycling is to be enjoyable. Gears enable cyclists to pedal at optimum cadence (the rate of turning the pedals) no matter what the gradient or other external influences on the bicycle. Each cyclist has his or her own optimum cadence, when efficiency is greatest and the effort required for cycling least. You should ride in the gear that enables you to maintain that cadence as much as possible.

In Britain gears are specified in inches, and equate to the diameter of a fixed (i.e. ungeared) wheel that would cover the same distance per turn of the pedals – for example, a gear of 40 inches is equivalent to pedalling a wheel of 40 inches diameter. In some other countries, the gear development is used, which is the distance, in metres, a cycle actually travels per turn of the pedals. Hence a 40-inch gear has a development of 3.2 metres.

A good range of gears is more important than the total number; some cycles have their gears very closely spaced. A bottom gear of 35–40 inches (2.8–3.2 metres) and a top gear of about 90 inches (7.2 metres) are suitable for riding in town traffic and up the hills encountered in most areas. However, to be able to tackle the really steep climbs in some localities, a bottom gear around 25 inches (2.0 metres) is desirable. With a gear of this size it is possible to mount hills as steep as 1 in 2.5 (40%), which is as steep as you will find on tarmacadam roads.

There are two types of gear mechanism: internal hub and derailleur. Hub gears are a little easier to use, more robust and need less attention, but are mechanically less efficient (except in one gear) and are difficult to service when they do go wrong. Three-speed hub gears provide too little range for most purposes, but versions with five or more speeds can be practical for utility riding or limited touring.

Derailleur gears are more versatile, being the easiest to adapt to your particular requirements. They are available in combinations from 5 to 30 speeds or more. In most cases two gear-change mechanisms are used: a front changer which selects between two or three chainrings, and a rear changer which operates on a cluster of cogs at the rear hub, called the freewheel. Derailleur gear changing requires more skill, but this is not difficult to acquire, especially with indexed gears, which, like hub gears, have pre-set lever positions for one or both changers. Further differences between hub and derailleur gears will be discussed in Chapter 5.

A rear derailleur gear mechanism

Correct adjustment of the gears is important for safety. Gear changing in traffic must be quick and precise; it is no place to stall or for gears to jump too far. Ensure that you can engage all usable gears (some overlapping gears should not be used, as Chapter 5 will explain) easily and reliably without the chain coming off.

To adjust derailleur gears, you have to alter the top and bottom limit stops of the front and rear changers so that the chain can reach, but not go past, the extreme gears, and there is an additional adjustment to synchronise the indexing. Hub gears vary, and should be adjusted in accordance with the manufacturer's instructions. In all cases, initial adjustments can be made with the cycle stationary and inverted, but some slight readjustment may be necessary to compensate for the greater forces present when pedalling.

Transmission

Moving parts benefit from cleaning and lubrication. The rule is little and often, but do keep lubricant away from brake blocks, gear levers and wheel rims. For efficiency and ease of gear changing, it is particularly important that the **transmission system** be kept in good condition. The chain gets rough treatment and should be re-lubricated each time it gets wet, and checked for wear every couple of months. To do this, pull the chain away from the front of the largest chainring with your fingers; if it will move more than the height of a tooth, it has worn too much and needs replacing. You may also need to replace the freewheel sprockets as old sprockets and new chains do not always work well together.

Checking for chain wear

Some bicycles are fitted with a chain guard, which can help to protect your clothes from grease or being caught up in the chain. Full chain cases are fully effective in this regard and also keep grit off the chain, prolonging its life. These attachments may be useful if you wish to cycle in ordinary clothes. However, if the chain is thrown off the chainwheel or freewheel (which can happen occasionally even on well-maintained bikes), it is more difficult to replace it.

A further transmission-system check is for play around the **bottom bracket** (1 in Figure 3.1). Grasp each pedal in turn and try to rock it from side to side. Any significant movement means a loose pedal, crank or bottom bracket. Then spin the pedals and cranks backwards. Any great resistance may indicate an overtight bearing.

Headset

A similar check for correct tightness should be made of the **headset**. The handlebar should be able to turn with no apparent friction, yet not be so loose that the bearings jar. With the front brake held on, rock the cycle back and forth. Movement should be restricted to that caused by the give of the tyres (or a suspension system, if fitted) and there should be no noticeable movement between the front forks and frame. A tight or a loose headset will make steering more difficult and may lead to an unsafe wobble at speed. It will also result in excessive wear of the headset cups and bearings.

Wheels

If you are buying a new bike, make sure to get one with **wheel rims** made of an alloy rather than steel, for the improvement in braking performance is marked, especially in the wet. Although it is possible to improve braking with steel rims by the use of special brake blocks, their all-weather performance does not match that of good blocks acting on alloy rims. If you have a bike with steel wheel rims, think seriously about replacing them.

In time, wheel rims wear thin, especially if you ride a lot in hilly country. Replace as soon as the braking surface is no longer flat.

Wheels should be checked for trueness from time to time, and whenever you hit something hard such as a pothole. To do this, invert the bicycle and spin each wheel in turn. An untrue wheel will be seen to wobble from side to side as it turns. Check also that the wheel does not touch either of the chain stays (7 in Figure 3.1); if it does, either the wheel is misaligned in the rear drop-outs or front forks, or the drop-outs or forks are bent.

Check the wheel fasteners – which may be axle nuts or a quick-release mechanism – for tightness. Develop the habit of checking the front wheel every time you start on a journey and whenever you retrieve a parked cycle, in case it has been tampered with. A loose wheel is a serious hazard.

Poor **hub cone** adjustment can also cause wobble and lead to excessive wear on the bearings. With a hand, try to rock each wheel from side to side at its rim. There should be no significant movement.

Broken or slack **spokes** can make a wheel untrue and weak. If left unattended, the wheel will progressively deteriorate in strength. Squeeze adjacent spokes of a wheel together with your fingers, one side of the wheel at a time. This will immediately detect a broken spoke, while the tension of all spokes should be about the same (but may differ between left and right sides of the rear wheel, which is usually asymmetrical). Any spokes that are obviously damaged should be replaced.

Tyres

The last important check is of the **tyres**. Worn tyres are likely to puncture more easily, while a smooth tread can be slippery on dirty roads. Of course, some cycle tyres are smooth when new, but these are really for racing, and something with at least a little tread is more practical for other purposes. Check not only the tyre tread but also the sidewall. Some tyres fail from a split sidewall long before the tread has worn away. Confirm, too, that the tyre is fully and symmetrically seated in the wheel rim, especially, if a tyre has been changed recently. A poorly seated tyre can be lifted by the inner tube, which may then explode.

Tyres must be inflated to the correct pressure. Most people would recognise the risk from explosion of over-inflated tyres, but few realise that under-inflation makes cycle control more difficult, as well as increasing drag and requiring more effort to ride. Low pressures may also lead to reduced tyre life and increase the risk of punctures and rim damage. The majority of people considerably under-inflate their tyres and the only way to be sure of the pressure is to use a pressure gauge. The maximum tyre pressure is usually printed on the tyre wall; for hybrid and touring cycle tyres, this will usually be 5–6 bar (70–90 pounds per square inch – psi). Although the maximum pressure should not be exceeded, the greater the pressure the more efficient will be your cycling on-road.

Tyre pressures should be checked frequently, as seepage occurs – particularly when there are large changes in temperature.

A routine maintenance check-list

Brakes

- Do the brakes operate with only a small movement of each brake lever?
- Are brake blocks worn down or not aligned along the wheel rims?
- Are the cables frayed, nicked or corroded?
  Apply a little lubrication to each cable at the brake-lever end when you do this check.
- Do the brakes apply smoothly, without juddering, squealing or locking a wheel? Do they also release properly?
- Are the brake levers tightly secured to the handlebar?

Wheels

- Are the axle nuts or quick-release mechanisms tight?
- Does each wheel spin freely, without rubbing against the frame or brake blocks?
- Are the wheels true?
- Can the wheel rims be rocked from side to side?
  If so, the hub cones are too loose.
- Are any spokes broken or loose?
- Are the rims damaged or wearing thin?

Tyres

- Is there still a good depth of tread on each tyre?
- Are there splits or cracks in the tread or side walls?
- Are the tyres inflated to the correct pressure?

Gears

- Do the gears change correctly and can you engage all available gears? Check also the limit screws so that the chain cannot override the freewheel or chainwheels.
- Does the chain rub when riding in any gear (except where overlapped gears make this unavoidable)?
- Are gear cables frayed, nicked or corroded?
- Are the gear mechanisms clean and lubricated?
- Are the gear controls tightly secured?

Transmission

- Is the chain too stretched? Does it need lubrication?
- Can you rock the cranks from side to side?
  If so, this may mean loose cranks or a bottom bracket in need of adjustment.
- Do the cranks and pedals rotate freely but without slack?
- Are the chainwheels securely fixed to the cranks with no bolts missing or loose?

Headset and handlebar	• Is the headset loose? Apply the test described in the section on headsets in this chapter.
	• Can the handlebar be turned freely, without catching? Is it attached securely so it stays aligned at 90° to the front wheel when turned?
	• Are the handlebar height and reach still right for you? The maximum height mark on the stem must not be visible.
Frame and forks	• Is there any sign of damage or weakness, particularly near ends and joints? Be suspicious of wrinkled paint.
Saddle	• Are the height and alignment still right for you? The maximum height mark on the seat post must not be visible.
Accessories	• Are all accessories firmly attached with no loose or missing nuts or bolts? Is anything broken, does anything rattle?
	• Do lights shine brightly or are batteries in need of replacement?

M-check

To make it easier to check all the parts of a bike, follow the shape of a letter M from the front wheel hub to the headset, then to the bottom bracket, the saddle and finally the rear wheel hub. Check all the components that you pass.

Check your understanding:

☐ Which type of bike is best for you and why?

☐ Which adjustments are essential for safety?

☐ What are gears for?

☐ Why should the tyres be kept close to the right pressure?

☐ What checks should you make of your bike and how often?

Chapter 4

What else do you need?

This chapter should help you to:

- ➔ choose the clothes to wear for the kind of cycling you wish to do
- ➔ decide which accessories might assist your cycling and enhance your safety
- ➔ consider whether you wish to wear a cycle helmet
- ➔ check that you are familiar with the *Highway Code*.

What to wear

Cycling is an energetic activity that, on the one hand, generates heat to warm the body through the physical effort exerted and, on the other hand, dissipates excessive heat through the cooling effect of the air to which the cyclist is directly exposed. The result is that a cycle is the perfect air-conditioned vehicle, warming its rider in winter and cooling in summer.

Clothing for cycling should be light and loose fitting. If you need to wear a suit or a uniform at work, you might consider changing when you get there. Everyday clothing is ideal for short journeys but more specialised cycling clothes can be beneficial if you want to ride further or faster. Special cycling shoes, in particular, make cycling easier and more comfortable.

Trousers suffer increased wear on a bike, particularly where they rub against the saddle. When the temperature is suitable, shorts are the most comfortable lower garment. If you do wear trousers, these should be close fitting at the bottom, or use trouser clips to gather excess material to the outside of the leg. Alternatively, fit a chaincase to the bicycle.

Trousers with flared bottoms, long skirts and long laces in shoes may all get caught in the chain, which is a hazard. Shoes with deep treads can be difficult to remove from pedals, and smooth-soled shoes can slip when you set a foot down. Avoid wearing all these when you cycle.

In winter, gloves or mittens will keep your hands warm, which is essential for control of the brakes. For short journeys in wet weather, a lightweight breathable rain jacket will keep you dry and cool. For longer journeys, more robust rainwear and windproof garments are available, and these are discussed in Chapter 14.

Toe clips and clipless pedals

Toe clips and clipless pedals can be a great safety asset once you have mastered using them. When riding in stop-go traffic they prevent shoes slipping from the pedals and enable quick restarting. They also greatly improve the efficiency of pedalling.

Clipless pedals (more correctly, clip-in pedals) have the best advantage, as they lock the shoe firmly to the pedal. They can only be used with special cycling shoes fitted with matching cleats, but a wide variety of shoes are available. Choose shoes with recessed cleats (e.g. mountain bike types) if you also want to walk in them.

Toe clips, on the other hand, can be used with any shoes. Wider clips designed for mountain bikes merely locate the toe of the shoe and are strapless, but toe clips usually have straps to hold the shoe down. For non-competitive cycling, the straps should always be kept loose. If you haven't used toe clips before, try just the right one first.

To use toe clips, engage one foot in its clip before you start off. The other clip will naturally hang downwards, which means that it will not interfere with you using the back of the second pedal for pedalling during the first few metres if you need to. As soon as you can, pause pedalling and knock the rear of the second pedal downwards with your toe, moving your foot slightly backwards and out of the way at the same time. The toe clip will rotate to the top, when you should move your foot quickly forwards and into the clip. With practice, you should be able to engage the second toe clip within half a revolution of the pedals after starting.

A clipless pedal. A cleat in the sole of the shoe clips into a sprung housing on the pedal. This is a combination pedal; it can be used without cleats on the other side.

To remove a foot from its toe clip, just pull it back. So long as you keep the straps loose, you will not find that using toe clips interferes with putting a foot down when stopping.

Clipless pedals are similarly easy to use but take a bit more getting used to. You clip the shoe directly into the pedal by stepping onto it. To release your foot, twist your heel and pull, which may require a little practice. The release tension can be adjusted, and you should start with this at minimum. Double-sided clipless pedals give faster and easier entry than single-sided ones and are preferable for urban riding with frequent stopping and starting.

The riders of recumbent cycles find clipless pedals especially useful, as there is a tendency for feet to fall out of toe clips.

Being seen

For safety on the road it is important that your presence is noticed by others. But that is not sufficient; for the way in which other road users react to you will depend not only upon the fact that they have seen you, but also upon who or what they perceive you to be and on how far away they think you are. For instance, a driver who mistakes your rear reflector for a reflective road edge marker may fail to pull out to pass you, and a driver will not manoeuvre so early if you are thought to be further ahead than you are.

To be really safe on the road, therefore, you must not only be seen, but you must be seen to be a *cyclist,* and your position must be judged accurately. Perspicuity – being clearly understood – is more important than simple conspicuity, and this is particularly so if you are riding along a road where cyclists are few and far between.

Unfortunately, some of the so-called visibility aids available for cyclists attempt only to achieve conspicuity, while some can actually convey misleading information about the other details which are so important for pinpointing a cyclist on the road. Before using any aid intended to make your presence more obvious, you should always consider just how well it portrays the complete picture.

Be careful, too, not to cause visual confusion by the use of too many different devices. Good perspicuity requires conveying simple, easy-to-decipher information about your presence; overdoing it may prove counter-productive.

Visibility aids

It is sensible for cyclists to wear light-coloured clothing at any time, but it is unproven that additional visibility aids have much advantage during the day. The way cyclists ride, and in particular their position on the road, has much more effect on how easily others see and react to them.

Special high-visibility jackets are available, but brightly coloured ordinary clothes are almost as effective, much cheaper and less obtrusive off the bike.

Reflective belts and sashes aid perspicuity, although only in a similar way to lights, for they do not clearly differentiate a cyclist from a motorcyclist or moped rider. They are most effective on dark country roads, especially around dawn and dusk, and in other poor-visibility conditions such as fog, but much less so during the day or under street lights. They are particularly useful if you need to wear dark clothing for some reason when you cycle.

One unfortunate side effect of the devices, however, can be that oncoming drivers are more reluctant to dip their headlights, for this reduces the intensity of the reflected image they receive back.

Reflective bands are available for arms and legs, and strips can be bought for the cycle and luggage. Fluorescent garments are also available, but these are of no use at night.

Lights

Good lights are essential for cycling at night, as well as being a legal requirement. In comparison with good, bright lights, no other visibility aid is anything like as easy for other road users to see. A single white light at the front and a single red light at the rear make a cyclist clearly conspicuous, and strongly suggest a two-wheeled vehicle. The relatively slow speed of a cyclist and a natural wobble would probably suggest to an observant driver that the vehicle is in fact a cycle and enable a good estimate of position, but ordinary lamps alone do not make a cyclist perspicuous at night.

Lamps which use light emitting diodes (LEDs) offer superior performance, reliability and economy compared with traditional cycle lamps that use filament bulbs. However, you get what you pay for: cheap lamps often have low light output and may also be much less visible off axis. Wide dispersion of light is important for cycle lighting.

British Standard BS6102/3 defines the minimum requirements for cycle lights, but some lamps not marked as conforming to this standard are just as good, while the best lamps available considerably exceed it. If you want to be sure that you have good lights, carry out your own tests! Your lights should be clearly visible at night from 200 metres (650 feet) ahead or behind and 50 metres (about 165 feet) to the side. Another consideration if you ride outside towns is that the front light should provide adequate illumination for riding on an unlit road.

Flashing lights can greatly help to improve the perspicuity of a cyclist – no other vehicle is allowed to use red or white lights that flash – but only if the light output remains sufficient, for a lamp in flashing mode will inherently have a lower total light output than the same lamp in steady mode. An advantage of LED lights is that batteries last longer; however, you should change batteries as soon as the level of illumination starts to diminish. If you're riding far, always carry spare batteries with you. Some of the best lighting systems use rechargeable batteries, but are more expensive. Care needs to be taken to recharge the batteries frequently and before any long trip.

Dynamo lamps are always ready for use and modern hub dynamos are much more reliable than older tyre-driven types. It is best to buy one with a backup battery so that the light doesn't go out when you stop in traffic.

Make sure that lamps are securely fixed to the cycle, either along its centre line or to the offside. They should point directly forward and back, with the front lamp angled a little to the left. A front lamp lights the road ahead better if mounted on the front fork or a front carrier than on the headset, but only do this if there is a lamp boss fitted. Direct the beam to fall on the road between 5 and 10 metres (about 15–30 feet) ahead. As some cycle lights are now very bright indeed, avoid mounting them in a way that might dazzle other road users.

Some cyclists use more than one lamp at front or rear to boost their lighting, but with good lamps, more than one light in either direction is unlikely to achieve much practical advantage.

Reflectors

A red rear reflector is a legal requirement at night, but in the presence of good lights it adds little extra information about a cycle or its progress. The main value of such a reflector probably lies in the modest amount of protection it affords people who ride without lights.

The front and spoke reflectors fitted to new cycles are in much the same category, although there is no legal obligation to retain them. Front reflectors are only fully effective if oncoming drivers do not dip their lights, which increases risk for a cyclist and should not be encouraged. Spoke reflectors are of very limited value. The movement of the reflectors will only convey their message to a driver who is some way off along a side road, and who is thus unlikely to be in conflict with you; they are unlikely to be seen in time from a vehicle closer by.

The only type of reflector that adds significantly to perspicuity in the presence of good lights is that which can be fitted to the pedals. When fitted, the up and down movement of the pedals is easily picked up by a headlamp beam, and the movement is unique to a pedal cyclist. The amount of up and down movement also conveys useful information as to how far away a cyclist is. Pedal reflectors are one of the most effective safety aids for cyclists at night. Unfortunately, despite it being a legal requirement for cycles to have two reflectors on each pedal (except for cycles made before 1985), many pedals cannot be so fitted, especially clipless types. Shoe heel reflectors are a useful substitute. Reflectors need to be kept clean and in good repair in order to retain their advantages.

Helmets

Cycle helmets attempt to limit the consequences of a crash. They do nothing to prevent a crash taking place; indeed, if not used properly or if their limitations are not appreciated, they may actually increase that risk.

Helmet wearing by cyclists is a controversial and often emotional subject. It is important to keep the risk of head injury in perspective. The chance of suffering head injury when cycling is low and similar to when walking or travelling in a car. Serious head injury when cycling is rare, and all the more so for people who learn to ride skilfully. People who cycle regularly live longer, on average, than those who do not, with less ill health, so cyclists are not especially vulnerable to any life-threatening injury. Moreover, when cyclists are injured, they are usually discharged from hospital sooner than other road users, suggesting that, on average, their injuries are less serious. Whatever the merits of helmets, their promotion often unjustifiably scares people from cycling through making the activity appear much more hazardous than is really the case.

A helmet works through absorbing some of the force of an impact by itself deforming. A liner of shock-absorbing material acts as a buffer which reduces the acceleration forces that reach the skull. In this way helmets can prevent minor wounds to the head. Once the liner is fully compacted (which does not require a great deal of force), it provides no further protection and all the residual energy passes directly to the skull. Thus the ability of helmets to afford useful protection in more serious crashes, such as those that involve motor vehicles, is very much less.

Despite the theoretical advantages of helmets, confirmation of real-world benefit has proved elusive, there being no reliable evidence that increased helmet wearing has reduced the actual risk of serious or fatal injury across cyclists as a whole. Some studies have concluded that helmeted riders are more at risk, at least for some types of cycling. At the same time, research predicting large benefits from helmet wearing has attracted extensive peer criticism for bias and errors.

Nevertheless, many helmet wearers believe that they have been saved from serious injury. This is a very common experience, out of all proportion to the actual number of head injuries suffered by bareheaded cyclists. There is some evidence that helmeted riders are more likely to engage in riskier cycling and therefore crash more often, and are more likely to hit their (helmeted) heads if they do. The breaking of a helmet is not by itself evidence that it has provided useful protection to the wearer, as it is common for helmets to fail prematurely before the inner liner has crushed. In such cases, little if any protection may have been given.

It is a serious mistake to think that wearing a helmet is at all a substitute for having a safe bike and learning to cycle properly. Parents, in particular, should take heed of this. The limited protection offered by a helmet can be easily negated if a cyclist compensates by riding less carefully or in places where risk is greater, or if wearing one interferes in any way with the attention that is given to traffic. There is evidence that some people, especially children, will take greater risks when wearing a helmet and that drivers sometimes take less care around helmet-wearing cyclists.

Buying and fitting a helmet

If you do decide to wear a helmet, try to buy one that meets the Snell B90 or B95 standards. The more commonly available British/European EN1078 standard is much weaker, sample helmets having repeatedly failed independent tests, with some helmets shattering at very low impact forces.

The protection afforded by a helmet is very much dependent upon achieving a good fit. Heads are different, especially in the position of the chin relative to the skull, and a helmet which is suitable for one person may be quite unsatisfactory for someone else. Always buy a helmet from a shop where there is plenty of choice and where the sales staff have the knowledge to advise.

Check for a snug and comfortable fit around your head, after making any internal adjustments. The helmet should sit low on your forehead and you should be able to see the edge of the brim at the extreme upper range of your vision. Adjust the straps so that there is no slack in any of them (but the chin straps should not be uncomfortably tight), and then try to slide the helmet off. If it does not stay firmly in place, it is unsuitable or incorrectly adjusted. Keeping the straps tight in use is extremely important. Not only can loose straps reduce the protection given by allowing the helmet to move on the head, but this in itself can lead to neck injury.

Correct fitting of a cycle helmet

Ensure that the helmet will not interfere with your head movement, your vision in any direction, your hearing or the wearing of spectacles or sunglasses. Check also for general comfort, especially the adequacy of ventilation. Inadequate air circulation can impair your attentiveness on the road. Many cyclists who normally wear a helmet take it off when climbing hills in hot weather, and this is preferable to overheating the head, which could be detrimental to safety.

Helmets have only a limited effective life, even with careful use, and damage is not always visible. It is the condition of the crushable inner liner that is most important, not the outer shell (if any). It is recommended that a helmet should be replaced every few years. If it is subjected to a hard drop or impact (inside or out) or becomes badly scratched, it should be replaced straight away. Chemicals, detergents, heat and sunlight can all reduce the strength of a helmet.

Bells, horns and sirens

The only situation in which the traditional bicycle bell is useful is when using paths shared with pedestrians. In quiet surroundings it can be a courteous and unobtrusive way of letting non-motorised travellers know you're there, although it is often equally effective, and sometimes better received, to slow down and say a polite 'Excuse me'. Be aware that some pedestrians are deaf and others wear headphones. A bell should never be regarded as a safety aid. If you are at risk of colliding with a pedestrian, keep both hands on the brakes and shout a warning.

In traffic, a bell is useless. Shouting can be effective, but on most occasions it is far better for cyclists to give all their attention to taking evasive action if another vehicle or a pedestrian is heading their way.

Horns have no purpose. On paths their sound is too abrupt, and as likely to frighten someone into your way as out of it, and in traffic they are as ineffective as bells.

Aerosol-operated sirens are available for cycles, and the louder ones can be heard inside cars. Their sound is more offensive than a warning and in most instances a cyclist should be busy avoiding a potential collision rather than sounding off about it.

Mirrors

Many people coming to cycling after driving a car perceive the use of a rear-view mirror as a safety aid. However, there are important differences between mirrors mounted on a car and those which can be attached to a cycle, and also between the amount and type of information that motorist and cyclist need to absorb from behind.

Cycles transmit vibrations from the road to a mirror much more actively than does a car. Also, cyclists must move their eyes much further to switch views between the road ahead and a mirror low on the handlebar. Even convex mirrors have a limited field of view. A cyclist needs to see clearly what is happening to the sides, and there are few occasions when looking behind in a mirror is sufficient. So mirrors are much less useful to a cyclist than to a motorist.

Turning your head gives much more information about what is happening all around. It also gives more accurate information. For cyclists, the third dimension is all-important; judging the closing speed and distance of a following vehicle is much less easy in the small two-dimensional image reflected in a mirror. Turning one's head has other advantages over a mirror, such as alerting a following driver that you might be about to change course, and eye-to-eye contact with drivers is an essential part of negotiation.

Of course, looking behind can sometimes be tricky in dense traffic on narrow roads. An advantage of a mirror under these circumstances is to detect gaps in traffic that could allow you to look behind. There are other occasions, too, when a mirror might usefully supplement your awareness of traffic, and this is fine so long as your attention is not diverted from what is ahead and on riding a straight course. It is a mistake to think that you can look ahead and in a mirror at the same time.

One situation in which a rear-view mirror is to be recommended is when riding a recumbent cycle. Here, it can be more difficult to turn one's body to look behind, and these machines sometimes allow the mounting of a mirror in a more satisfactory position. Mirrors can also be very useful to riders who for a variety of reasons, such as an arthritic neck, may have difficulty turning their head to look directly behind.

Eye protection

Seeing where you are going is essential, not only for coping with traffic but to avoid riding off the road. Insects and airborne debris are potential hazards if trapped in an eye, although it is rare for both eyes to suffer simultaneously. Various eye shields, visors and glasses are sold to give protection, and could be useful if you find this a persistent problem. You should make sure that your peripheral vision is not obstructed.

Highway Code

The *Highway Code* is an important document containing a lot of sound advice about sharing the roads. You should use it to become familiar with the traffic regulations and the meaning of road signs and markings. Only a minority of the rules contained in the *Highway Code* have the force of law (where the word 'must' is used), but its other advice may be taken into account by a court when trying to establish blame for an incident.

The *Highway Code* is a generalist guide, dominated by consideration of motor traffic, and it does not always reflect a good understanding about cycling. As a result, its advice for cyclists is sometimes simplistic, impractical or controversial. You should bear this in mind and not regard it as a definitive summary of best practice.

Insurance

There are three types of insurance that should be considered by a cyclist: cycle insurance, legal assistance and third party.

Cycle insurance covers the theft of your bike or damage to it in the event of a crash or other mishap. Cycle theft is a serious problem is some places, so if the loss of your machine would be of financial concern to you, ensure that it is insured. Policies invariably require cycles to be locked securely when left. This is always a sensible precaution and you should buy a D-lock for best protection. There may also be restrictions regarding cover for household members, maximum value, use abroad etc.

Legal assistance cover will pay for you to have help from a solicitor if you have a crash and need to claim compensation. This cover is less important than it used to be as many solicitors now offer their services on a no-win, no-fee basis. Although that means that you are only likely to get their support if your case is expected to be successful, insurers often impose similar conditions. Insurance cover will more often be of benefit if you cycle abroad, as international claims for compensation can be more complicated.

The likelihood of a claim against a cyclist for causing injury or damage to someone else is very, very small – considerably less than the claims experience of motorists. Nonetheless, having third-party cover is a responsible thing to do, although it is not mandatory.

The most economical way to obtain insurance for cycling is through a household insurance policy if the cover is already suitable or may be extended to be so. You should read the small print carefully to check the limits on the cover provided, as policies vary greatly in this respect.

The second option is to consider membership of one of the national cycling organisations, which include legal assistance and third-party cover as a benefit of membership, and cycle policies as an optional extra.

A few commercial companies also offer insurance packages for cyclists. It's more difficult, however, to get a policy for only one type of cover and the cost may be disproportionately high.

Check your understanding:

☐ What clothing is suitable for your kind of cycling?

☐ What are the main clothing-related hazards to avoid?

☐ What are the best ways to ensure that you are seen when cycling at night?

☐ How much protection can you expect from wearing a cycle helmet?

☐ When did you last read the *Highway Code*?

Part II
Cycling with
skill and
confidence >

Chapter 5

Basic cycling skills

This chapter, along with practice in cycling, should help you to:

- prepare for making a journey by cycle
- control your bike and make simple manoeuvres
- use your gears
- be aware of others and communicate with them through looking and signalling.

Good cycling is a skill that is easy to acquire given the right approach and some practice. Very few people are unable to cycle. One of the keys to safe cycling is that machine and rider operate as one: you should master the control of your bike so well that it becomes automatic, leaving you to give your full attention to the traffic and other hazards, or even to enjoy the countryside. Good control is also efficient and satisfying, with all manoeuvres carried out smoothly, silently and purposefully. It is no coincidence that a skilled cyclist keeps relaxed and does not suffer from road strain. Other road users will give you fewer problems if you are confident and in control.

The following skills start with the most basic. Plenty of practice in these techniques is essential and is best acquired away from traffic in a quiet car park, playground or similar open space. If you have not cycled before, you may find that progress is slow at first. This is not unusual, so do not be disheartened. Once you have mastered the basics, you should find that you progress more quickly.

①②③
These symbols indicate that this topic is a key skill that must be acquired in order to attain Bikeability, the National Cycle Training Standard, Level 1, 2 or 3.

① Mounting and dismounting

If your bike has a low top tube (e.g. ladies' models), stand just left of the bike, hold the handlebar with both hands, pull on the brake levers so that the machine does not move, lift your right leg and step over the bike.

With other models, hold the handlebar with both hands, pull on the brake levers, and then swing your right leg over the saddle to the other side. You may need to practice getting your leg sufficiently high, but you can reduce the height of the bicycle a little by leaning it towards you as you mount.

Having mounted, continue to hold the handlebar with both hands. You should keep the brakes applied and the front wheel pointing straight ahead until you are ready to start, as this will stop the cycle moving under you. Keeping your left foot on the ground, put your right foot on its pedal and move this counter-clockwise to a position a little forward of its highest position. Looked at from the right side of the bike, the correct 'pedal ready' position is at 2 o'clock relative to the chainwheel. Then sit on the saddle and make yourself comfortable. You will find it easier to keep stable in this position if the bike is tilted a little to the left.

On some bikes, such as mountain bikes, you may not be able to sit on the saddle with a foot on the ground due to the height of the pedals. In this case you will have to learn to lift yourself onto the saddle after you start off and to leave the saddle just before you stop. Lowering the saddle may help you to achieve these skills but it should be raised again later.

To dismount, hold the handlebar, apply the brakes and keep the front wheel pointing straight ahead while you reverse the procedure for mounting, tilting the cycle a little to the left as you do so. Your left foot should be close to the bike and stable on the ground throughout so that you can comfortably transfer your weight onto it.

Practise getting on and off the bike until you can do this with ease.

① Holding the handlebar

Straight handlebars

Straight handlebars may have only one position for holding. Grip the handlebar firmly, but not too rigidly, with your fingers over the brake levers, ready to apply them. Modern levers are designed to be operated with only two fingers, allowing the others to maintain a grip on the bar.

Bar ends and aero bars provide some straight handlebars with one or more alternative holding positions, which are often similar to the upper positions of dropped handlebars, described below. However, if these add-ons do not allow immediate access to the brake levers they should not be used in traffic.

Dropped handlebars

There are four ways to hold dropped handlebars (Figure 5.1), and you should be able to move between these positions easily and without wobbling. The first thing to realise is that, contrary to popular opinion, you will not often use the 'dropped' position (Figure 5.1c), unless you wish to cycle as a sport, riding as fast as possible on roads where good speeds can be maintained, in which case this is the most efficient position in terms of minimising wind resistance. In general, though, the dropped position is the least comfortable and generally the least practical in traffic. Nevertheless, the position can be useful when confronted by a strong headwind, so you should practise it.

The normal position for town riding, or for any other occasion when you may need to brake quickly, is to hold the tops of the brake levers with the thumb on one side and the fingers on the other (Figure 5.1a). The brakes are usually applied with the hands remaining in this position and the fingers reaching out for the levers about halfway down. This is a powerful braking position as the arms are straight, braced by the brake levers, which act as a stop to your body moving forward. With this posture you are least likely to be thrown over the handlebar when braking sharply. However, people with small or weak hands may not be able to do this easily (although smaller brake levers are available) and will need to brake from the drops. If this applies to you, always remember to allow extra braking time for the movement from top to drops – or you may find it easier to use a straight handlebar.

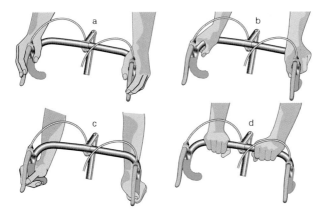

Figure 5.1 *Holding dropped handlebars*

a   Normal position in traffic
b   Relaxed position away from hazards
c   Position against a strong headwind
d   Alternative position for quiet roads

The usual way to hold dropped handlebars where there are no hazards is to grasp them on top, just back from the brake levers where the bars run parallel to the direction of motion (Figure 5.1b). You should be able to slide from here to the levers smoothly and quickly.

The last position (Figure 5.1d) is used as an alternative when riding longer distances, in order to relieve pressure on the hands. Here the straight section of the handlebar either side of the stem is grasped with the fingers in front and the thumb behind. This position is the slowest for moving to the brakes, so you should move back to one of the others at the slightest hint of a hazard. However, it is a good position to use while you perfect your balance, as the hands are closest together and the bike is at its least stable.

ⓘ Stopping and braking

You must know how to stop a bike safely before you make it move. Once you know how to stop, you can avoid almost any situation that might otherwise cause you to fall, and this should help you to gain confidence that you are in control of your machine.

Begin by doing the following exercise, running with your bike. You should stand to the left side of the bicycle, and hold the handlebar with both hands over the brake levers. You will find this easier to do, and you will be less likely to hit your ankle with a pedal, if you lean the bike slightly towards you. Now run forward with the bike for a few metres and then quickly apply the right (front) brake lever. You should find that the bike stops very quickly, but that the rear wheel jumps off the ground.

Now repeat the exercise, but apply the left (rear) brake lever. Do you notice the difference? On this occasion the bicycle stops much less quickly, but both wheels stay on the ground.

The lesson to be learnt from this is that the two brakes have quite different effects. If you apply only the front brake, the bike will stop quickly but you may be thrown over the handlebar. On the other hand, applying only the rear brake will stop you more safely, but not very quickly.

To stop a bicycle quickly and safely, you need to apply both brakes and to do so simultaneously. Practise doing this running with the bike until you can bring the bike to a stop quickly and under your full control.

At the same time get a feel for the power of the brakes so that you stop quickly but not too abruptly. You will stop most comfortably and safely if you pull the brake levers steadily but quite slowly.

ⓘ Starting to move

Before you start, put the bicycle into a low gear. On a derailleur-geared bike, you can do this without riding by lifting the back wheel off the ground and manually turning the pedals as you move the gear lever(s). With hub gears, move the lever(s) first and then check that the gear is engaged by turning the pedals. Next, mount the bike as described previously so that you are seated on the saddle (if possible) with the right pedal in the 'pedal ready' position.

Getting a helping hand

A friend or parent can help a trainee to learn how to start, stop and balance in a similar way to a cycle training instructor.

To practise starting and stopping, the helper should face the trainee from in front of the bicycle and grip the handlebar either side of the handlebar stem. The aim is to keep the bicycle going straight and upright as it moves forward. The helper, of course, will have to walk backwards. In this way the cyclist can concentrate on locating the feet correctly on the pedals, pedalling and braking.

To practise balance, the helper should grip the bicycle from behind the cyclist, either under the saddle, by the seat post or by a carrier, if fitted. Alternatively, the cyclist could be held around the waist. This way of holding will allow the rider to have full control of the handlebar and brakes, while the helper is there to prevent the bike leaning too far and to assist in sudden stops. As the cyclist gains competence, the helper should loosen the hold on the bicycle and then gradually move their hand away altogether.

To start moving, release the brakes (but keep your fingers over them), push down firmly with your right foot and at the same time lift the left foot onto its pedal. Freewheel for just a metre or two and then stop as explained above.

When you stop, you should keep both feet on the pedals until the bike has come to a halt, then quickly move the left foot to the ground, tilting the bike a little to the left as you do so. For best stability, set your foot down close to the bike. Your right foot should stay on its pedal unless and until you are ready to dismount.

Make learning fun as you teach a child how to ride

Starting with the other foot

Some people, particularly if they learnt to cycle in a right-hand-drive country, start with their right foot on the ground and the left foot on the pedal. When stopping, they put their right foot down first. If you feel comfortable about this you may decide to continue this practice. However, in left-hand-drive countries it is usually more practical to adopt the procedure described above.

Cover your brakes!

From the beginning, develop the habit of keeping your fingers over the brake levers whenever you are on the bike. This will keep the bike firmly under your control and enable you to stop quickly at any time. You will also find that an open hand makes your upper body less tense.

Only when you are cycling in quiet conditions away from potential hazards should you hold the handlebar away from the brake levers.

Ride most of the time with your hands lightly over the brakes

① Balance and steering

The next stage is to achieve balance on the moving bicycle. Practise this, if possible, in a large flat area that is clear all around.

Mount and start the bicycle as described above, but this time keep the pedals turning. A couple of strong pushes on the pedals at the beginning will help you to gain momentum, which will make balancing easier. Always keep your hands over the brake levers so that you can stop at any time.

Fix your eyes on a distant point, not on the surface ahead, and your aim at first should be just to stay upright. Don't try to keep to a straight course, but steer as necessary to maintain balance. If you start to tilt to the left, steer to the left to correct, and if you start to tilt to the right, steer right. This may seem counter-intuitive at first. Don't overdo the correction, however, which needs only to be small. As you become more proficient, you will start to correct for balance as much by shifting your weight from side to side as by turning the handlebar.

Try not to be tense – control is always easier if you are relaxed. If you find yourself going too fast, a gentle touch on the rear brake should be sufficient to keep speed under control. For really good balance, you should master riding slowly.

When you have achieved balance, practise steering a straight course. Steering straight is aided by a smooth pedalling action – follow a straight line marked on the surface or some natural mark to perfect this. A good cyclist will wobble less than 2.5 cm (1 inch). When you can ride straight, practise turning to left and right. The aim is to make the bike go where you want it to go. As you turn you will begin naturally to lean into the turn, which is the way cyclists make most changes of direction.

Practise steering accuracy by riding between closely spaced lines such as these formed from twigs

It is important to be able to steer accurately, placing your wheels precisely where you want them in order to avoid potholes and stones. Fortunately, this can be achieved quite easily, as our normal stereoscopic vision has the remarkable ability to be able to judge whether an object lies straight ahead to an accuracy of better than 1°. You will go where you look.

To practise accurate steering, mark two chalk lines on the ground about 30 cm (12 inches) long and 8 cm (3 inches) apart. Ride between the lines repeatedly until neither the front nor the rear wheel touches them at normal riding speed. This is most easily judged by a friend standing nearby. As soon as you have mastered this, decrease the spacing to 5 cm (2 inches) and then to 2.5 cm (1 inch). When you can achieve this accuracy consistently, you will be an important step closer to harmonising the movements of bike and body.

① Pedalling

Pedalling should always be carried out with the ball of your foot, never with the instep. This is the most efficient pedalling position and it is easier to achieve if you use toe clips or clipless pedals. These enable you to pull a pedal up as well as to push it down, and can increase pedalling efficiency by up to 50%. The use of toe clips and clipless pedals is described in Chapter 4.

Another important aspect of pedalling is to 'ankle' the pedals round: do not simply push them down. This means pivoting the foot at the ankle so that the toes are pointed slightly upwards at the top of the stroke and downwards at the bottom. In this way you should aim to apply pressure to each pedal with your foot for about three-quarters of its circle of travel (Figure 5.2). Acquiring a good pedalling style will help dispel the myth that cycling is hard work.

Figure 5.2
Pedalling position and ankling

① More about braking

You should always be able to move your hands quickly to the brake levers and to apply them with just the right amount of force to slow or stop in the distance required. This means that you must get to know the 'feel' of your brakes, and that you keep them adjusted so that this feel remains constant over time. Practise applying different amounts of force to the levers, and learn the total distances before you are brought to a halt, as well as the initial distances before the brakes start to have effect. It is particularly important to practise this under both dry and wet conditions, as there will be a marked difference between the two distances when both rims and road are wet.

There is another element that must be included in the total stopping distance that has nothing to do with the brakes, but which can be significant. This is the reaction distance – how far you travel between seeing an incident which requires you to brake and responding to it. Reaction time varies between about a second and 2.5 seconds, depending upon how alert you are; and at 32 km/h (20 mph) you will cover nearly 23 metres (75 feet) in 2.5 seconds!

Table 5.1 gives typical total stopping distances of cycles for extreme states of weather and rider on roads with different gradients. Note how much greater the distances become under imperfect conditions. All distances relate to alloy-wheel cycles; in wet weather, steel-wheel machines can take up to twice as far to stop.

Table 5.1 Total stopping distance on a cycle

	16 km/h (10 mph)	24 km/h (15 mph)	32 km/h (20 mph)	40 km/h (25 mph)
Gradient, 0%, level				
Dry and alert	6 m	11 m	17 m	24 m
Wet and tired	15 m	27 m	41 m	57 m
Gradient, 5%, down				
Dry and alert	6 m	11 m	18 m	25 m
Wet and tired	17 m	30 m	47 m	67 m
Gradient, 10%, down				
Dry and alert	7 m	12 m	19 m	27 m
Wet and tired	20 m	37 m	58 m	84 m

You learnt previously the difference in effect between the front and rear brakes (see 'Stopping and braking' above). Put simply, the rear brake is for slowing down and the front brake is for stopping. Getting to know the action of each brake on its own, at an early stage under controlled conditions, could prove useful should a brake cable fail. However, for safety, you should normally use both brakes, applying them simultaneously. Practise this until it becomes second nature every time. As far as possible, brake only when steering straight.

A closer look at braking and skidding

By far the greatest amount of stopping power comes from the front brake, but if this is used too harshly, the cycle will pivot about the front wheel and you will be thrown over the handlebar. However, if you need to stop quickly, most of the stopping power must necessarily come from the front brake.

The tendency of a bike to tip forwards when you decelerate takes weight off the rear wheel. The quicker you stop, the less useful the rear brake becomes and the more easily the rear wheel will skid. A cycle takes more than twice as far to stop using only the rear brake compared to using only the front brake, which will usually stop the machine just as quickly as using both brakes. Nevertheless, you should always apply the rear brake, at the same time as the front brake, so that a slight skid at the rear will warn if you get close to the hazard point at which the bike may tip. If you are stopping gradually, brake firmly at the rear to start with, then reduce pressure as you squeeze the front brake lever harder. In an emergency stop, keep the rear brake applied lightly.

A rear-wheel skid is quite easy to control; a skid at the front, almost impossible. Fortunately, it is very difficult to make the front wheel of a typical bicycle skid under most conditions. Weight transfer onto the front wheel will keep it on the road right up to the tipping point. A front-wheel skid can occur when the road is very slippery due to ice, spilt diesel, leaves, loose gravel or certain types of smooth paving when wet, or if you turn while you brake. You should learn to recognise these conditions so that you may ride more slowly and won't need to stop as quickly. Make more use of the rear brake when you do stop.

Although of limited use for stopping, the rear brake is most useful for keeping your speed in check when riding downhill, before a sharp bend, at the approach to a junction, and generally in traffic and near pedestrians.

Even if you do use both brakes, too rapid braking can still be risky as one or more wheels may lock. Judging when this may occur will take time. Meanwhile, don't try braking more hastily than you know is safe unless you really have no choice.

For a more detailed description of what happens when you brake, see the box on braking and skidding.

① Turning

Steering control is now further developed as you practise making turns. In practice, for many changes of direction, 'turning' is the wrong term to use, as the front wheel is only turned when you want to follow tight corners or when travelling very slowly. At other times the handlebar remains almost straight and the cycle moves around a bend by being leaned in that direction in order to counteract the centrifugal force on the wheels. The degree of lean necessary is proportional to both the tightness of the turn and to your speed. Practise making turns of increasing tightness and at increased speed. You will soon find that you make the correct amount of lean automatically. Don't overdo the leaning, particularly if the surface is not firm, or your wheels may slip from under you.

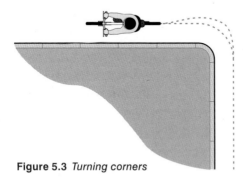

Figure 5.3 *Turning corners*

The tightest turn that you will commonly make is a left turn at a road junction. Find a junction on a quiet road and notice how the kerb is radiused around the corner. You should be able to approach the corner and ride around it while keeping your rear wheel parallel to the kerb all the time (Figure 5.3). The front wheel will inevitably turn more widely at normal speed and you should learn the exact amount of oversteering necessary. This practice becomes even more important if you ride a tandem or pull a trailer as the amount of oversteering is then more significant.

Before making a tight turn, apply the brakes to check speed and to bring the bike under your firm control.

Practise making turns at different distances from the kerb where the camber (arch) of the road – and hence the kind of control necessary – may differ. Occasionally, you will encounter more acute angles, and you should practise turning as sharply as you can to both the left and right.

② U-turns

A useful extension of your turning practice is to see how tight a U-turn you can manage. You should certainly be able to U-turn within a normal two-lane road. Safe U-turning requires low speed, a low gear to help you keep balance, a generally upright position and the ability to stay relaxed. Take particular care if your feet (or toe clips) can touch the front wheel or mudguard, as this could lock you into the turn, resulting in a fall. In such cases a shunting movement of the pedals, to keep them clear of the front wheel, is necessary.

① Avoiding obstacles

Having acquired the skill of riding as straight as possible, it is now time to learn how not to! You will, for example, need to avoid potholes and other obstacles.

Place three small objects or chalk marks on the surface of the ground, 4 metres (13 feet) apart in a straight line. Weave between them, passing alternately to the left and to the right. You should aim to veer as little as possible from the straight line – swerving in traffic could put you into the path of following vehicles.

Having succeeded in avoiding obstacles 4 metres (13 feet) apart, gradually decrease the spacing to about 0.5 metre (1.5 feet). As the spacing reduces, you will find that it will not be possible to make the rear wheel follow the front; this does not matter too much, as you are more vulnerable to toppling over from deflection of the front wheel by an impact than from deflection of the back. Also, although you should be able to negotiate the first spacings reasonably quickly, as spacing decreases, so must your speed.

For isolated or widely spaced small obstacles, it is possible with some practice to keep both the body and handlebar moving in virtually a straight line while the cycle wheels move from side to side. As the wheels are much narrower than the rider, this can result in virtually no deflection of the cycle and cyclist's combined path. To achieve this, approach a single object in a straight line until you are very close. Then turn the handlebar suddenly – just a little – so that your front wheel misses the object, but without leaning first in the same direction as

Practise avoiding obstacles

you would normally. Your body will start to tilt in the opposite direction, but you counter this by steering back towards that side as soon as your front wheel is past the object. You will need to oversteer somewhat in order to compensate for the unusual body angle, but then you straighten both the handlebar and body to continue on your original course (Figure 5.4). There is no doubt that this technique needs practice, for you will have to make movements which are at first unnatural. Having learnt it, though, you will not only be able to avoid holes and stones, but you will also be able to make quick turns more easily in an emergency.

Figure 5.4 *Advanced obstacle avoidance*

① Using gears

You use gears to maintain as much as possible a steady rate of pedalling (known as cadence) irrespective of the physical conditions under which you are cycling. It is thus possible to climb quite steep hills using no more energy than when cycling on the level, by selecting a low gear. To achieve this benefit, however, you will travel more slowly. Conversely, a high gear allows you to cycle more quickly when it is physically easier to do so, such as when the wind is behind you. Pedalling should always be comfortable, and changing gear as conditions alter is the principal means of ensuring this.

Wherever you cycle, you should always start off from stationary in a low gear to make it easier to apply the additional pedalling force that is needed to get you going. As conditions become easier, you change up in gear. When riding in town traffic, good use of your gears will make the frequent starting, accelerating and stopping less tiring than would otherwise be the case.

The technique for changing gear differs according to whether you have internal hub or derailleur gears, and according to the type of gear control.

Change down before you stop

In order to be ready for an easy restart, always change down to a lower gear each time before you stop.

Hub gears

Hub gears can be changed when you are freewheeling or stationary, but not when applying pressure to the pedals. This has both advantages and drawbacks. You do not have to think about changing down approaching traffic lights, or anywhere else where you might have to stop, because you can do so after stopping (although it is still good practice to anticipate a change). On the other hand, you must change down before hills in order not to lose too much momentum while you ease off pedalling.

To change hub gears, simply move the gear lever at the same time as you pause pedalling. In some cases rotating the pedals backwards slightly can make for an easier change. Some hub gears require the operation of two levers to cover their full range, but in all cases there are quite definite notches for the levers for each gear, and changing should be accurate so long as the gear has been set up correctly.

Derailleur gears

In contrast, derailleur gears can only be changed while you are pedalling, which means that you must anticipate occasions when you might have to stop and would need to be in a lower gear. However, you will not lose too much momentum changing down to climb hills. To change gear, you continue to pedal, but ease up a little on the pressure applied. This will decrease the tension in the chain and make for an easier and quieter change. Then simply click the gear control between positions. If the gears have been correctly adjusted, changing should be accurate.

There are many types of control for operating derailleur gears, known variously as gear levers or shifters. In all cases there is one control on the right side of the bike to change between the freewheel sprockets and – if there is more than one chainring – another on the left side to change the chainring.

Hybrid bikes are most often fitted with trigger shifters. These are part of a combined gear and brake lever mechanism and have two levers each for controlling the gears. They are operated by the thumb and forefinger. One lever changes to a higher gear, the other to a lower gear, and in this respect the left trigger usually operates contrary to the right. Designs vary. Some integrate the shift mechanism with the brake lever: squeeze to brake, flick up and down to shift. Some move only one gear at a time, others can shift by up to three gears if you push the trigger further. In any case they can be fired rapidly in succession to move quickly through the full range of gears. Trigger shifters provide very efficient gear changing which can take place without moving the hands from the brake levers. This makes them ideal for riding in traffic.

Grip, or twist, shifters are fitted as an integral part of the handlebar. They are operated by rotating the handlebar end with the full hand, in one direction to go up in gear, in the other to go down. It is not possible to operate these and the brakes at the same time, but they do provide a gear changing mechanism that most people find easy to use.

Cheaper and older flat-handlebar bikes may have thumb shifters: small, simple levers mounted on top of the handlebar, pushed one way by a thumb, pulled the other way by a finger.

Modern cycles with dropped handlebars usually have something similar to the flat bar trigger shifters described above, in which the brake levers swing inwards to shift to a larger sprocket or chainring. Usually there is a smaller lever to shift the other way.

Other cycles with dropped handlebars may have gear levers on the down tube and you must take a hand from the handlebar to operate them, which makes them less suitable for frequent gear changes in traffic. Each lever is moved in one direction to change up in gear, and the other to change down. You should operate both the front and rear levers with the same hand, usually the right. Although a little awkward at first, this method allows you to move both levers simultaneously if necessary, and you can also make any compensatory adjustments with the other lever more quickly.

On some cycles the front shifter, and sometimes also the rear, will not be indexed. The gear lever is held in position by friction alone, with no predetermined positions for each gear. These require more practice to change accurately, involving the ears as well as the hands and feet, but can result in very fast gear changes. You should move the gear lever until you have gone just beyond the gear you want and then bring it back slightly as the chain settles into place, finely adjusting for minimum noise in the transmission system. You may have to readjust the front mechanism slightly when changing the rear, and vice versa, because the overall chain line will alter.

With derailleurs that have more than one chainring, there will usually be some overlap between the ranges of gears that each chainring provides. The front changer will nevertheless deliver a bigger step-change than shifting at the rear. You should therefore normally use the rear changer when you want a small change in gear and the front for a big change. If you need to make a small shift but have run out of gears at the back, change at the front then immediately (or simultaneously) shift one or more rear gears in the opposite direction.

Try to avoid using the innermost rear sprockets with the outermost chainring and vice versa, as these gears are inefficient, noisy, cause rapid wear and risk the chain falling off if you back-pedal.

With triple-chainring systems, the middle chainring is frequently used for normal riding and the two others provide over- and under-drive for less frequently encountered conditions.

All systems

Whatever gear system you have, don't ride in a noisy gear; it is inefficient and accelerates chain wear. A gear system in good condition and properly adjusted should be quiet to use.

When changing to a lower gear, you should be able to do this one gear at a time. When changing to a higher gear, though, it is not unusual to have to move two or more gears at a time. This is not normally important, but can be a nuisance when ascending hills, when fine gear changes are needed. However, as the gradient gets easier, it is not difficult to pedal in a lower gear than ideal for what will usually be only a short time. Alternatively, you can compensate for a change to too high a gear by changing immediately back to a lower one.

The hardest gear change to make smoothly is when you are only partway up a long hill and the gradient has eased just a little. It can then be difficult to reduce pressure on the pedals sufficiently for a smooth change, while riding in too low a gear would become increasingly tiring. In this case, pedal faster than usual over a short distance in order to achieve sufficient additional momentum to reduce pedal pressure so that you can change gear without your speed falling to less than that at which you started. A similar technique can be used to change to a larger chainring.

Get to know your own gears and practise changing them until you can select the gear you want quickly, smoothly and quietly.

⚙ Cadence and sprint speed

Cadence is the number of times a cyclist turns the pedals in one minute. A steady, comfortable pedalling rhythm is essential for efficient cycling, while increasing one's cadence strengthens the leg muscles and enables more rapid acceleration. Increasing cadence also makes it easier to increase your sprint speed – the maximum speed that you can attain over a short distance, such as through a roundabout.

Racing cyclists know well the benefits of having a high cadence, but there can also be important safety advantages for everyone. Generally speaking, you are at your safest in traffic if you can move at a speed comparable to that of the other vehicles. Increasing your cadence and sprint speed will allow you to achieve this more often, particularly at those places where it matters most – junctions with complex manoeuvring. It will also be easier to restart quickly in a low gear at traffic signals and roundabouts, and to get yourself out of trouble if you are on a potential collision course.

 Increasing cadence and sprint speed are two of the most positive steps a cyclist can take to enhance safety.

A good cadence to aim for is about 80, while a sprint speed of 32 km/h (20 mph) will enable you to tackle most traffic situations with ease. To increase your cadence, select a gear lower than you would normally use for a given road and simply force yourself to pedal faster in order to maintain your usual speed. Gradually, your leg muscles will become accustomed to the higher rate and your cadence and strength will increase.

⚙ Looking behind

Up to now you will have practised maintaining good balance while looking ahead and with both hands on the handlebar. However, it is also important for you to be able to control your machine without looking where you are going and with only one hand! You need these skills to be able to look behind and then to signal before manoeuvring. Looking back is a key communication skill that is essential for your safety.

Looking behind

When you are confident about keeping a straight course, practise looking behind. Keep both hands on the handlebar – the normal position in traffic – and then move your eyes as far as you can and turn your head and shoulders until you can see behind you.

You will soon realise that most of the steering control now comes from the hand on the 'blind' side. The other hand is essentially for steadying. Although in the majority of instances you will wish to look over your right shoulder, practise looking over the left shoulder, too, as this can sometimes be very useful.

Look before you signal or move

When you are cycling, you should always look behind before you signal a movement that might conflict with someone else. You need to be sure that the movement would be safe to carry out prior to indicating that you wish to make it.

You should also look behind in the direction in which you intend to move just before any change in your position on the road, so that you are certain that there is still sufficient space available for you to enter.

① Control with one hand

Lift each hand in turn from the handlebar while riding straight ahead: first by just a little, and then move it well away to the side of your body. The other hand must compensate for the imbalance by pressing a little harder on the handlebar and at a slightly different angle. Move the free hand to and from the handlebar until you can make this adjustment easily. Riding with one hand is easier if you do not ride too slowly.

When you can do this, practise looking behind to the same side as you lower your hand. This is the most difficult action to perfect in terms of keeping the bike travelling in a straight line. However, it allows a greater turn at the waist and hence better visibility of what is happening behind than when you keep both hands on the handlebar. This movement takes time, so should be avoided when there is traffic ahead.

② Signalling

Now focus on lifting an arm to give a right- or left-turn signal. Always signal with the full arm straight out and fingers pointed so that there can be no doubt about your intentions (Figure 5.5).

Figure 5.5
Signalling

a Intention to move or turn right

b Intention to move or turn left

c Slowing down or stopping

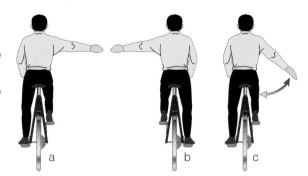

a   b   c

The slowing-down or stopping signal, in which the right arm moves between the body and a position 45° to the horizontal, is not used often but has advantage in some situations and you should practise it.

For each signal, you will notice that the compensation necessary by the other arm is slightly different.

① Listening

An essential skill for understanding what's going on around you is listening. Here the unencumbered cyclist has an important advantage over most other drivers, as traffic noises are considerably muted inside a motor vehicle. Your ears should be active all of the time, unscrambling the background din for any noise that requires your attention. You will soon get to know the obvious sounds, such as the screeching of brakes or fierce acceleration, but detecting the change in pitch of a car engine as the driver decides to pull in behind you or to come out across your path will require some practice.

Listening is a skill that should be used to complement looking, not to substitute for it. Some potential hazards make little noise and looking about you enables communication with other road users in a way that listening alone does not. Nevertheless, there are many occasions when listening can give a warning long before a hazard comes into view.

Good hearing for a cyclist is vital. If you wear a hat, keep it clear of your ears, and never listen to audio equipment when you are cycling.

① Collision-avoidance techniques

A careful cyclist will aim not to get into situations which could result in a collision with anyone else; certainly, there are many situations in which potential crashes can easily be avoided. Watchfulness and anticipation are the primary collision-avoidance techniques and are all that should be necessary for the great majority of the time.

However, because a cyclist is vulnerable to the actions of others, and there are many drivers on the roads today who do not appreciate the problems cyclists face, there may be times when you will have to react quickly to an error by someone else. You may have to decide how to react in only a fraction of a second, and the precise action required will vary from situation to situation. Nonetheless there are certain last-moment collision-avoidance techniques which you can learn and practise, to deal with a potential conflict.

There are three responses to an emergency:

- brake sharply
- accelerate
- change direction quickly.

Braking

The most instinctive response is to brake sharply, but this is often not the best thing to do. The problems with braking are: firstly, cycle brakes are inefficient; secondly, their sudden, sharp application is liable to lock a wheel or rip a cable – in either case you may go over the handlebar; thirdly, you end up stationary in the conflict zone, which is not good if a car is still coming towards you.

Braking is usually only the best way to avoid a collision if you have sufficient safe space before you, and you are reasonably confident of being able to stop within that space, without toppling. If you do brake quickly, brake hard with the front brake but with normal severity at the back. As you brake, throw your weight backwards in the saddle, which will reduce the braking distance and improve your stability.

Accelerating

Often you can avoid a collision most easily by accelerating rapidly away from it. The aim is to get away from the conflict zone as quickly as possible. Although motor vehicles are capable of much faster maximum speeds and acceleration rates than cyclists, it is surprising just how quickly a cyclist can move when it matters, particularly if a high cadence has been acquired. This is often sufficient to get you out of the way of a car which fails to give way at a roundabout or which looks likely not to stop when coming out of a side road. Developing the skill of judging the speed of other vehicles will allow you to decide if there is likely to be time to outpace someone. If so, just pedal as fast as you can – there may be no time to change gear!

Changing direction

Making a sudden change of direction is usually the best response to unsafe turning movements by other vehicles at junctions. It can also be useful for avoiding potholes and other hazards, but these will be discussed more fully in Chapter 7. If a vehicle pulls out of a side road across your path, but you are not sufficiently advanced to be able to accelerate out of the way, make a quick diversionary turn towards the offside of the car (Figure 5.6a). This, of course, will put you at some risk from any following traffic, but in practice although a driver may pull out without seeing a cyclist, this is less likely if another vehicle is coming. In any case, good observation on your part should suggest in advance that this situation might happen, leaving sufficient time to slow down and look behind. Holding the primary riding position, as will be described in Chapter 7, will mean that you are more likely to be seen, and that your avoiding manoeuvre need be less severe if you are not.

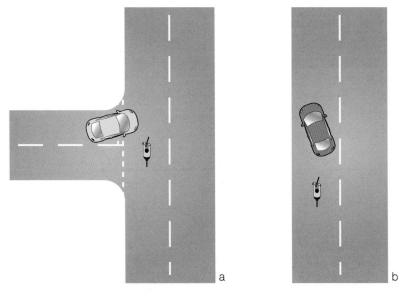

a   b

Figure 5.6 *Diversionary turns*

Less easily avoided is the situation when a car overtakes a cyclist and then suddenly pulls into the kerb to stop (Figure 5.6b). Sometimes drivers behave in this way just to get themselves out of a fast stream of traffic. A cyclist may not be able to match the car's deceleration and, once the car has stopped, a door may be opened into your path. Maintaining a position away from the kerb will help to minimise the swerve into traffic that may then be necessary.

A similar situation, known as a left-hook and one of the commonest causes of collisions with cyclists, is when a driver overtakes a cyclist and then turns left across the cyclist's path at a junction or entrance. If this happens so close to the junction that braking is not practicable (often you can detect the situation arising by the sound of the car slowing down as it overtakes and you can then start to brake early), the only response is to make a tight left turn into the same road in order to keep to the left of the car (Figure 5.7). Tight left turns are hard to do and a little hazardous to practise. The idea is that the first movement you make is to turn the handlebar *right*, towards the car. This throws the body to the left, and when, a split second later, the handlebar is turned left, the body is already leaning and the turn will be that much tighter. The same technique is applicable if a car from the opposite direction turns right across your path. In neither case is it wise to veer right instead of left, as that could lead to a head-on collision.

On occasions a combination of two of the three avoidance techniques may be best, perhaps starting with braking and then steering past an obstacle once you are going slowly enough to do so, or accelerating again to respond to a change in a driver's behaviour.

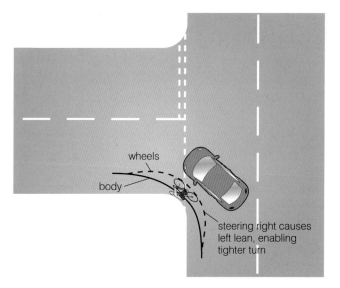

Figure 5.7 *The quick left turn*

Being prepared

For a skilled cyclist, crashes are very, very rare. Nonetheless, despite all you do to avoid it, it is prudent to be prepared for a crash. In collision with something, or if the cycle slips, a cyclist is invariably thrown into the air, if only for a second or two. The greatest potential risk is that the head will hit something hard, such as the ground. By comparison, other injuries are relatively unimportant. Action to minimise or control injury requires great presence of mind, but it could help if you've thought about it beforehand.

Insomuch as you have any control over the orientation of your body, try to keep upright for as long as possible. This will lessen the chances of your body or head going under another vehicle. Then look for your knees! The effect of this should be to turn your head inwards, which will minimise the likelihood of your skull hitting the road. If you are sufficiently alert to roll yourself up into a ball, so much the better.

Even if you have landed without any apparent serious injury, take your time getting back up. Move carefully, checking all over for injury, then sit still for a while to recover from the shock. It is unwise to carry on while still dazed. When you have recovered, check your bike over carefully for any signs of damage, looking particularly at the wheels, frame and brakes.

Check your understanding:

☐ Describe in detail how you would slow down and then stop a bicycle.

☐ What should your actions be before starting off?

☐ When should you change gear and how is this done on your bike?

☐ Can you look behind and then signal while maintaining a straight course?

☐ Describe the three collision-avoidance techniques.

Chapter 6
Sharing the roads

This chapter should help you to:

- ❯ appreciate that safe cycling is primarily about adopting safe strategies for sharing the roads
- ❯ recognise the importance of attitude and judgement in keeping you safe.

A common reason given by people for not cycling is that sharing the roads with motor vehicles is unsafe. Bikes and cars, it is thought, are incapable of mixing safely. From this follows the argument that to maximise their safety, cyclists should keep (or be kept) out of the way of motor traffic as much as possible.

In fact, nothing could be further from the truth. Cars and cycles can mix well and they usually do. A considerable number of people cycle regularly in traffic with very little difficulty. As you will read in the chapter on cycle facilities (Chapter 13), no alternative to the general road network has yet been devised which is as safe or advantageous overall for cycling.

Cycling safely on the roads is not simply a matter of luck, nor does it depend solely upon the behaviour of the drivers of motor vehicles, although cyclists are certainly always vulnerable to the actions of others. Safe cycling is also a matter of adopting sensible strategies, for in practice, most drivers cooperate with cyclists who follow the rules of the road in a confident and disciplined manner.

Feeling at ease on the roads is largely a matter of gaining confidence, whereas being safe requires both expert control of your machine, and also the ability to 'read' the road and to predict and respond to the behaviour of others. Other sections of this guide deal in detail with developing these skills.

Another equally important aspect of road sharing is the development of psychological skills for understanding why other drivers behave in the way they do and seeking to achieve a helpful relationship with them.

Attitude

Having the right attitude towards your cycling and others is extremely important if you are to cycle well and safely. Without the correct frame of mind – having an awareness of both your rights and responsibilities – you will give yourself unnecessary problems by encouraging others to make mistakes or by annoying them needlessly. Research suggests that cyclists who are tolerant of others have a significantly lower risk of conflict.

The first thing to realise is that very few drivers are deliberately aggressive; they are simply intent, like you, on getting from one place to another with the minimum of trouble. Drivers hardly ever choose to have a collision with a cyclist. Having said that, people often do stupid things. Probably the most common driver error is impatience. Unfortunately, people are often taught to pass the driving test rather than to acquire safe driving skills. Very little is taught about sharing the roads with non-motorised users, or about the particular difficulties faced by people such as cyclists. If you study this guide well, you will achieve a greater level of skill and understanding than the average road user of any kind.

It is also true that some aspects of modern vehicle design increase the difficulties motorists have in controlling their vehicles safely on all-traffic roads. The amount of power under a driver's command is considerable and features such as anti-lock braking and the fast rates of acceleration and braking now possible encourage some drivers to travel at speeds greater than those at which they are competent, and tempt them to take more risks because it is now easier for them to get *themselves* out of trouble.

Road design, too, can cause problems for drivers. Many motorists find busy roundabouts and complex intersections as intimidating and difficult to use as do many cyclists. So much of their attention is devoted to finding the correct route and looking out for others who might conflict with them that there often isn't a lot of attention left to spot a cyclist. Drivers may also be pressured by other traffic into making quick decisions based on limited information.

With both vehicle and road design, engineering improvements can improve safety as well as convenience, but some drivers abuse these advantages without necessarily thinking of the consequences for others. As a cyclist you need to be aware of all these limitations of drivers and to allow for them.

Do not let yourself be annoyed by others, however stupid their actions. This will take your attention from the road and could lead you from a near miss to more certain conflict. Develop the ability to curse and then forget. One of the great advantages of cycling is that the physical effort involved can help to dispel anger and frustration quickly and harmlessly. The same doesn't apply to someone sitting motionless in a car, who may continue to resent some thoughtless action of yours long after you have forgotten it. However, if you get annoyed, it is a good idea to seek a positive interaction with someone else to help to dissipate the tension.

Likewise, don't retaliate with abuse or a siren; you may cause greater trouble for the next cyclist the driver meets. Of course, if someone has acted aggressively towards you with intent, note the registration number and make a report to the police, although the chances of proceedings following are slim unless there is a witness.

Riding around with a feeling of superiority to others is also foolish. A halo offers no protection against the bad driving of others; indeed, bad driving may even be encouraged by such a 'holier-than-thou' attitude on the part of the cyclist.

A sensible attitude to adopt when cycling is that of an equal to all others on the road. Do not be submissive to others, and exert your rights if this does not put you too much at risk. Be equally prepared, however, to yield to the rights of others and to show tolerance and understanding of the difficulties that all road users have. You should also appreciate that even a cyclist is capable of causing injury or nuisance to others.

Curiously, the biggest mistake made by many cyclists is that they are too submissive when sharing the roads, somehow feeling that they must always give priority to motor vehicles. It is precisely this attitude that causes many of their difficulties in traffic. You need to appreciate that, as a cyclist, you have as much right as anyone else to be on the road, with as much right to an easy journey. Although a lack of caution is certainly unwise, so is a lack of confidence. If you keep giving way or hesitate when the right of way is yours, you will not only get nowhere fast, but the resulting confusion may well put you more at risk than if you'd been more assertive.

Courtesy in using the roads leads to greater safety for everyone. Try to show courtesy and patience when you can, and give a brief 'thank you' wave if someone does you a kindness. It is remarkable the goodwill that this can generate.

Judgement

Good judgement of road conditions and of the behaviour of others is important if you are to cycle positively and confidently. Judgement is largely a matter of experience and is closely related to observation, which will be discussed more fully in Chapter 7. But much can be learnt simply by looking critically at the actions of others, both motorists and cyclists.

Go to a busy free-flowing road junction, such as a simple give-way junction or a roundabout. Watch closely how drivers behave. Although you can never recognise for sure a good driver – which is why any judgement needs to have an adequate margin for error – there are certain tell-tale indicators of poor driving. Close overtaking, weaving and the failure to give way to others are obvious faults. Much bad driving is noisy: fierce braking and acceleration, inappropriate speed, impatient turning. Cars with embellishments and souped-up engines can suggest aggressiveness on the part of their drivers, but don't assume that all bad driving is aggressive. Many drivers are simply lazy, tired or incompetent and react too slowly. Too many older drivers have poor eyesight. Identify carefully the errors you see being made and try to imagine how best to react if you were cycling amidst such behaviour.

Try to stand in such a way that you can see the faces of drivers who should yield right of way. Where do they look and for how long? What distractions are there of their attention? Are they all confident in their actions or are some experiencing problems? The answers to these kinds of questions should help you to appreciate the reality of modern traffic conditions, the degree of competence of drivers and the difficulties that even the least vulnerable of road users endure. This knowledge should help you to cycle in a way which minimises difficulties for others, so that you, in turn, may have the maximum potential for a safe passage.

Look at traffic approaching the junction. Where is it maintaining speed and where does it slow or accelerate? Where would be the best place to move to the centre of the road for a right turn and what would be the likely effect on following vehicles? Try to get a feel for the capabilities of motor vehicles. Note how far it takes a car, a bus and a lorry to stop, both when driven well and driven badly. Estimate in advance how long it will take different vehicles to stop – and then see if you were right! Use the average length of a car (about 5 metres/16 feet) or the length of the road centre-line markings (usually 4 metres/13 feet at junctions) to help quantify these distances.

Note the sounds produced by different rates of acceleration and braking, as these can give you a good idea of your vulnerability to traffic when you are cycling. Note, too, how much room different vehicles need in traffic lanes of various widths, and judge whether you could safely share the same lane.

Having obtained a good assessment of general traffic conditions, look at the way cyclists you see ride. What are their skills and faults and, in particular, which of their actions increase or reduce risk? Which cyclists make the best progress through the junction and seem the most confident? How does the treatment given by others vary from one cyclist to another?

If you analyse these situations carefully, your confidence in traffic should be given a boost. It can be worth repeating this exercise at different locations.

Check your understanding:

- ☐ Why do other drivers sometimes act badly towards cyclists?
- ☐ Suggest some general ways to maximise your safety when sharing the roads.
- ☐ What characteristics of traffic should you particularly look out for?
- ☐ Is it possible to detect a safe driver?

Chapter 7

Riding along

This chapter, along with practice in cycling, should help you to:

- ❯ develop your skills in observation and anticipation
- ❯ recognise the critical importance of good positioning in keeping you safe.

② Starting off

The first thing is to decide where to start. In choosing a suitable place you should consider your own safety, that of others whom you might impede, and whether or not from a purely practical point of view it is a good place.

Bad places are close to a junction, on a tight bend or near the crest of a hill, between or immediately after parked vehicles or on steep uphill gradients. Good places are on straight roads where you are clearly visible from behind, and along a side road or drive from which you can turn left. It is worth wheeling your bike a short distance to a better place if there is one.

An important point is to start from where you can see and be seen. This may mean starting from the kerb or road edge, but if there is continuous parking that you cannot avoid, you may have to place your bike further out in the road before mounting. If this is the case, position the bike on or just beyond the line of parked vehicles but where you do not obstruct the traffic flow.

As you mount, apply the brakes, which will prevent you moving before you are ready and will also provide a quick, automatic check every time you start to ride that your brakes are in good order. If possible, sit comfortably on the saddle before you start in order to minimise swerve as you gain balance.

Starting off: hold brakes on while you check behind

Start in a gear lower than your normal riding gear so that you can get away quickly. With derailleur gears you should have anticipated this the last time that you stopped, and changed down. If you didn't do this, you will either have to change down now by lifting and rotating the rear wheel, or you must be prepared for a slow start for which you will require a longer gap in traffic.

Look over your right shoulder for vehicles behind. As a suitable gap appears – you should aim not to interrupt the flow if possible – glance forward in case a pedestrian has suddenly stepped out in front of you or a car is pulling out or turning across your path. If clear, check backwards again, and then, looking ahead, start to move off. As soon as you have achieved good balance, you should glance behind once again so that you are absolutely sure what, if anything, is following, particularly if there are parked vehicles ahead to pass. This multiple checking forward and back should become a habit every time you start off, so that you cannot be caught unawares if something or someone suddenly appears from an unseen nook, however unlikely it might seem.

Generally, there is no need to signal when you start off, unless you have to intercept traffic, but the golden rule with all signalling is to do so if it might help yourself, other traffic or pedestrians without itself putting you at risk.

If there is a continuous stream of traffic, one advantage of a cycle is that you can often start when a wider vehicle would have to wait. This applies when the road is sufficiently wide that in moving off you will not interfere with moving traffic, and there are no parked vehicles immediately ahead.

② Stopping

There are two normal types of stopping: stopping when you want to, and stopping when you have to. There is also emergency stopping, which was covered in Chapter 5 as a collision-avoidance technique.

When it's your choice, always stop in similar places to those from which you can safely start. Keep clear of road junctions, tight bends and other places where you might impede traffic. Stopping very close to a junction is a common error by cyclists, especially when riding in groups, and one which is most frustrating to other road users as well as being hazardous to everyone concerned. If you must stop near a junction to read a sign or map, always do so a few metres back where you will not affect visibility; and always stop at the road edge, not in the middle of the road.

One difference in the law as it applies to cyclists and motorists is that bicycles (without sidecars!) may stop where there are double white lines on the road. Treat this privilege sensibly; it is still unwise to stop on a bend or where other vehicles might be obliged to cross the centre lines.

Before stopping, be sure to change down to one or two gears below your normal riding gear, as this will make restarting easier. If an uphill restart is likely, change down still further. If you are riding downhill on a derailleur-geared bike, you can change gear by pedalling with the brakes applied as you move the gear lever.

Descents apart, you should usually aim to stop without using your brakes, except for their final support as you set a foot down. This will give a smooth and gentle stop, save unnecessary brake wear and can reduce hand fatigue by a noticeable amount on long journeys. Brakeless stopping requires the ability to judge just how far you will freewheel once you stop pedalling, and you should practise this.

If you need to stop where there is continuous parking, or if for some other reason you must stop within the traffic stream where other drivers might not expect this (such as in being the first to give way at a pedestrian crossing), you should give the slowing-down signal as an indication of your intentions. If you then intend to dismount, stop at a gap in parking or as far to the left as is practicable, allowing for the fact that you will need space to dismount. Take care not to pass so close to parked vehicles before you stop that you are vulnerable to a door being opened.

Involuntary stops occur frequently in traffic – at junctions, pedestrian crossings, other controls and in traffic queues. You need to be able to use your brakes quickly. Try to anticipate the likelihood of stopping as much as possible by looking ahead, so that you can change down in gear. Rapid restarting is important in traffic, so if frequent stopping is likely, stay in a low gear.

You should normally stop in the centre of the traffic lane. This puts you in the position where you are most likely to be seen by other drivers and where they will be least likely to pass you unsafely when restarting. However, although the centre-of-the-lane position will make you clearly visible in the inside rear-view mirrors of most cars, you may well be in the blind area of larger vehicles. The solution is to allow extra space in front and to move right (not left) a little, until a mirror is clearly visible. You should never stop closer than 2 metres (nearly 7 feet) behind a preceding vehicle; with larger vehicles increase this distance. If there is any hint of a vehicle reversing, you will then have sufficient room to move out of the way.

 **If you cannot see a mirror of the vehicle in front, that driver will not be able to see you.**

Vary your stopping position, if necessary, so that you are visible in a mirror of the vehicle in front

If you need to interrupt the traffic stream to move to the centre of a lane, look behind for a safe gap and then signal your intention using a brief moving-right signal. Always make sure that there is sufficient room for the manoeuvre before you make it. Make eye contact with a following driver if you can. This shows that the driver has seen you and reassures the driver that you know they are there.

Whenever you stop in traffic, get ready to restart straight away. With one foot on the ground and – at least for short stops – remaining seated on the saddle, get the other foot and pedal in the 'pedal ready' position as quickly as you can. Toe clips and clipless pedals make the changing of pedal positions very much easier.

② On the move

Riding along, particularly in towns, entails a lot more than turning the pedals and manoeuvring at junctions. Not only must cyclists control their own vehicle, they must also continually compensate for the actions of others. Whereas a motorist whose concentration wanders may suffer nothing more than a dented car, a cyclist is much more at risk of personal injury and needs to be the most vigilant driver on the road. Although you should not hesitate to take your priority of passage when this applies, you should always act on the assumption that others will not respect it. Keeping relaxed but alert will enable you to deal best with any situation that occurs.

Observation, anticipation and positioning (discussed below), are the most essential skills to develop in traffic. After these comes conservation of momentum: when a cyclist provides all of the motive power from personal effort, it is a pity to waste it needlessly. The principle is to keep your momentum going by being sufficiently aware of conditions ahead that you can compensate for them by changing speed, rather than by stopping and restarting. Usually this will mean slowing down, but sometimes a burst of acceleration can serve the purpose instead. Because a cyclist does not usually impede the passage of other vehicles, it is possible to determine your own pace more easily than other drivers, who are often subject to pressure to keep up with the traffic flow.

The principle of maintaining momentum leads to two related considerations:

▶ You should use your brakes as little as possible. Not only does their use waste valuable pedalling effort, but cycle brakes do not perform as well as those of other vehicles. It is better to use your brakes only when essential.

▶ If you need to slow down because of traffic conditions ahead, you should either cease pedalling completely or change to a lower gear. It will usually be less tiring, particularly on longer journeys, to use a lower gear than to alter your cadence, and there is the added advantage that you will be better prepared for stopping and restarting should it prove necessary.

② Observation and anticipation

Thinking ahead and planning every move is the hallmark of a skilled cyclist. For this, good observation is essential. If you cannot see and read exactly what is going on – in front, to your sides and behind – it will be impossible for you to plan the safest and fastest manoeuvre in any given situation. It is not enough to see every detail; you must also assess what you see and anticipate what might follow, and then form a riding plan accordingly. For a cyclist, observation is not only about seeing; it is also about hearing. Many vital clues to the traffic situation are most easily assimilated by the ears.

The purpose of observation is to give you time to react to any actual or potential hazard. Because of this need for reaction time, the degree of concentration necessary is proportional to both the complexity of the traffic situation and its surroundings and the speed of traffic. Although you should always adjust your speed so that you can adequately observe the conditions around you, as a cyclist the level of concentration necessary will usually depend more on the speed of the other vehicles than on that of your own. You should realise, however, that as your speed increases you will need to concentrate further ahead and the foreground will become less distinct. You may also need a greater stopping distance for a given speed than a motor vehicle.

Local knowledge can help considerably in anticipating problems, but equally, familiarity can easily lead to a sense of false security. Always be guided by the prevailing conditions.

Observing traffic and people

While riding along, look ahead as far as possible, but try to concentrate on an area up to two or three vehicles ahead and spanning the full road width. Observe the obvious: vehicles turning into and from your road; the approach of junctions; parked vehicles and traffic queues. Note other drivers' signals, but never rely on them! Always wait for supporting evidence such as a reduction in speed or a change in direction.

Of equal importance, you should observe the small details which give such valuable clues to the less obvious:

▶ The presence of people in a parked car – a door might be opened or the car might move off.

▶ Exhaust fumes coming from a stationary vehicle – an even more likely sign of imminent departure.

▶ A bus stop ahead – will the bus behind overtake and then pull in?

▶ Children playing at the roadside – a child or a ball might come into the road.

Near junctions, keep an eye on the wheels of vehicles in front – many drivers do not signal turns. Likewise, drivers in side roads and at roundabouts often take advantage of the approach of a cyclist to enter the traffic stream, with little appreciation of the speed of the cyclist. Again, check for wheel movements. Sometimes a stern glance in their direction is all that is necessary to make an encroaching driver respect your right of way, but this is an acquired art, to be used only if you still have the ability to get yourself out of trouble.

Near shops be wary of delivery vans – the driver may be concentrating on unloading and not see you. Likewise, the attention of the driver of a crowded car might be distracted, while dogs in vehicles are often a menace to a

Shopping streets are busy places and there's a lot to look out for. Use positioning to advantage to give yourself time for these checks.

driver's concentration. Shadows on the road, reflections in shop windows and vehicle lights at night can all give important clues of potential hazards. Don't keep your eyes *only* on the road ahead!

From time to time – and at the approach to any junction on your side of the road – it is important to glance over your shoulder so that you know what's happening behind you. Note what types of vehicle are following (cars, vans or lorries), how far behind the first one is and approximately how fast it is going.

Before looking behind, at this or any other time, always ensure that it is safe to do so. Check first that you are not so close to a vehicle in front that you would ride into it if it stopped suddenly, and that no one is about to cross your path. When looking behind, it is also important that your actions are not misinterpreted by others. Some drivers seem to think that because a cyclist has looked behind and seen them, they may immediately overtake. All too often the opposite is true, for the cyclist has looked behind as there is a hazard ahead. There are two possible responses to this:

▶ If conditions permit a longer look back, look the driver full in the face and establish eye contact. This will often cause the driver to be more careful.

▶ Otherwise, it is useful to acquire the knack of looking behind discreetly, so that you can obtain the information you need without making it obvious that you have seen a following driver. To do this, move your eyes to the extreme but your head as little as possible.

Risk from impatient drivers can be minimised by closely watching their actions and adopting a prominent position

Rearward observation is usefully complemented by listening, especially in quieter traffic conditions. Learn to differentiate between normal sounds and those that warrant your attention. A common hazard at junctions is for a driver to overtake a cyclist and then to turn left sharply across the cyclist's path; another frequent problem occurs when a driver decides to overtake and then pulls in to stop. By detecting the change in pitch of a car's engine as the driver uses the accelerator, brakes, or changes gear, you may gain an important warning that these manoeuvres might occur, at a time when it is still safe to take compensatory action.

Look, too, at oncoming traffic. Is it going to turn across your path or encroach upon your space by overtaking? Again, wheel movements are more reliable indicators of actions than signals. Take particular care of the driver who has just given way to a car immediately ahead of you – that driver may restart without noticing you. Take heed, also, that the greatest hazard is not always the most obvious one. For example, the second driver emerging from a side road may just follow the first without adequately looking in your direction.

Look at the pedestrians you approach, particularly children who may suddenly rush across the road. Are dogs on a lead and under control, or are they boisterous and likely to act unpredictably? Other cyclists, especially children, can also create problems.

Roads and their surfaces

The actions of other people are not the only things to observe. Roads themselves require attention. The position of trees, hedges and other side features can enable you to judge more easily the severity of bends and gradients. If the most distant point that you can see along a verge on either side of the road remains fixed, an approaching bend or hill is severe. If the point changes as you progress along the road, the bend or hill is more gradual. Take advantage of every opportunity to observe your surroundings. Breaks in hedges, for example, can sometimes give you a better view down a side road some way before a junction than it may be possible to obtain closer to it. The movement and lights of other vehicles might also help.

Traffic signs are important aids to observation and it is important that you understand the meaning of signs and markings. Even those which are not directly applicable to cyclists may give useful information about the way motorists might behave, and at night, on unlit roads, signs are particularly useful as warnings of what is coming. Although a cyclist will generally have more time to react to a sign than a motorist, you should nevertheless quickly observe and understand it, and then look beyond for the potential hazard. It is the message that is important, not the sign!

Cyclists and the riders of other two-wheeled vehicles need to be particularly careful in scrutinising the condition of the road surface ahead. The presence of potholes and other surface irregularities is an obvious hazard, and you will need advance warning in order to avoid them. But learn, too, to identify the different surface coverings which can give trouble: examples include snow, ice, oil, mud, loose stones, gravel and wet leaves. Oil and diesel fuel are often present on the road at the approach to other hazards; they are visible on dry roads, but often not when wet, although diesel's distinctive smell can be a useful clue. Similarly, ice can be very hard to recognise in advance, and extra care needs to be taken when its presence is at all likely. Some surface types themselves create problems. Stone setts, metal studs and many types of blockwork require care. Wooden surfaces can be very slippery. Concrete can hold surface water, and all these surfaces can trap ice long after it has disappeared elsewhere and in a way that cannot be seen easily.

Take note, too, of the weather. Wind not only affects cyclists but also high-sided vehicles and caravans. Spray thrown up by passing cars can affect your braking performance, even if it is not raining.

Responding to hazards

Having identified any hazard, the decision as to what you should do about it depends upon what can be seen, what can't and the circumstances that might reasonably be expected to develop. It is important not to react just to what you have seen and not to rush into any situation just because the driver in front does. Frequently, too, you will meet more than one hazard at a time, which may be related or quite independent of one another. You must prioritise the hazards on the basis of their significance, in order to direct your attention to best advantage.

What do you observe?

What should you notice cycling along these roads, what might the
implications be and how should you respond? Answers on next page.

Answers to observation quiz

Upper picture

▶ Pedestrian crossing – will the lights change? Check traffic behind, move to the primary riding position and keep fingers on brakes.

▶ Children waiting at crossing – will they step into the road prematurely? Leave plenty of space.

▶ Poor road surfaces with both longitudinal and transverse trenches. Look out for vertical edges and effect on bike control. Ride clear of worst defects – nominally using the primary riding position will give you space to manoeuvre in traffic.

▶ Parked cars ahead – move out to pass. Stay in primary riding position from the crossing and watch out for opening doors.

▶ Car emerging from side road – will it encroach on your path? Be ready to respond to its movements.

▶ Traffic queuing ahead – junction or bend in road ahead (notice building line). Insufficient space and visibility to filter past: join end of queue and stay in primary riding position.

Lower picture

▶ Roundabout ahead. Check traffic behind, move to primary riding position in centre of tarmac lane (keep clear of the edge blockwork, which could affect steering control). Signal left or right if you are not going straight ahead.

▶ Be prepared for ramp up to roundabout (indicated by chevron markings). The road surface is a little uneven at the top – cross where it minimises discomfort.

▶ White car is turning right across your path – give way. Keep track of where the car behind it goes (it is not yet signalling but you cannot assume it will go straight ahead). Scan continually all the entry roads and watch, too, for pedestrian movements.

▶ Change down in gear and reduce speed to arrive at the roundabout when there is a gap in traffic, if possible. If not, you must stop and wait until a suitable gap arrives.

▶ Roundabout has a textured surface around its centre, the nature of which is not yet distinct. Keep away from this in case it affects bike control but take heed that other drivers seem to be cutting across.

▶ Anticipate possibility of edge blockwork on the exit you intend to take, similar to that on this road. Keep away from it, if present.

▶ Parked cars on the far side of the roundabout – keep to the primary riding position at least until these have been passed.

▶ Someone has just started to cross the road ahead, behind the oncoming cars. Be ready to cooperate.

The responses to many hazards will be found elsewhere in this guide, but there will always be some situations where reactions cannot be learnt in advance. You should realise that, as you learn, mistakes may be made. It is therefore essential that all your decisions have a sufficient margin for error.

② Positioning

It has already been said that positioning is one of the most important traffic skills for a cyclist to acquire, yet it is precisely here that most cyclists perform badly. Many people fail to position themselves properly because of their fear of traffic yet, ironically, it is this very fear that probably puts them most at risk.

There are two basic objectives of proper road positioning:

▶ To increase your margin of safety by riding where you can obtain the best view, where you can best be seen by others and your movements predicted, and where you may deter movements by others which could increase risk to yourself.

▶ To allow you to ride as direct a route as possible, conserving your energy and making control of the bicycle as simple as possible.

Good road positioning is _not_ about keeping you out of the path of other traffic as much as possible.

Contrary to popular belief, keeping away from traffic is not always the best way to maximise your safety. Many people dislike riding in close proximity to other traffic because of a fear of being hit from behind. In fact, this type of collision is one of the least likely and sometimes the result of the cyclist swerving carelessly into traffic. You should not worry about rear hits if you cycle competently.

On the other hand, riding where other drivers can see you clearly is likely to reduce your chances of having one of the much more common types of collision, which occur during turning or crossing manoeuvres. More collisions happen because drivers cannot see a cyclist or cannot anticipate the actions of the cyclist than because they do see but fail to take notice.

Positioning – A key skill for both adults and children

Of all cycling skills, road positioning is probably the most important, for it is through their position on the road that cyclists can exert the greatest influence on their safety in traffic.

Children should learn to position in the same way as adults. The risks introduced by poor positioning are the same irrespective of age, and so are the solutions.

An important rule of road sharing is that no one should unnecessarily impede the passage of anyone else. However, you are quite justified in restricting the movements of other vehicles where this is important in protecting yourself, and you should not hesitate to do so when necessary.

Motorists primarily give attention to that part of the road where there is risk to themselves: they are not nearly so good at noticing anything outside their path. This zone of maximum surveillance is often very narrow, especially at higher speeds – it does not extend to much more than the moving traffic lane that the driver is following, plus the moving traffic lanes that are most likely to conflict with the driver's own movement. For you to be safest as a cyclist, you must normally ride within this zone of maximum surveillance, not outside it.

The standard riding positions

To understand positioning, you must understand the concept of a moving traffic lane – that part of the carriageway along which through traffic is moving *at the present time*. It is a dynamic concept, changing continually with place and traffic conditions. A moving traffic lane meanders past parked vehicles and other obstructions, and does not necessarily coincide with any markings on the surface. On a free-flowing road where markings are present, the moving traffic lanes are typically centred on the marked lanes, but do not embrace their full width. The moving traffic lane itself also varies a little in width, according to the types of vehicle present at the time.

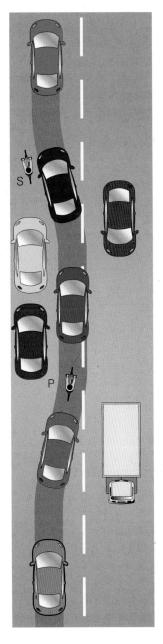

Away from junctions you should ride in one of two standard positions (see Figure 7.1), according to circumstances. The **primary riding position** is in the centre of the leftmost moving traffic lane for the direction in which you wish to travel. Here you will be well within the zone of maximum surveillance of both following drivers and those who might cross your path, and you will have the best two-way visibility of side roads and other features along the road. The road surface will usually be flatter here than it is nearer the edge, with fewer potholes and other problems, and this will afford easier control of your cycle. You should be able to maintain the straightest and fastest course without the need to deviate at side roads.

It is often the best position, too, on roads where there is no following traffic and on multi-lane roads where the traffic flow is light.

Because the primary riding position can result in some inconvenience to following drivers, it is reasonable to ride further to the left when this could help others, *so long as your own safety is not thereby impaired*. At these times you should adopt the **secondary riding position**, which is about 1 metre (3 feet) to the left of the moving traffic lane if the road is wide, but not closer

Figure 7.1 *Standard riding positions*

The moving traffic lane (shaded) meanders to pass the parked vehicles. Cyclist P is adopting the primary riding position, cyclist S the secondary riding position.

than 0.5 metre (1.5 feet) to the edge of any road. Riding closer to the edge will leave you with no room for manoeuvre in the event of an emergency, while increasing the need to make unpredictable movements which could lead to a crash. You might also have to endure the discomfort and possible hazard of drain covers, edge damage and the debris which tends to collect at the side of the road – and there is no reason why you should have a less comfortable journey than anyone else. Riding too close to the edge will also make you harder to see by drivers coming out of side roads and drives.

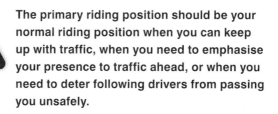

The primary riding position should be your normal riding position when you can keep up with traffic, when you need to emphasise your presence to traffic ahead, or when you need to deter following drivers from passing you unsafely.

Follow the traffic, not the edge of the road

The secondary riding position is always relative to the moving traffic lane, not the road edge. Riding further left, even if there is space, will reduce your ability to be seen by other drivers and the notice they will take of you.

Only on long stretches of road where there are no side roads, drives or other entrances and you are travelling slowly (perhaps up a hill) should you allow yourself to ride further to the left than the secondary riding position, but always keep at least 0.5 metre (1.5 feet) from the edge. Conversely, if you are travelling quickly, keep further out.

On lightly trafficked roads where you use the primary riding position, keep aware of conditions behind you, using both eyes and ears. Always check behind when you see oncoming traffic, a bend or other hazard ahead. As soon as you sense a following vehicle, plan your move to the secondary position, so long as it is safe to do so. You should make your move neither too early nor too late, but gradually, in a way that causes no inconvenience to the other driver or to yourself. Because the move is done gradually and the position change is usually small, signalling is not necessary.

On busy roads, it will be necessary to keep to the secondary riding position most of the time. There is no point in oscillating back and forth, as this will be more tiring for you and might confuse others. However, there are many occasions, even on busy roads, when you should use the primary position in order to benefit from the increased margin of safety that it provides.

Change to the primary riding position when the road surface near the edge is bad, perhaps because of a poorly reinstated trench. Motorists are often less aware of surface conditions and may not appreciate the real hazard or discomfort these can cause for cyclists, so this change of position will need to be signalled well and made carefully. Where a really bad surface extends well into the road, move further out still, but try not to allow sufficient room on your left for anyone to pass.

You should use the primary riding position when riding on narrow or winding roads and at other types of narrowing (such as in traffic calming schemes)

Figure 7.2 *Improving visibility on tight left-hand bends*

A is the additional angle of forward vision you get from moving towards the centre of the road.

where overtaking could be unsafe. When you ride in this position, looking back lets a following driver know that you are aware of their presence and may encourage them to cooperate. However, where such conditions persist, as on some country lanes, do try to let traffic pass as soon as a suitable opportunity occurs, even if this requires you to slow down a little. You can never be sure whether a driver behind is becoming impatient and might take a chance when it is the least safe for you.

On tight left-hand bends, moving to the primary riding position will not only discourage unsafe overtaking, but can also improve both your forward visibility and your chances of being seen by drivers from both behind and ahead (Figure 7.2). Conversely, on right-hand bends the secondary position may improve visibility if there is little likelihood of you being passed. A further advantage of changing position at bends is that this can help to reduce the severity of the bend and make bike control easier.

Exceptions to the advice on positioning

Further situations where a particular position should be adopted will be described in subsequent sections of this guide. There is, however, one important general exception to the rules for holding the primary riding position – when there is a significantly increased risk of being hit from behind. Bad visibility conditions such as fog, heavy mist or fine, persistent rain significantly increase the risk. Late evening, especially on country roads, is another time to observe caution: drivers who have been drinking cannot be relied upon to control their vehicles safely. At each of these times, it is prudent to keep further left and to take special care near junctions.

You may also find it difficult to move to or maintain the primary riding position along narrow main roads where traffic is fast and continuous. Your only option here is to ride as best you can and reduce speed at hazards if you cannot move out. At all times, make sure you have good control of your bike by grasping the handlebar firmly, but you may get more clearance from traffic if you do not steer too straight a course.

② Cycle lanes

As you will read in Chapter 13, the presence of cycle lanes can complicate the traffic situation and increase risk for cyclists. Safe cycling requires cyclists to keep close to the moving traffic lane where they are easily seen by other drivers. Cycle lanes, however, remain inflexibly fixed adjacent to the kerb irrespective of traffic conditions. Cyclists who keep within them can easily escape the notice of drivers from both behind and ahead.

On any multi-lane road, drivers make use of the full width of the lane in which they are travelling, expecting traffic in adjacent lanes to keep out of their path. Their speed is also determined primarily by traffic conditions in their own lane and not to their side. It is a common experience that cyclists are often overtaken closer and faster in cycle lanes than would be the case if they were sharing space with other traffic.

In the UK, there is no legal obligation on cyclists to use cycle lanes and you should do so only where it is safe and to your advantage. As far as you can, ignore the presence of a cycle lane in determining the best position to ride on the road, but be extra careful if you decide to ride outside it, as some drivers may resent this. All movements out of a cycle lane require the same lane-changing technique that is applicable to multi-lane roads of any kind (see Chapter 9).

Forward clearance

In normal moving traffic a cyclist does not have to worry too much about keeping clear of vehicles in front, but in towns and other places where traffic speeds are low it is a necessary consideration. Getting too close to the back of another vehicle creates two problems. You may be less visible to the driver (for example, you may not be visible in mirrors), and you will be very vulnerable if the driver suddenly puts on the brakes. In addition, the closer you are to the vehicle in front, the less you will be able to see beyond it (Figure 7.3).

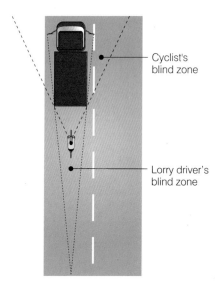

Cyclist's blind zone

Lorry driver's blind zone

A good clearance to maintain is about 2 metres (nearly 7 feet) for every 5 km/h or so (3 mph), with an absolute minimum of 3 metres (10 feet). Holding the primary riding position will deter overtaking into this space by anyone behind, but move right of this if necessary to be visible in the mirror of the vehicle in front.

Figure 7.3 *Forward clearance*

Riding too close to a vehicle in front reduces your visibility, and others' visibility of you.

Check your understanding:

☐ What should you ensure if you stop in traffic behind another vehicle?

☐ What are good ways to maintain your momentum?

☐ Describe some of the key things to look out for as you ride along.

☐ What are the objectives of good positioning?

☐ When should you adopt the primary riding position?

Chapter 8
Everyday movements

This chapter, along with practice in cycling, should help you to:

- ➔ understand when and how to signal
- ➔ overtake other vehicles and be prepared when others overtake you
- ➔ recognise the serious hazards posed by long vehicles
- ➔ carry out safely left and right turns from and into ordinary roads
- ➔ use traffic signals and advanced stop lines.

The movements and strategies described in this chapter are the basic building blocks of cycling that should be known by anyone who cycles. Learn them well, for they will make your cycling safer, easier and more enjoyable.

② Signalling in traffic

Many of the movements you make on the road have the potential to conflict with or inconvenience other road users. Signalling is used to communicate with others in a standard way, so that they are aware of what you intend to do. A signal is not an instruction to anyone else, only a warning of the movement you wish to make. It conveys no right of way, and you should be quite sure that a movement is safe to make, without unduly inconveniencing anyone, before carrying it out. For this reason, a signal should always be preceded by looking about you, particularly behind.

There are two kinds of signal applicable to cyclists: safety signals and courtesy signals. Safety signals should always be carried out and are used in situations where you cross the path of other traffic (or pedestrians) and you or others are thus vulnerable to any misunderstanding about what you intend to do. If you cannot give a safety signal because this in itself might adversely affect control of your machine (such as in descending a very steep hill when you need both hands on the brakes), you should delay manoeuvring until you are sure there will be no conflict. Unless otherwise stated, references in this guide to signalling refer to safety signals.

Courtesy signals cater for those circumstances when, alas, signalling can impair rather than enhance your safety. For example, due to the behaviour of a significant minority of drivers, signalling a left turn is not always as desirable for a cyclist as it should be. Some drivers, themselves turning left, take any indication that a cyclist ahead of them is doing likewise as an invitation to overtake at the junction. In so doing it is common for them to cut across the cyclist's path in an unsafe manner. Even the primary riding position does not protect a cyclist completely against this behaviour. With courtesy signals you must use discretion: be courteous to others and signal if you can, but do not do so if it might compromise your own safety.

Signals should always be clear and unambiguous. For example, if you signal right to overtake parked cars close to where there is a right turn, your signal might be interpreted as an intention to turn right by someone a little further on who then decides to pull out in front of you. Very often the timing and duration of signals can be used to minimise ambiguity.

The hand signals you should use when cycling are illustrated in Figure 5.5. You will find additional notes concerning the use of signals by cyclists in other sections of this guide. The general principle, however, is to signal when, and for as long as, a signal can convey useful information to another road user, not forgetting pedestrians. You should therefore signal before making an unpredictable movement and maintain this until all those who need to know have understood your intentions. You can usually tell by their subsequent actions or by their expression when you look directly at them. Then you may withdraw the signal to complete the manoeuvre as quickly as possible. You should always return both hands to the handlebar before making a turn in order to be in complete control of your cycle in the event of any problem with the surface.

> **Communicate by looking**
>
> Giving hand signals is only one way of communicating with other road users. Looking directly at drivers, when this is possible, is another important way to establish understanding and cooperation.

② Overtaking

Overtaking is a manoeuvre you will have to use often, and one for which correct positioning is important. In most cases, cyclists only overtake stationary vehicles and other kerbside obstructions, but there are always potential hazards, such as a door opening into your path or a vehicle moving off as you pass.

Choosing a sufficient gap in traffic and keeping well clear of vehicles you pass are key skills in overtaking

Start to prepare as soon as you first see a need to overtake by keeping track of the progress of vehicles following you, so that you are always aware of the space available. Well in advance – as much as 100 metres (about 330 feet) on free-flowing roads – take the first opportunity to move smoothly to the overtaking position, which is at least 1.5 metres (5 feet) clear of a parked car (in case a door is thrown open) but further out from a lorry or bus. Moving out should not be difficult, as drivers behind you will be making the same movement. Signal right at the start of the manoeuvre if there is another vehicle close behind, but often signalling is not necessary when overtaking within the same traffic lane.

As you close in on a parked vehicle, be alert for tell-tale signs of imminent movement, such as exhaust fumes or occupants visible through a window. Check too that there does not remain space to your right where you could be overtaken, but not safely; move further out if necessary.

If you do not have to cross a marked traffic lane in order to overtake, you will have right of way over the vehicles following you, although you should take care that this is respected. On the other hand, if it is necessary to cross a lane marking to overtake, you must give way to traffic already in the second lane before entering it. This may require you to slow down a little until a suitable gap arrives (change down in gear and keep looking behind), or even to stop. For busy roads, Chapter 9 will describe how to negotiate your way into the traffic stream.

If there are a number of stationary vehicles to pass, maintain a straight line past all of them, keeping at least 1.5 metres (5 feet) from any. Don't weave back and forth, and do not move left if there is only a short gap in parking. Drivers may take advantage of any apparent opportunity for them to pass, and you could have difficulty moving back. You will also be moving out of their principal area of surveillance and putting yourself more at risk; remember that parked cars can easily mask a cyclist who is out of the moving traffic lane. Try not to worry if keeping to the lane seems to impede following traffic – it is not safe for it to pass.

If there is a longer gap in parking – about 30 metres (100 feet or so) or more – move to the secondary riding position (just left of the moving traffic lane) if this would allow others to pass you safely, but make sure that you move out again well before the next parked vehicle. Of course, where the moving traffic lane meanders, you should follow it.

When overtaking, look out especially for pedestrians, children, cats and dogs that might move out between parked vehicles. This is another reason for not getting too close. High-sided vehicles pose a particular problem in this respect, as you will not be able to see over them. When passing such a vehicle, move further out than usual, slacken speed and be ready to brake. Take similar precautions near obvious attractors of children, such as ice-cream vans and school buses.

If a driver starts to pull out in front of you, slow to let the driver go if possible, but if it is too late to do this, accelerate to get past, steering right. However, if a driver is only signalling an intention to pull out, it is usually better for a cyclist not to give way. Do, however, move as far away as you can and keep an eye on the movement of the vehicle's front wheels.

Sometimes your side of the road will be largely or completely blocked. The most difficult situation is when a cycle could pass a stopped vehicle without straddling the centre line, but a car couldn't. Under these circumstances the driver of the obstructing vehicle (a bus at a stop, for example) might not expect anyone to be able to pass and could take insufficient care when restarting.

If your side of the road is completely blocked, it will be necessary to cross the centre line in order to overtake. Be sure that there is nothing coming in the opposite direction before proceeding. It is better not to overtake a long vehicle in this way if it has only stopped temporarily.

There are times when cyclists need to overtake moving vehicles – other cyclists, tractors, milk floats, even slow cars and lorries. Before doing so, be quite sure that overtaking is really necessary. There is little point overtaking a slow truck near the top of a hill if it will soon speed up and then overtake you!

Also, ensure that you have both sufficient speed to overtake, and sufficient safe distance in which to do so. A cyclist's ability to accelerate is limited, and even a gentle hill can make all the difference. Always look ahead of the vehicle to be overtaken for bends, obstructions and other hazards – overtaking will often take longer than you think.

Once you have decided to overtake, adopt the normal overtaking procedure, ensuring that the driver of any vehicle to be overtaken can see you in a mirror. If that vehicle speeds up as you pass – it should ease off to let you by – slip back. Until you have passed half the length of the vehicle, you can change your mind if necessary and slip back quite easily. After that, you should normally continue, particularly if you are being followed by someone else. Of course if some new hazard appears, easing back may still be the best reaction.

If there was only a small difference in speed between yourself and the other vehicle, do not pull in too quickly after overtaking. The sideways movement will reduce your forward speed and you could then be hit from behind.

Never overtake a moving vehicle on the left side within the same traffic lane.

Being overtaken

Because other drivers often do not appreciate the risk that they can present to a cyclist when overtaking, it is necessary for a cyclist to be alert to this problem. The use of positioning to deter overtaking when it is not safe has already been described, and by adopting the recommended riding positions you will leave yourself room for manoeuvre if someone passes too close. It can also be useful to look back at a vehicle that is about to overtake as this can encourage the driver to pass more slowly and to leave more room.

Even if you are overtaken very close with no escape room, you are unlikely to be hit so long as you maintain a straight course. This primarily requires a cool and confident approach to your cycling.

High-sided vehicles create special hazards when overtaking, particularly when it is windy. As they pass you they may provide a break from the wind, but this is followed by eddy currents which can easily force a cyclist off course and cause a spill. The suction effect of large vehicles can be considerable. To minimise the problems, pedal to increase your stability as you are passed, but do so with the brakes applied if necessary in order to keep your speed down. Hold the handlebar firmly, ready to resist any change of direction, and crouch low. Strong crosswinds can deflect a high vehicle across the road significantly, and this can create a hazard for all other road users.

Caravans towed by cars can be similar in their effect to long and high-sided vehicles. Their drivers – who are frequently much less experienced than lorry drivers – often only allow for a car's width when overtaking. Treat caravans with caution, and be alert for extension mirrors protruding from the side of the car.

The greatest risk to a cyclist from overtaking comes not from traffic behind, but from ahead. When a cyclist is travelling alone on one side of a road, some oncoming drivers use the opportunity to overtake vehicles ahead of them, encroaching upon the cyclist's path. If such an overtaking procedure starts when you are close, there is little you can do about it except to keep left and hold on firmly. However, the manoeuvre will often commence well ahead, perhaps because you haven't been seen. Here, with care, you can take deterrent action. After ensuring that there really is no one behind you, pull out further right, but be ready to go quickly left. It can take some nerve to steer towards an oncoming car and to hold this position for long. More often than not, the oncoming driver will soon realise that you are there and that there is a potential risk, and will move in. However, if the driver is intent on holding course, go left in good time and hold on tight.

Long vehicles

Long vehicles, including buses and cars towing trailers and caravans, create serious dangers for cyclists during overtaking and turning manoeuvres. Collisions with these vehicles are too often fatal. You should exercise the utmost caution when cycling near to a long vehicle and leave nothing to chance.

Figure 8.1
*Turning path of a
long vehicle at a
road junction*

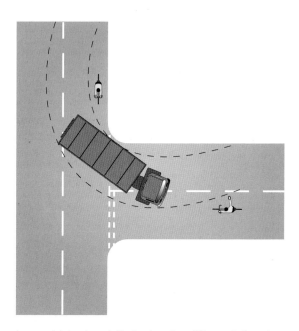

Risk is greatest when long vehicles turn left at a junction (Figure 8.1) and on left-hand bends. In both cases the middle of the vehicle moves further left than its ends, and the driver will need to steer well to the right to avoid colliding with an adjacent cyclist. However, the driver of a long vehicle may be unable to detect a cyclist alongside their vehicle. On an articulated lorry the driver's side mirrors turn with the cab, not with the trailer, and the two parts of the lorry will be at different angles during a turn. The driver will not be able to see along the sides of their trailer in the mirrors.

If you see a long vehicle coming up behind on the approach to a left turn or a bend, you can encourage the driver either to give you more room or to wait until it is safer to overtake by moving further out yourself. Signal right briefly before doing so.

If it is you that is coming up behind a long vehicle ahead, be certain not to put yourself in a position where you could be at risk from that vehicle moving. Stop and wait behind.

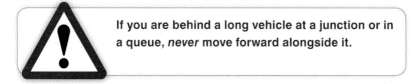

If you are behind a long vehicle at a junction or in a queue, *never* move forward alongside it.

Take care, too, if you are leaving a road into which a long vehicle is turning in the opposite direction, for it may well swing over your side of the road (Figure 8.1).

There can be hazards with being overtaken by a long vehicle even on straight roads as sometimes drivers do not allow adequately for the speed of a cyclist. The front of a long vehicle may pass with plenty of clearance, but the tail end of a trailer can swing back to the left too soon and threaten a cyclist who has progressed further than was anticipated. This is a particular problem on busy, narrow roads when overtaking takes place during relatively short gaps in oncoming traffic. To help the situation, it is wise for a cyclist to ease off pedalling when being overtaken by a long vehicle, and to be ready to brake if necessary in order to keep clear of the rear end.

Major and minor roads

The descriptions of manoeuvres that follow use the terms major and minor to describe roads at junctions.

A major road is the through road as depicted by the road markings at the junction, and on which traffic normally has priority. It is not necessarily a main road or a busy road.

A minor road is any other road that intersects with the major road and from which the exit is controlled by give-way or stop signs or markings. Traffic leaving a minor road does not have right of way and must wait until there is a gap in traffic and it is safe before entering the major road.

② Passing side roads

When approaching a minor road or driveway on your side of a through road, always look as far as possible into that road to check for vehicles at or approaching the junction. Do this as early as you can. Look behind, too, to see if a following vehicle might be turning left. If you are absolutely sure that there is no hazard, you can maintain your current position. But if you are unsure – perhaps because visibility is not good – or if there is any vehicle which could cut across your path as you approach, move to the primary riding position until the junction is passed.

Never assume that, just because a vehicle has stopped, it will remain stationary, and in particular, don't trust drivers who approach a junction fast and then brake fiercely – move out!

Keep clear of side roads, especially if a vehicle is waiting or approaching

The primary riding position will:

- ▶ maximise the chances of you being seen and of your speed being appreciated
- ▶ improve your own visibility of conditions ahead
- ▶ provide an enhanced zone of safety should a driver cut across your path
- ▶ help to dissuade a following driver from overtaking and then turning left.

It is, of course, necessary to make the movement from secondary to primary position with care. Don't wait until you are at the junction – start to prepare the move as soon as you see a hazard or suspect that conditions might make a decision difficult. Check behind for a sufficient gap in traffic, signal right briefly if anyone is close, and then change position. So long as your secondary position was correct, the relatively small movement to the right that is necessary should not be difficult. Indeed, in most circumstances, if you start to move early, the deviation will be so slight that neither a gap in traffic nor signalling will be needed.

Side roads crossed by cycle lanes

If there is a cycle lane marked across the mouth of a side road, always ignore it. Such lanes pass through the very place where risk of collision is greatest and where cyclists are least able to protect themselves. You should never allow your safety to depend upon another driver obeying the rules.

Ride as you would if the cycle lane were not present. If there is a vehicle approaching the junction or you are not sure, keep well away from the give-way lines.

② Turning left off a major road

The left turn from a major road into a minor road is the simplest turning manoeuvre for a cyclist to make, but there are still consequences to be considered.

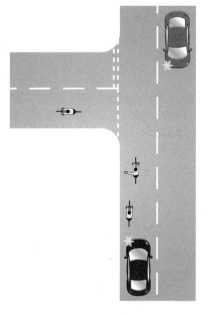

Figure 8.2 *Turning left off a major road*

If you need to deter overtaking, and always where there is a turning lane, turn left from the primary riding position.

Where a turning lane is bounded by kerbs on both sides, use the primary riding position

If visibility is good in all directions and you know that you will neither have to stop at the junction nor be followed by any other vehicle turning left, you can turn left maintaining a secondary riding position, if that is how you approached the junction. In all other circumstances, you should first adopt the primary riding position, however odd it may seem to move right in order to turn left (Figure 8.2).

It is a common mistake for cyclists to keep too far left at all turns.

Before you turn, check that another cyclist or a motorcyclist is not coming up close behind you and with whom your turn might conflict if they try to come between you and the kerb. Glance behind over your left shoulder to be sure.

As you turn, look out for other vehicles which may cross your path from the right. Normally you will have the right of way, but at some turns where there is a specific turning lane, road markings give priority to the right, and you must heed this. Check for pedestrians crossing the road and give way to them if you can (but see Chapter 10). Then look into the road into which you are turning to check for parked cars or anything else on the left to be passed. If you will need to overtake, start to move to the right straight away to pass in one smooth movement. You should not allow other drivers to pass you in the same traffic lane until you are sure that it is safe for them to do so.

As mentioned previously, the left-turn signal should usually be considered a courtesy signal. If someone else could conflict with your movement, either do not signal (but take extra care if there are pedestrians), or signal left only immediately before you turn and when it is unlikely to increase risk to yourself. However, if there is a cyclist or motorcyclist behind with whom you might conflict, the left-turn signal becomes a safety signal and should be given as early as is necessary to check their movement.

If there is a separate left-turn lane at a junction, use it, but always ride in the primary riding position within it to deter overtaking. If there is an island at the junction between a single turning lane and the rest of the carriageway, take particular care that you are not squeezed at the point where the island starts. Again, the primary riding position will give you room for manoeuvre, while a brief moving-right signal at the approach to the island can discourage a driver from overtaking and cutting in front.

② ③ Going ahead at junctions

This section is about crossing more important junctions when you are travelling on a major road and there is a significant amount of crossing or turning traffic. Passing minor side roads was described previously in this chapter, and how to go ahead from a minor road will be described later.

You should always adopt the primary riding position through junctions of this kind and maintain it until you leave and it is safe for others to pass (see Figure 8.3). Although you should keep yourself aware of the complete traffic situation throughout the manoeuvre, your attention at the approach to an important junction should be particularly concerned with ensuring that others do not overtake and then cut in front of you to turn left.

Sometimes a short moving-right signal can be useful for emphasising to following drivers that you are exercising your priority to go ahead, particularly where a left deceleration lane (i.e. one which is built out from the main carriageway) is provided. Although it is best not to confuse others if at all possible, giving a moving-right signal, even though you are not intending to go right, can encourage drivers to take more care than might otherwise be the case. As in all cases, you must ride to suit the circumstances and to ensure your own safety.

As you get closer to the junction, concern yourself first with traffic crossing or turning right across your path, and then with vehicles pulling out from the left. If at all possible, take the priority which is yours and, by changing your position or signalling or both, discourage others from usurping it. However, always ensure that you leave yourself a sufficient margin of safety to allow

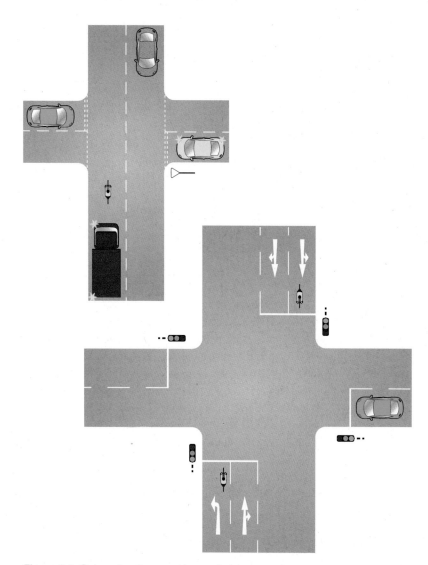

Figure 8.3 *Going ahead on a major road at crossroads*

If you use a left-turn lane to go ahead, move to its right side; otherwise, adopt the primary riding position.

for the aggressive driver who flouts all the rules, and try to avoid making any movement too suddenly. Take extra care if you are masked from any drivers by turning traffic or congestion and always keep your fingers over the brakes.

> **An important general rule for junctions is to regard any give-way or stop markings on a road which intersects with the one you are on as indicating a zone of heightened risk, for it is at these places that most collisions between cycles and motor vehicles take place. Always give a wide berth to give-way and stop markings.**

If there is a left-turn lane which, because of its design, is unlikely to be used other than by traffic turning left, you should keep out of it when intending to go ahead and use the left-hand ahead lane. Maintaining the primary riding position should avoid any ambiguity as to where you are going. Indeed, it is always best to use the appropriately marked lane for going ahead if this is possible, but there are times when such action can result in unacceptable risks for a cyclist under real-life traffic conditions. The most common occasion is where there is a left-turn lane marked on the road, but with no physical separation from the ahead lane(s). The problem in using the correct lane in such circumstances is simply that many motorists do not, and you could easily find yourself overtaken on the left as you cross the junction. A cyclist is vulnerable to traffic passing on both sides at the same time and you cannot look rearwards to both sides at once. The solution, therefore, is to keep to the left-hand lane at these junctions, but to occupy a position to its right-hand side in order to suggest to following drivers that you might not be making the marked turn. You should take care, however, not to leave sufficient room to your left for anyone to pass.

If a turning lane is controlled by a separate filter traffic signal, you should not use it for ahead movements. And if there is more than one marked left-turn lane, use the right-hand of these to go ahead if necessary. Never use a lane further to the left. Often the second or third lane will be marked for both left-turning and ahead movements and you should use the leftmost lane that is so marked. Whenever you do use a lane away from the left side of the road, bear in mind the possibility that someone might pass on your left, and do not move back towards the left side until you have checked that there is no one there.

If possible, use the correct marked lane to go ahead, and always do so if there is a left-turn filter signal. Stop in the primary riding position.

Another type of ahead movement requiring care is where the road required lies straight ahead, but the road you are on turns left (Figure 8.4). This is in fact a right turn and you should use the procedures described in the next section for making it. Take care, however, not to get too close to the centre line before being sure that there is no oncoming traffic, as this might be going fast and cut the corner. It is better to stay back, even if this means temporarily blocking following vehicles.

Figure 8.4
*Going ahead off a
major road*

② Turning right off a major road

The right turn is the most complicated turn for cyclists, as it is necessary to cross every lane of traffic. However, by following the correct technique, right turns can be carried out with little risk on all but the fastest of roads. This section describes the technique when turning right off a major road into a more minor one.

One of the first requirements is to identify just where the right turn is to take place. You will need to have this information much earlier than for a left turn. In the absence of good local knowledge, direction signs can be useful, but on faster roads these will often occur too early for a cyclist to start manoeuvring. The movement of traffic ahead can provide more useful clues as to where to turn. If you get too close before moving right, you will have to stop on the left and await a suitable gap in traffic before proceeding.

 Never swerve suddenly or cross moving traffic at too great an angle or without making the proper preparations.

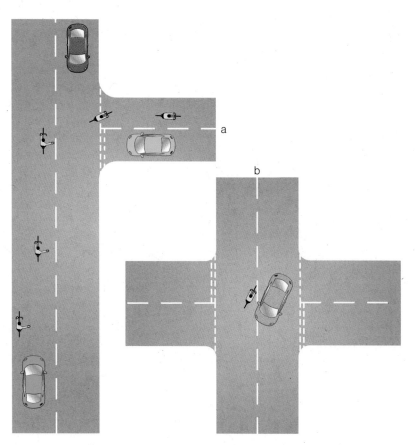

Figure 8.5 *Turning right off a major road*

This diagram is not to scale; in (a), you should allow much more space for the manoeuvre.

If the road from which you are turning has only a single lane in each direction and traffic flows are light, turning right is quite easy. From about 100 metres (about 330 feet) before the junction, keep track of the movement of any following vehicles by looking behind at least twice. Look, too, at oncoming traffic in case it might be about to cross the centre line for any reason. At about 50 metres (about 140 feet), look behind again and select a sufficient gap in traffic. Signal right clearly, and move smoothly but quickly towards the centre of the road (Figure 8.5a). Keep an eye on following vehicles as you cross, but transfer more of your attention towards the traffic coming towards you. As you approach the junction you should be about 1 metre (3 feet) from the centre line, but always be prepared to change position if other vehicles come too close.

To turn right, position towards but not too close to the centre line and watch oncoming traffic

If you are turning with other traffic, take up a position along the centre line of those vehicles, in order to deter overtaking. If there is a marked right-turn lane, use it and adopt the primary riding position. Where there is more than one right-turning lane, use the leftmost one.

If there is any traffic approaching which could conflict with your turn, wait at the junction opposite the centre line of the minor road. Continue to signal while you wait. On lightly trafficked roads it is often possible to adjust your speed in order to avoid arriving at the junction at the same time as anyone else. When there is a sufficient gap in traffic, turn right as quickly as you can.

If the minor road has only one lane in your direction of travel, your position on entering it should be between the centre of that lane and the middle of the road. Do not enter too far to the left or you may encourage a following driver to overtake you in the turn or you may have to move out again to pass an obstruction. On the other hand, take care that no one can pass to your left, or that a driver leaving the minor road does not come out into your path. Remember, too, to keep well clear of the hazard zone near the give-way or stop lines.

If the minor road has more than one lane in your direction, enter the left-hand lane between its centre and right side – do not cut across the other lanes. Whatever the road, take up the primary riding position after entering it until you are sure that there is nothing to overtake and it is safe for you to be passed.

The technique described for entry to another road can be applied to all types of right turn. However, if the major road is busy, the approach will be more difficult and involves use of the more advanced technique of negotiation. This will be described in Chapter 9.

Sometimes at a crossroads you will be turning right at the same time as another vehicle from the opposite direction. In the UK, the normal rule here is that you first pass each other right side to right side and then turn (Figure 8.5b). In some places, however, road markings or local practice indicate that such turns should be made left side to left side without passing. Stick to the normal rule unless markings indicate to the contrary, but always be alert to the fact that others may act differently. In all cases, be very careful if a queue of vehicles waiting to turn masks your visibility of oncoming traffic. Nose out inch by inch until you can see better.

Use the primary riding position in situations such as this to deter impatient drivers from cutting across your path

A different type of right turn is where the marked priority road turns right but another, more minor road goes straight ahead. This is not really a right turn at all as you will have priority over traffic on the minor road, but don't count on it! In some places, traffic going ahead can be in the majority, and local drivers rushing to get home might not expect a cyclist to be going right. If you are unsure as to whether your priority will be respected, adopt the primary riding position and signal right. Watch out for traffic ahead and behind.

② Leaving minor roads

The movements described so far have assumed that you start on a road which has priority, either continuing along the same road or turning onto one of lower priority. The reverse movements – from a minor road onto or across a major road – differ in that you will usually be less at risk before the junction, but more at risk while passing through it. Whichever way you are going, the object of positioning is the same – to deter anyone behind from overtaking you in an unsafe manner, and to give you the best view of major road traffic.

If there is only one lane in your direction, occupy the primary riding position for any movement. If there are two or more lanes, occupy the primary riding position in the appropriate lane. If a single lane is wide enough, mentally split it into two lanes and ride in the primary riding position for the direction in which you're going. Never get too close to the centre line as this puts you at risk from traffic turning into your road.

Unless there are traffic signals, the junction will be controlled with either a give-way or a stop sign directed at your road. If there is a give-way sign you do not need to stop if there is a clear passage, but you must be prepared to do so if necessary. Therefore, approach slowly, changing down in gear, to give yourself plenty of time to survey the traffic situation. Where possible, it is better not to stop, as you will waste valuable momentum; just as important, you will cross the major road more slowly after a restart and therefore be at risk for longer. However, unless you are quite sure that it is safe to proceed, you should stop. Where there is a stop sign, you have no choice. Such signs are usually placed where visibility is bad, at least from a motor vehicle. Sometimes visibility is better for a cyclist, but you should always obey the sign.

Adopt the primary riding position according to your direction of travel to deter anyone from trying to pass within the junction

From time to time you will find that a driver on a major road offers you the right of way when it is not yours. Such an invitation may take the form of a wave for you to proceed, the flashing of headlights, or simply an obvious slowing down or stopping. This friendly gesture should, if possible, be accepted, but don't do so too readily. Although one driver may be willing for you to proceed, another driver may not, or the latter may simply have not understood the intentions of the first. Whenever you are offered priority, first check in all directions that it really would be safe to accept. If so, say a polite 'thank you' by raising a hand briefly (or by nodding and smiling) as you proceed. However, if to accept would place you at risk, refuse the offer by waving the driver past. Some offers of right of way, though well intended, can complicate manoeuvring and are best declined.

When the way is clear, proceed across or turn as desired, occupying the primary riding position on the second road, at least until it is safe to do otherwise. When turning right don't cut corners; imagine an island at the point where the centre lines of the two roads would meet, and turn around this, keeping left. By doing this, you will ride the shortest distance across the major road and be at risk for the minimum time.

If going ahead or right at a crossroads, watch out for traffic from the opposite direction. Wherever it goes it affects, and has priority over, your right turn. If it turns right it should give way to you going ahead, but don't rely on this. Sometimes, drivers deliberately cut in front when turning right, either to minimise their own time at risk or because they misjudge the speed of a cyclist.

When crossing a dual carriageway, it will usually be possible for you to treat it as two separate roads, pausing in the middle if necessary. Because a cycle is shorter than a car, this is often an easier movement for a cyclist than for a car driver. Sometimes, too, it will be necessary to wait in the middle of a multi-lane non-dual-carriageway road. If you do this, you should wait with your cycle in a similar position to that which you would adopt if turning right from the major road – in this position you will take up less space yet still be able to see and be seen. Obviously this will not be necessary if you can be protected by the cover of another vehicle making the same movement. If you are held up while turning right by a queue of traffic from the opposite direction, wait in the furthest lane of the major road so that you will have the minimum distance to cross after restarting (Figure 8.6).

No-priority junctions

Most junctions of any importance have priority markings in one direction or another in order to regulate the flow of traffic and maximise safety. However, there remain some junctions with no indication of priority, particularly in residential districts and on country lanes.

At T-junctions, the acknowledged order of priority is that straight-through vehicles crossing the T go first, followed by those turning into and then out of the stem of the T. In effect, the priorities are the same as if there were give way markings to favour the through road.

At unmarked crossroads the situation is more complicated, and there is no clear priority at all. There is no universal priority-from-the-nearside rule in Britain as in some other countries. The only guideline is that crossing traffic from any direction usually assumes precedence over traffic turning. The answer is to treat whichever road you are using as one where you should give way, and to proceed cautiously. In practice, traffic flows at these junctions are usually so light that problems do not often arise.

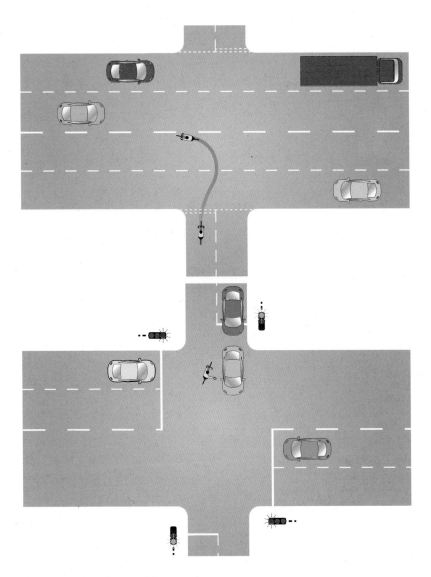

Figure 8.6 *Crossing multi-lane roads*

If you need to pause when crossing, take up a position as if you were turning right off the major road.

If you are held up by oncoming traffic when turning right, wait in the furthest lane.

② ③ Traffic signals

Traffic signals provide one of the safest ways for cyclists to cross busy junctions. The law relating to traffic signals is the same for cyclists as for other drivers and signals must always be obeyed. It is especially foolish for cyclists to ignore red lights as this increases greatly the risk of a collision.

It should not be thought, however, that the presence of signals necessarily makes for a safe junction. A combination of the complexity of movements, the tendency of some drivers to proceed before or after the green light and the frequent presence of large numbers of pedestrians can easily lead to situations where collisions happen.

From a cyclist's point of view, the greatest hazard is not being seen by other drivers. With their concentration attracted by the signals, a cyclist can be overlooked, so it is necessary to make yourself as conspicuous as possible through positioning.

To go straight ahead or turn left, occupy the primary riding position at the approach to signals, whether they be at red or green. To turn right, ride in the centre of the right-hand lane if there is one. In all cases, do not allow any other vehicle to share the same lane to the side of you. This will maximise your chances of being seen from both behind and ahead, and also protect you from close overtaking as the signals change. On multi-lane roads, the general lane-taking advice already given for junctions applies.

Approaching signals, change down in gear unless you think that you can keep going. If you're proved wrong and have to stop, brake hard if it is safe to do so and change down quickly. Although Chapter 11 will discuss the special circumstances of filtering in congested streets, it can be risky to creep up the inside of queues at signals as you will not be easily seen by drivers.

 **Never pass a bus or long vehicle in the same lane in a signal queue.**

A red signal means you must stop, while if it's green you may pass, but only if it is safe to do so. Look out particularly for pedestrians making a last-minute dash across the road, or the driver who jumps the change to red in the other direction. You should also not pass unless the junction is sufficiently clear that you can go straight through, but this will seldom be a problem for a cyclist.

A single amber signal means that you should stop unless you are so close to the stop line that to pull up might cause a collision. Because of a cyclist's vulnerability, you should be careful about this one – don't pull up so sharply that a following vehicle could run into you. You should be able to tell from the sound of its engine whether or not a car behind is likely to stop; if not, keep going yourself.

The red and amber signal also means 'stop', being merely an indication that green is to follow. Traffic should not move at all on this signal, but it often does, and it is recommended for cyclists to use this phase to gain balance. In this way you can get off to a quick start on the green, and you will be less likely to be overtaken unsafely in the junction. You can do this quite legally if you make a point of stopping just a metre (3 feet) back from the stop line, for that distance should be quite sufficient for you to push off and balance before the signals change to green. Do not do this, however, if it might antagonise pedestrians; you should always wait for pedestrians to clear the road before moving.

Watch out for filter signals, and do not use a filter lane unless you are turning. In Britain, but not in most other countries, the illumination of a green left or right arrow indicates that vehicles turning in that direction are protected from oncoming traffic.

A final point on traffic signals concerns their actuation – the mechanism that makes them change to green in your favour. Often this is no problem for cyclists, there being plenty of other traffic about to do the job for you. But late at night or early in the morning, things may be different, and yours may be the only vehicle on the road. If you don't want a delayed journey, it will then be necessary to ensure that you change the signals yourself. Most modern signals are actuated by induction loops, buried under the road surface – their location is marked by box-like patterns in the tarmacadam. Be sure to pass over these. If there's no other traffic about, you can maximise your chance of being detected by riding along the lines of the box instead of just across them.

Some signals do not respond to cycles. Most are capable of doing so, but their sensitivity may be incorrectly set. If you find that you can't actuate a change to green in your favour and there's no other traffic on your road, be very cautious about how you proceed – traffic on the other arms of the junction won't expect you to be moving. You may be able to proceed more easily if you walk. If you face this problem regularly at a particular location, report the fault to the local council.

Advanced stop lines

At some junctions controlled by traffic signals, advanced stop lines permit cyclists to stop ahead of other traffic. A cycle lane is usually provided at the approach, by which cyclists may filter past waiting vehicles. This lane may either be by the kerb or between other traffic lanes.

This 'advanced stop line' is approached by a central cycle lane. However you reach the waiting area, wait in the primary riding position so that traffic doesn't pass you closely when the lights change.

The benefits of an advanced stop line are that it puts cyclists where they are easily seen by other drivers while waiting for the signals to change to green, and it gives them a head start when the change takes place, allowing cyclists to clear the junction and build up speed before being passed. You need to be in a low gear to take best advantage of this head start. These are advantages in congested streets and where turning movements are common, especially for slower and less confident riders. There is also the added advantage of not having to wait close to the exhaust pipe of a motor vehicle.

These advantages during the red phase of the signals must, however, be set against possible risks at other times. Cyclists who manoeuvre into the waiting area for cycles as the lights change from red may be vulnerable to other vehicles moving forward. At no time should you cut sharply in front of other traffic. If you are in a cycle lane when the lights change to red and amber, negotiate your way back into the traffic stream.

It is always unsafe to use a kerbside cycle lane to reach an advanced stop line and then to turn right by riding across the waiting area.

 Never turn right in traffic directly from the left side of the road.

If you intend to turn right, position normally towards the centre of the road, as if the cycle lane were not there. Move forward to the advanced stop line if it is safe to do so, but otherwise stay with the traffic. If you find it difficult to move across the road, wait by the advanced waiting area and move across it just after the lights change to red.

If you are going straight ahead or left, you shouldn't enter the cycle lane unless there is a clear advantage – refer to the general comments about cycle lanes in Chapter 13. When the signals are at green, staying in the general traffic lane may avoid the need to leave and then re-enter the traffic stream, which can be safest and quickest, too.

If you decide to use a cycle lane to reach an advanced stop line, always proceed cautiously in case a car door is opened into your path. Passengers sometimes alight from cars waiting at traffic signals and often take less care opening a door than drivers. When you reach the waiting area, move away from the side of the road to the primary riding position to maximise your safety when traffic restarts, but be cautious of other cyclists who come alongside to your left.

②③ Roundabouts

Roundabouts are to be found on all kinds of roads, and most cyclists will need to encounter them from an early stage. Many roundabouts on local roads pose no great difficulty for cyclists, but others, which are not always easy to distinguish by design, are associated with increased risk. For this reason, advice on roundabouts is grouped together in this guide in Chapter 9. You should read through this and apply it to the roundabouts that you meet.

Roadworks and diversions

Minor roadworks are much the same as any other form of obstruction – you pass using the usual techniques for overtaking, taking particular care in case the road surface is uneven or muddy. Where works involve a long length of road, one or more lanes may be closed, all traffic being channelled into the remaining space. On two-lane roads a shuttle lane is often created, traffic using the lane first in one direction and then the other. Control may be by traffic signals or by manual 'Stop–Go' boards. These situations can be hazardous for a cyclist if following vehicles try to squeeze past in too narrow a space, or if oncoming traffic proceeds before you are clear. The rule is to ride as you would on a road of corresponding width; occupy the primary riding position unless it is safe for you to be passed, having full regard to the condition of the surface. Try not to worry about delaying other traffic but, on the other hand, do pass along the lane as quickly as you can.

Use the primary riding position in situations such as this where it would not be safe for you to be passed. Watch out for mud on the road and other hazardous surfaces.

More substantial works sometimes require the closure of a road in one or both directions, and the diversionary route can add significant extra distance, perhaps via busier roads. In most cases, cyclists are still able to pass a closure, if only by dismounting, but it can be a gamble to ignore a diversion sign if you do not know what's ahead. If possible, ask someone living locally. In the country, look carefully at a map for the likely location of a closure. If there is a bridge which might have fallen or a new road under construction, your path is more likely to be blocked. Otherwise, you will probably be able to proceed. However, you should not ride against the flow on a road signed for one-way working.

Taking the wrong route

Everyone makes mistakes and there will be times when you will take the wrong turning or use an incorrect direction lane at a junction. This may be because you are a stranger in the locality or because traffic conditions make it difficult to follow the correct route.

If possible, follow through your mistake and then make a correction. Only if you are absolutely sure that there could be no inconvenience or risk to yourself or anyone else should you change lanes at a junction, turn from the wrong lane or change direction in an unexpected manner.

The simplest form of correction is often to proceed through a junction, then stop and, when clear, make a U-turn. In one-way streets, a series of left or right turns may solve your problem, or it might be easier to dismount and walk to the correct road.

Check your understanding:

- [ ] When is signalling essential and when can it be safer to exercise discretion in doing so?
- [ ] What should you look out for when overtaking another vehicle?
- [ ] Is it ever safe to pass a long vehicle in the same lane?
- [ ] What are the principal risks to be aware of when approaching road junctions?
- [ ] How should you position yourself when approaching traffic signals – with and without advanced stop lines?

Chapter 9

Busier roads and faster traffic

This chapter, along with practice in cycling, should help you to:

➤ apply a standard system of cycle control to any manoeuvre

➤ negotiate with other drivers to make more difficult manoeuvres easier and safer

➤ understand how roundabouts and gyratories impact on all drivers and thereby enable you to ride in a way that minimises risk

➤ adopt suitable strategies for handling high-speed junctions of all kinds.

There was a time when the ordinary right turn was considered to be the most complicated manoeuvre that a cyclist had to make. Since then, the preoccupation of traffic planners with accommodating growth in motor traffic has led to a host of new problems for cyclists as they strive to share roads which were never designed for them. Add to this an increase in faster and more aggressive driving, and it is scarcely surprising that many people are deterred from cycling by today's road conditions.

Once more, this guide makes no excuses for the trends in road design which have led to the current situation. But in the real world there are techniques which cyclists can learn to maximise their safety and reduce to a minimum the problems that they encounter. Such techniques were previously seldom taught, cyclists usually being advised to do what is often impractical and to avoid difficult locations.

The best way to tackle any difficult problem is to break it down into more manageable parts. For example, although you may share a busy junction with more than one hundred other vehicles, you will rarely have to interact with more than one or two other drivers at any one time. Success in the more difficult manoeuvres comes by tackling each situation step by step, riding to suit the current circumstances, while making preparations to your advantage for what is to come.

Two important assets in handling difficult situations are the standard system of cycle control, which assists a cyclist in identifying the best actions to take, and negotiation whereby a cyclist can elicit protection from other road users.

Take heed that these skills are not for the novice. You will need to have practised and mastered all that has been taught so far before progressing to these advanced techniques. A good cadence and sprint speed (see Chapter 5) are particularly useful for carrying out the techniques in this chapter. Having said that, most reasonably agile people should be capable of acquiring these skills which, when exercised correctly, are much less hazardous than might at first seem.

A standard system of cycle control

Cyclists are particularly vulnerable to errors of judgement, whether their own or those of someone else. The standard system of cycle control – known as IPSGA from the initials of its phases – provides a systematic approach to handling hazards in a logical way that assists decision-making, maximises safety and minimises stress.

> IPSGA was developed by the police for their own drivers and motorcyclists and is also taught by the Institute of Advanced Motorists. Here it has been adapted so that cyclists, too, can benefit from its advantages.

There are five phases of IPSGA:

Information

Absorb information by keeping aware of what's going on all around you through looking and hearing. All that has been said in Chapter 7 about

observation and anticipation applies here. Always check behind you before
changing speed or direction. Keep aware, too, of the road surface ahead.
Continually process your observations to plan how to deal with the hazards
you have identified, and give information to others (by signalling and looking)
before you cross someone else's path and at other times when this might be
helpful. Processing information continues throughout all the other phases of
IPSGA, to update your strategy as the situation develops.

Position

Position your cycle to maximise your safety and to minimise the amount
of physical effort you need to provide. Always check that there is sufficient
clear space into which to move.

Speed

Adjust your speed to suit the circumstances. You may need to accelerate
in order to be able to integrate with traffic, or you may need to slow down
in response to a hazard ahead. At other times, you may not need to alter
your speed at all. To slow down, freewheel if you can, using the brakes only
when necessary.

Gear

If you need to accelerate, consider changing to a higher gear. If only a short
burst of acceleration is required, it may be sufficient to alter your cadence
and not the gear. If you need to slow down or stop, changing to a lower gear
will make subsequent acceleration or restarting easier.

Acceleration

If you had to slow down, accelerate back to your riding speed. If you
increased speed to integrate with traffic, ease off pedalling. Change gear as
necessary to regain optimum cadence.

The system is intended to be used flexibly. Although you should consider all
its phases on the approach to every hazard, you may not need to use every
phase in a particular situation. If new hazards arise as you proceed, you may
need to start again at an earlier phase.

IPSGA can be applied to all manoeuvres, including those discussed in previous chapters. It should be practised until its use becomes automatic. Some examples of using IPSGA are presented in this chapter.

③ Negotiation

A bicycle is small and lacks the power of other vehicles. But that doesn't mean you can't take your place in traffic and carry out complex manoeuvres safely. Negotiation is the technique by which you get other road users to cooperate and protect you as you ride. It is a skill which requires confidence, with respect to both control of your machine and your relationship with other road users. It is also a skill which is at variance with how many people perceive you should cycle – far from advising you to keep away from other traffic, it requires that you deliberately seek to integrate with it.

Negotiation recognises that you are the driver of a vehicle with as much right to proceed safely and quickly as any other. It relies upon establishing cooperation between you and other drivers in order to facilitate your progress

Negotiation requires confidence, but carried out systematically using IPSGA it is an effective means of traversing cycle-unfriendly road layouts. Observation, signalling and positioning are the key skills required.

and to protect you from the hazards that might otherwise arise. It makes other drivers want to assist you by appealing directly to a basic human instinct – responding with help when it is specifically requested. In other words, you try to influence the actions of others to your best advantage.

The following example illustrates the use of negotiation and IPSGA when you need to pull out into a moving traffic stream in order to pass an obstruction. Subsequent sections will explain the use of the technique in more complicated circumstances.

Overtaking by negotiation

Chapter 8 described the basic method of overtaking – reducing your speed in order to await a suitable gap in following traffic and then pulling out into the space. This is fine on two-lane roads where you have right of way or on lightly trafficked multi-lane roads, but on busier roads where you need to change traffic lanes you could wait a long time before there is a sufficient gap. Instead, you need to negotiate with following drivers to let you in when the right of way is not yours.

To do this, move to the right side of your lane well in advance of the obstruction and look behind for a gap in traffic that is a little longer than average (Figure 9.1). Apart from giving you more space to manoeuvre, a longer gap often suggests that the driver behind is less hasty, and therefore more likely to let you in. Unless the gap is long, never try to intercept another two-wheeler, a bus or a lorry, as it might be more difficult for the driver to slow down to give way.

As a gap approaches – if possible, while the previous vehicle is still overtaking you – signal right and move to about 0.5 metre (1.5 feet) to the left of the next moving traffic lane. This should be a clear indication to the driver behind that you wish to slip in front, but you have not yet moved to a position which puts you at any great risk. If traffic speeds are not too high, you may also be able to engage eye contact with the driver, which can be helpful.

Next you must decide whether or not the driver is responding to your request, or whether it would be better to try again with someone else. You must make this decision very quickly, for any delay in accepting may result

Information *Read diagram down from the top.*
Keep track of following vehicles and anyone
ahead of you (including pedestrians). Watch
out for surface defects. As you get closer to the
obstruction, look for signs of occupancy, such
as exhaust fumes, wheel movements or anyone
visible through a window.

Position

In plenty of time, move towards the right side of
your lane. This should not be difficult as drivers
behind will also be moving out. Seek out a
sufficient gap in traffic, move up to the lane line
and signal right. Watch and listen for a driver to
let you in, then move quickly to the primary riding
position in the new lane.

Speed

Adjust your speed to merge as seamlessly as you
can with traffic. If you have to wait for someone
to let you in, slow down a little but be ready to
accelerate quickly to restore your speed as soon
as an opportunity to merge arises.

Gears

At any time that you need to alter your speed,
consider changing gear to maintain optimum
cadence.

Acceleration

Maintain the primary riding position until you have
completely passed the obstruction. Move back
left when safe to do so and return to a comfortable
riding speed.

Figure 9.1 *Negotiation in overtaking*

*This diagram shows the sequence of events,
but is not to scale.*

in a change of mind by the driver. In practice, most drivers do respond positively to a clear and confident negotiation request, and typically indicate this by slowing a little to let you in. Listen carefully to the sound of the engine. If the driver agrees to let you in, move quickly to the primary riding position in the new traffic lane and complete the overtaking procedure. If you can give a friendly 'thank you' wave to the driver, so much the better.

If the person following decides not to let you in, move back to the right side of the previous lane and repeat the whole procedure with someone else. It will usually not be long before someone accedes to your request.

A variation of this technique can be used to start off on a narrow road where the stream of traffic seems unlikely to cease. In this case, scoot your cycle to just outside the moving traffic lane, aligning it at about 30° to the traffic flow. Wait for a gap a little longer than average, signal right and edge forward slightly. When a driver accedes to your request, start off as quickly as you can; otherwise move back.

③ Complex right turns

When turning right from a busy road, it is not so easy to reach the centre as it was in the case of the simpler right turn described in Chapter 8. You still need to take stock of following and oncoming traffic at least 100 metres (about 330 feet) before the junction, but when you come to start your movement you will need to proceed more cautiously and make use of IPSGA and negotiation (Figure 9.2).

Move towards the right side of your lane by negotiating with drivers behind. You do this by signalling and moving towards traffic when there is a sufficient gap to enter. Wait for a positive response to your negotiation request and then merge quickly, at first taking up the primary riding position. If your request is denied, wait and repeat the procedure with another driver. It's always worth giving a courteous 'thank you' wave to drivers who cooperate.

Information

Read diagram down from the top.

Continually look all about you, take information and identify hazards (including surface defects). Keep aware of what is happening behind and to your right throughout, but as you approach the turn prioritise your concentration ahead. How far ahead is the junction? What can you see there? Is anyone else turning?

Position

Move first across your lane, negotiating with drivers behind as necessary. Ride close to the lane line but not sufficiently advanced as to encourage anyone to pass on your left. Hold this lane until you can move on.

Negotiate to move into the second lane, holding the primary riding position there until you reach the turn.

Plan on stopping (towards, but not too close to, the centre line of the road) but be ready to go as soon as there is a sufficient gap in oncoming traffic. Then turn quickly, taking up the primary riding position in the new road.

Signal clearly all moves across traffic.

Speed

Adjust your speed to mesh with gaps in traffic while negotiating, then merge as quickly as you can. Vary your speed, too, to arrive at the junction when there is a gap in oncoming traffic if you can, so that you do not need to stop at the turn.

Gears

Consider changing gear at any time you alter your speed, but it is sometimes easier to maintain the same gear and increase your cadence for short bursts of acceleration.

Acceleration

Give way to pedestrians crossing, then accelerate to your preferred riding speed if safe to do so. Maintain the primary riding position until it is safe for you to be overtaken.

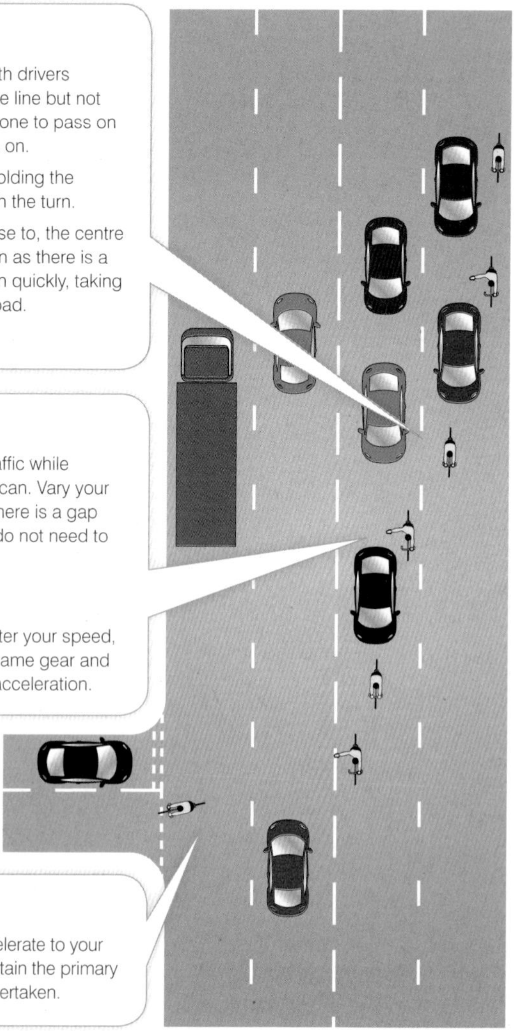

Figure 9.2 *Right turn by negotiation*

This diagram is not to scale.

> ⚠ **It is essential to hold each lane until you can enter the next. Never try to ride across more than one lane of traffic in the same movement.**

Where you need to cross more than one lane, negotiate to move into each lane in turn, holding your present lane through prominent positioning until you can enter the next. Bear in mind that traffic may be travelling faster in successive lanes, which will require you to seek longer gaps for crossing.

In the last lane, ride in the primary riding position until you reach the turn. If there is a marked turning lane, ride in its centre. Otherwise, decide if there is enough room to allow following drivers to pass if you move right a little, but keep away from the centre line in case an oncoming vehicle straddles it. If another vehicle is turning with you, it can be useful to seek its cover, but don't ride in anyone's blind spot.

The main requirement in negotiation is patience coupled with a methodical approach to your actions. Do not be rushed because a following driver becomes impatient. More often, a driver who has let you in will be happy to shield you until you can move further, so long as you do not delay unnecessarily. Cyclists are often less delayed when crossing traffic than motorists, as their all-round vision is better and they can accelerate away more quickly as long as they have selected a suitable gear.

A skilled and agile cyclist should be able to negotiate with traffic in order to make multi-lane right turns as described for traffic speeds up to about 64 km/h (about 40 mph). Where speeds are higher or the cyclist is less agile, the technique can still be applied if there are sufficiently long gaps between vehicles and visibility is good. Where circumstances are less favourable, it may be safer to stop on the left side of the road and wait for an interruption in the traffic flow in which to cross. If you do decide to stop in this way, do so a little way short of the junction and engage a low gear ready to accelerate away quickly. You may also choose to cross as a pedestrian but this is usually only safer where there is a protected crossing.

②③ Roundabouts

Roundabouts are places where cyclists can be especially at risk. It is important, however, not to overstate the problems of roundabouts for cyclists. Many roundabouts operate safely for both cyclists and other road users, and cyclists too can benefit from the ease of movement that roundabouts allow. Unfortunately, it is not always easy to predict which roundabouts are most likely to present problems, for more depends on local circumstances than on any particular facet of roundabout design. Thus a large main road roundabout may sometimes be less of a problem than a small roundabout in a residential area. Driver temperament and traffic flow (ferocity more than speed) are often deciding factors.

Because of the difficulty of categorising roundabouts in terms of risk when cycling, all are treated together in this section. You should aim to gain a general understanding of the problems that may be present so that you may apply the advice as appropriate to individual circumstances. Most of the causes of roundabout collisions are predictable. If you learn to ride in a way which makes conflict less likely, you will find that you can cope with the great majority of roundabouts with very little difficulty.

General considerations

It is helpful to analyse the problems that cyclists face when using roundabouts, for this should increase your awareness of where the main hazards lie, and thus enable you to ride in a way that minimises these.

Roundabouts should be safer for everyone, as they reduce the number of conflicting movements compared even with traffic signals, requiring drivers to give attention to traffic from only one direction at a time. Unfortunately, some motorists use the increased safety to allow themselves to drive faster or less carefully, and this can cancel out any benefit to the less well-protected road user. Discipline at roundabouts is often poor.

The biggest threat to cyclists is when riding on the circulating road as you pass an intermediate entry – over 70% of cycle crashes on roundabouts happen at the mouth of an entry road. Frequently, drivers fail to cede your right of way at these places, sometimes because they haven't noticed you.

Good positioning by a cyclist is extremely important at a roundabout, and the following sections will detail the preferred positions for negotiating the different designs. The most important rule to bear in mind when riding around any roundabout is:

Keep well clear of the give-way markings, for they depict the zone of greatest risk.

Following on from this is another rule of considerable importance:

Always keep away from the outside edge of a roundabout, no matter which exit you are intending to take.

Riding near the edge takes you close to the high-risk zone of the give-way markings and makes it more difficult for drivers to see you. At roundabouts in particular, drivers are above all looking out for other motor vehicles. As a cyclist, you are at your safest if you ride where a car would be driven for the same manoeuvre. Near the edge, you may also be masked by signs and background features, and you are very likely to be cut across by drivers exiting left – another of the most common causes of collision.

Even when you do ride in a similar place to a car, drivers approaching a roundabout can still have difficulty seeing you. This is exacerbated by the very philosophy of a roundabout, which encourages drivers to keep moving as much as possible, reducing the care that they might otherwise take. Some designs may also permit high speeds.

In fact many motorists themselves fear roundabouts, while plenty of others find it difficult to cope when there is a lot of traffic or when several main routes converge. Their main concern is to get through the junction as quickly as possible. Attention is concentrated on watching out for threats to themselves (which does not include anything as small as a cycle), controlling their vehicle amidst the complex weaving which often takes place, and finding their way to the correct exit. In addition, drivers often have to make a number of gear changes. That doesn't leave a lot of time to look out for other people.

At larger roundabouts the entry roads may bend to the left as they meet the circulatory road, sometimes considerably. Circulating vehicles already on the roundabout are therefore often more behind than to the right of a driver approaching the give-way lines, and this makes it much more difficult to see them. A bicycle can easily be overlooked (Figure 9.3). At the same time, if the driver is concentrating to the right, it will be harder for that driver simultaneously to monitor traffic in front, such as a cyclist passing too close. Slower cyclists are particularly vulnerable here.

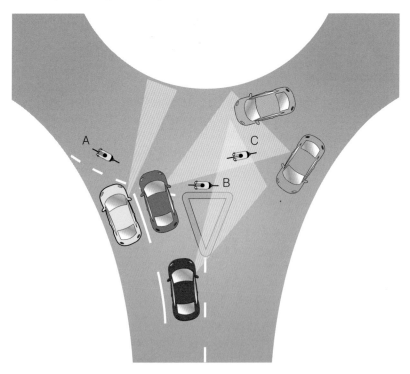

Figure 9.3 *Typical arcs of concentration of drivers entering a roundabout*

Cyclists A and B are difficult to see and very vulnerable. Cyclist C is more visible and has greater room for manoeuvre.

In all these cases, keeping well away from the edge will at least give you warning of a driver not ceding right of way, and will allow a few metres in which you can take avoiding action. But bear in mind that it will take any driver longer to give way if you are seen when the driver is accelerating away from the give-way lines than when braking while approaching them. Many drivers cannot move from accelerator to brake quickly. Another way of avoiding trouble at less busy roundabouts is to pace your riding so that you don't arrive at an entry road at the same time as another vehicle. A small adjustment to your speed will be all that is usually required.

Even if all drivers were perfect, roundabouts would still give problems to cyclists. A fundamental rule for any two-wheeler is to avoid braking on a curve, particularly if the surface is wet or icy. But at roundabouts this may be necessary. The entries to main-road roundabouts are also among the main places where large deposits of oil and diesel fuel are to be found, adding to the problems of control. Additionally, surface defects are more of a hazard if you are not riding in a straight line. On a roundabout there are many demands on your attention.

At a roundabout, a cycle's inherently poorer acceleration and gear changing mechanisms are at their greatest disadvantage compared with those of cars. You are usually at your safest moving on a roundabout if your speed is high and is as close as possible to that of the other traffic. For this you need to be in a high gear. However, you, as others, should give way to traffic already circulating on the roundabout; at best this will mean slowing, but it may mean stopping. In order to move away again smartly you will need to be in a low gear. As you can't change gear when stationary on a derailleur-geared bicycle, you may face a dilemma as to which gear to use – there is much more uncertainty than at traffic signals.

Make a judgement of the conditions as you approach the roundabout, based on the traffic flows at the time. If it seems likely that you will be able to move straight onto the roundabout, perhaps by adjusting your speed slightly to find a gap in traffic, stay in a high gear. If circumstances change, you may then have to make an abrupt stop, but if at all possible keep going and accelerate out of trouble.

If giving way seems likely in advance, approach in a lower gear and more slowly. Make a final judgement when you are about 5 metres (15 feet or so) from the give-way line. If clear, accelerate rapidly by increasing your cadence to a higher rate than normal and then change up in gear, if you can.

If stopping is necessary, brake hard until you are only just moving and then change down in gear. So long as you have practised the skill of low-speed riding and gear changing, you should be able to complete this before reaching the line. On roundabouts it is essential that your gears are reliable and correctly adjusted; it is no place to stall.

If at all possible, keep moving, albeit slowly, rather than stop at a roundabout, so that you will have more momentum to proceed when the way ahead is clear. Even with good acceleration, you may find after a stop that another vehicle appears to your right before you have scarcely crossed the give-way line. If possible, you should not stop again having crossed the line, but it is essential to be guided by circumstances – drivers who appear fast are never to be trusted, although a stern look in their direction can often make them yield, as they should.

Take special care if you cannot see over the centre island, which will decrease the warning you have of another vehicle approaching. The theory is that this makes drivers take more care, but too often they simply go fast and take the risk.

Single-lane roundabouts

These small roundabouts are found mainly in residential districts and on other minor roads. They pose little problem for cyclists where traffic flows are light, but on busier roads they always need to be treated seriously.

The greatest hazard is that some drivers race a cyclist to the roundabout, cutting sharply across the cyclist's path in order to enter. Drivers often do not realise how great a cyclist's speed can be, and as a result there is often insufficient space to complete the overtaking manoeuvre safely. The likelihood of being overtaken in this way seems to be greater where there is no entry island, but if there is an island and a driver still overtakes, it can act as a further hazard by creating a squeeze point.

It can be difficult for a cyclist to know the intentions of a driver behind. Can you ride normally and comfortably, or should you accelerate or brake in order to prevent or counter a potentially unsafe manoeuvre? Sharing a road where there is a series of these roundabouts can be a very strenuous business, even if there's only one car following. Although a cyclist often maintains a constant speed, a car will generally be faster between roundabouts but slower through them, and the continuous to and fro between car and cyclist can lead to uncomfortable pressure and a feeling of vulnerability.

When approaching a single-lane roundabout, take up the primary riding position in good time, and at least 20 metres (60 feet or so) in advance

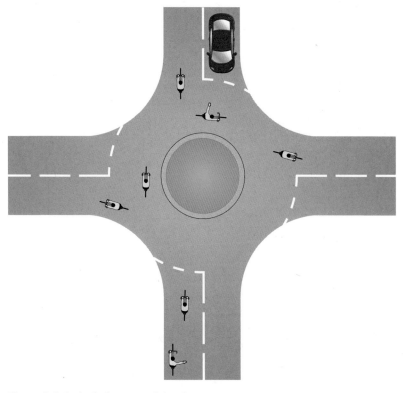

Figure 9.4 *A single-lane roundabout*

See text for full signalling details.

(Figure 9.4). You should do this whether you are going ahead or turning left or right. You must do your best to dissuade any driver from overtaking until you are safely through the junction. Give warning of the move if there is following traffic (or if you are unsure), with a short moving-right signal.

If you are going straight ahead, give way to traffic from your right as necessary, and then ride the shortest route through the roundabout. Don't waste time keeping parallel to the edge, but do ensure that no one can pass on either side. A straight course will not only get you out of the roundabout as quickly as possible; it will also be the safest if the surface is slippery or if you need to brake suddenly. If there is traffic coming from the opposite direction or there is a pedestrian nearby, give a courtesy left signal as you approach the exit road, but be cautious about doing this if there is a vehicle close behind for it can be taken as an invitation to overtake.

For a similar reason, if you are turning left, signal your intention with a courtesy signal only just before you start to make the turn. Keep in the centre of the lane until you are out of the roundabout. You must always give way entering a roundabout even if turning left, and at small roundabouts it can be especially hazardous not to do so.

When turning right, signal your intentions early, and ensure that this is seen by oncoming drivers. Although you should keep a good distance from the entry roads you pass, you should not get too close to the centre island. This would mean a sharper turn, and might also encourage someone to pass on your left side. A position just to the right of the centre of the circulatory road is usually best, going straight to your exit from opposite the previous entry.

When turning right it can be difficult to maintain a signal as you turn as both hands should be on the handlebar. It is easy for an oncoming driver not to realise your intentions until you are close in front. The solution is to signal intermittently. Critical times to signal are when entering the roundabout, and as you approach intermediate exits.

Multi-lane roundabouts

These are found on busier roads. As well as a wider circulatory road, the entries to these roundabouts are often two, three or more lanes wide, at least for the final distance leading into the roundabout. Although some examples on roads with low traffic speeds pose no great problems, these roundabouts are often a place of great difficulty and increased risk for cyclists, as a common purpose of their design is to increase junction capacity and keep vehicles moving.

The two principal hazards are traffic entering at intermediate roads, and weaving movements as drivers jostle to get to their desired exit. Once you have entered, you cannot usually go back!

As you approach a roundabout on a busy road, make your presence known early by occupying the primary riding position (Figure 9.5). In general, you should start to do this as soon as you pass the advance 'roundabout ahead' sign, but on high-speed roads, where signing distances are greater, wait until you are about 75 metres (about 250 feet) from the junction, though earlier if you are turning right.

If you want to turn left, keep to the primary riding position in the leftmost moving traffic lane all the way through the roundabout. As at other left turns, give a courtesy signal if you can, but don't if it might encourage someone to

Prominent positioning is all-important at large roundabouts where it is otherwise easy for cyclists to be overlooked. Negotiation can also be a very useful asset.

Information
Read diagram upwards from bottom.

More than anywhere else, you need to keep alert to what's going on all around you on a roundabout, looking continually in all directions. Use what you see to identify the most important risks at any time. Look, also, at drivers, so that they notice and protect you.

On the approach, focus most on the vehicles behind and to your side. But as soon as you're in the correct lane, concentrate ahead to the roundabout to track what's happening. Going round the roundabout, focus on the entry roads you pass and on vehicles whose paths may cross yours.

Give information through signalling each time before you move across traffic.

Apply IPSGA at least twice on a roundabout: at the approach and when on the circulatory road.

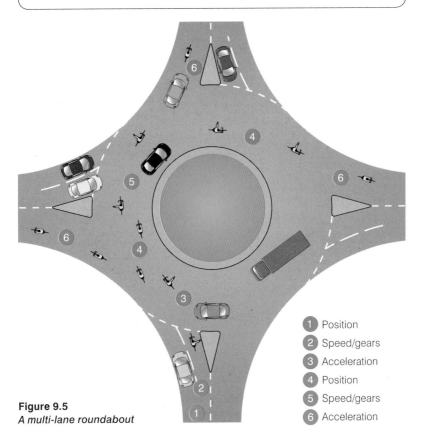

Figure 9.5
A multi-lane roundabout

1 Position
2 Speed/gears
3 Acceleration
4 Position
5 Speed/gears
6 Acceleration

Position

Move to the centre of the lane for your direction of travel in good time, negotiating to cross traffic as necessary. Hold the lane all the way to the roundabout.

Speed

Move as quickly as you can to position, then modify your speed to try to arrive at the give-way lines when there is a gap in traffic so that you can keep going.

Gears

If you are sure you will not need to stop, maintain your current gear. Otherwise, change down so that you can stop and restart easily.

Acceleration

When it is safe to enter the roundabout, move directly to the centre of the moving traffic lane used by other vehicles for the same manoeuvre. Ride as quickly as you can, increasing cadence rather than changing gear if other vehicles are close.

Position

Ride in the centre of a moving traffic lane whichever way you're going – keep well away from the give-way lines.

When turning right, spiral out from the inner to the outside lane as you pass the previous entry, signal left and keep aware of vehicles on that side. Negotiate if necessary.

Speed

Maintain a steady speed throughout the roundabout.

Gears

Avoid changing gear on the roundabout. Alter your cadence instead.

Acceleration

Watch out for pedestrians and traffic ahead. Maintain the primary riding position until it is safe for you to be overtaken. Get back to your normal cadence, changing gear as necessary.

overtake you before it is safe to do so. Make sure that you give way to traffic already circulating and watch out for cyclists or motorcyclists on your inside.

To go ahead (or to the second exit where the junction is more than a crossroads), ease gradually on the approach to a position to the right side of the left-hand lane, but take care that no one can pass to your left. If there are only two entry lanes, maintain this position up to the give-way line. Where there are three lanes, move to the middle of the centre lane, but be wary of the possibility of someone overtaking on your left. Where there are four or more lanes the situation can be more difficult. If in doubt, use the centre of the second lane from the left, but as far as possible keep just within the path of other vehicles which appear to be making the same manoeuvre. In any event, try not to get hemmed in or masked by traffic on either side.

At less busy roundabouts, wait your turn, as necessary, at the give-way line in the usual way. On very busy roads, however, you could wait for a long time, while the risk to yourself can only increase if you hold up following drivers too long. Try, therefore, to seek the shelter of another vehicle, preferably one that is unlikely to accelerate away too quickly. Buses and lorries are good choices, but watch out that you are not so close to them as to be at risk when they turn. Keep out of their blind spots. Otherwise look for a driver who is driving more slowly and carefully.

Once you have entered the roundabout, proceed as quickly as you can, adopting a position to the right side of the left-hand circulatory lane, which may or may not be marked. This will give you the shortest and quickest ride through the roundabout, and will keep you as far as possible from intermediate entry roads.

Turning right at a multi-lane roundabout (or going beyond the second principal exit where several main roads join) is more difficult, particularly on fast-flowing, heavily trafficked roads. It needs great care, confidence and, preferably, the ability to attain a sprint speed of about 32 km/h (20 mph). Approach the roundabout in the middle of the right-hand lane, reaching this position by following the same techniques which would be applicable to a conventional right turn from the same road. Normally, you should not leave sufficient room on your right for anyone to pass, but where there is a lot of traffic turning right, it can be advantageous to adopt a position just to its left and to use the shelter of those vehicles for making the turn. Always make the most use of others for protection at any busy roundabout. Once on the circulatory road, ride to the left of the centre of the right-hand lane (whether marked or not) until you are opposite the entry before your exit. Then spiral out of the roundabout in a gradual curve (don't make any sudden turns), finally adopting the primary riding position on the exit road. It is usually best not to signal right on the roundabout, but do signal left clearly (this is a safety signal) before you begin to cycle out of it.

During any roundabout manoeuvre, you must keep your eyes and ears alert, monitoring other traffic all the time. Be ready to respond – with a quick move to the left or right, with braking or acceleration – to the slightest threat to your course. On multi-lane roundabouts, negotiation has an important role to play in persuading drivers to assist you. The technique is similar to that you would use when carrying out a complex right turn, but at a roundabout you may have to negotiate with drivers on both sides, sometimes at the same time, and the whole procedure needs to be carried out more quickly. As usual, you indicate your intentions by signalling, backed up with a small 'please let me in' movement, completing the move once someone has agreed. Very often a driver who has let you in will continue to protect you, but don't trust anyone else!

Where you pass an entry road be wary, particularly of traffic in the furthest lanes from you. A closer driver may have seen you and be waiting, but that driver's vehicle may mask you from another. If there is any possibility of someone moving into your path, move right. If you are going to the next exit, signal left (a safety signal) as you pass the entry road. This can deter drivers from edging out too far, but be ready to get your hand back quickly to the handlebar.

A hazard point when you leave a multi-lane roundabout can be where the exit road swings left to regain the original course of the road. The problem is particularly noticeable when the road reverts to a single lane in each direction, for it is here that the exit lanes merge. This relatively sharp deflection can act as a pinch point between drivers accelerating away and a cyclist to their left. Deter drivers from getting too close by keeping away from the road edge, preferably by holding the primary riding position until the hazard is passed.

Mini-roundabouts

A mini-roundabout is one with a flush or slightly raised central marking, but no kerbed island. It may be single- or multi-lane. The mini-roundabout is generally used where there would be insufficient space to install a larger roundabout, and is designed so that large vehicles, which cannot negotiate the sharp turn, may go straight across the centre. Generally, mini-roundabouts have a good safety record for cyclists, but this may be in part because they are found on roads of 48 km/h (30 mph) average speed or less.

One problem for cyclists is that cars sometimes drive straight across the central marking and they may do this at speed, particularly where the roundabout is placed at a T-junction and there is no deflection on the approach. Some drivers may overtake you on the roundabout.

Keep as far as you can from approaching vehicles when negotiating a mini-roundabout while looking out for poor road surfaces. Signal right turns on the approach, but return your hands to the handlebar before turning.

A second problem with mini-roundabouts is that the width of the circulatory road is often limited, and the give-way markings can be very close. There is little warning for a cyclist, particularly when making a right turn, if a driver fails to cede right of way, and correspondingly little room to take avoiding action. Drivers are often confused as to who has right of way at mini-roundabouts.

A further problem you may encounter with turning right at single-lane mini-roundabouts is that, having entered the roundabout, it is often not possible for a cyclist to continue signalling; the turn being so tight that both hands are needed on the handlebar. It can happen that a driver approaching fast from the opposite direction does not see an advance signal and so goes ahead, believing the cyclist not to be turning. On these roundabouts, there is very little room for error on anyone's part.

Negotiate a mini-roundabout in the same way as you would an ordinary single- or multi-lane roundabout, but watch out particularly for the problems discussed above. If turning right, change down in gear to enable you to accelerate away quickly after a sharp turn; give further signals if you stop, when you cross the give-way line and before you start to turn. If in doubt, let an erratic driver go first and be cautious of large vehicles, which may not be able to stop quickly.

Should you, too, ride across the centre of a mini-roundabout? You are always safest at junctions if you keep to the path taken by other traffic, so if other vehicles commonly cross the centre then you should consider doing the same. Also, some mini-roundabouts require very tight turns to avoid the centre, which may be impractical for a two-wheeler and hazardous if the surface is uneven, greasy or wet or if there is an adverse camber. As always, be guided by circumstances, but roundabouts are not practical places to set examples.

Multiple roundabouts

These comprise two or more roundabouts placed close together and sometimes immediately adjacent to one another. The roundabouts may be ordinary, mini-, single- or multi-lane (Figure 9.6).

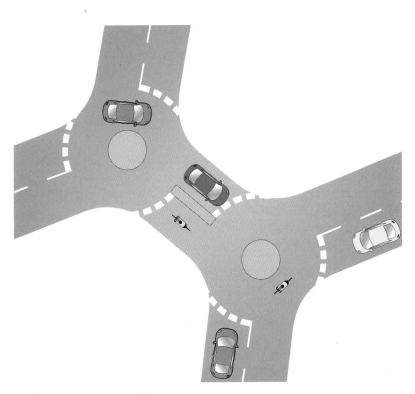

Figure 9.6 *Multiple roundabouts*

At first sight, these junctions appear merely to multiply the difficulties of their constituent roundabouts. Although this may be so at some locations, and the greatest care always needs to be exercised, at other places the general confusion caused by the complex junctions seems to reduce traffic speeds and leads to greater care by all concerned. Under these circumstances, a cyclist can sometimes move through the roundabouts more easily than other drivers.

Another, rarer, type of multiple roundabout is where there is a ring of mini-roundabouts around a large roundabout which can be travelled in either direction. These, too, need to be treated with caution.

Gyratories

Like large roundabouts, gyratory systems can be difficult for cyclists to negotiate. In this context, a gyratory means a much enlarged roundabout, with entries and exits flared to facilitate movement (Figure 9.7). Sometimes there are buildings, or even other roads, in the centre. Gyratories are usually to be found on main roads. The circulatory traffic system, comprising just a ring of one-way streets of more or less conventional design, and typical of the type found within older town centres, is much less of a problem, although you must take care to keep to the correct lanes.

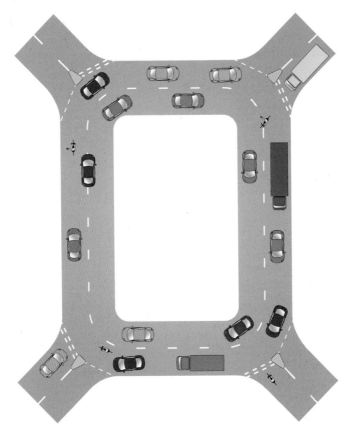

Figure 9.7 *A gyratory*

The main difference between a gyratory and a roundabout is that with a gyratory, the distance between the converging roads is greater. The same difficulties confront a cyclist approaching a gyratory or riding past intermediate entries as exist at a large roundabout, but there is the added problem of the extra distance to be ridden amidst weaving traffic, which often moves quickly. While to take the first turn left is no great problem, to ride in any other direction will mean that you will need to be in the centre of the road for an appreciable time, with traffic passing on both sides. This can be daunting, particularly for the slower rider. Worst times are in moderate traffic flows; when there is a lot of congestion, speeds are usually lower.

It is hard to give general advice on negotiating gyratories, as the difficulties can vary so much from place to place and time to time. As far as possible, you should adopt the same positioning as at a roundabout, but best of all try to spot the actual paths taken by other vehicles going in your direction and ride within that path. If you are going to a minor exit towards which traffic flows are light, use the path to the following exit but veer left early. Take great pains to make your presence obvious to others. Signal right as you approach intermediate exits to emphasise that you are not turning left (you need not actually be going right). Try to 'adopt' a driver to give you shelter for at least the most difficult sections by use of the negotiation technique, but be wary if that driver leaves you.

There may be occasions when it would simply be too hazardous to follow the path taken by other traffic. This applies especially to slower riders, but even the fittest can be in difficulty if the gradient is against them or the road very wide. Under these circumstances, you may have little option but to follow a route nearer the outside, but to do so needs the greatest care. Except to turn left, do not ride closer than about 3 metres (10 feet) from the edge of a gyratory, and keep well away from give-way lines. To cross intermediate exits, it may be best to pull in for a while to await more favourable traffic conditions, or simply to be sure what following vehicles are doing. Remember that restarting will be slow, so allow time for this.

Slip roads

These are found at split-level junctions on trunk and principal roads, and enable traffic to join or leave the main road at high speed. Cyclists going ahead on the main road are at great risk at such junctions, and when crashes do occur they tend to be very serious.

It is not just the speed of traffic which causes the problems, although this certainly increases the severity of any collision. Drivers on an entry slip road concentrate their attention to the right, in order to select a gap in traffic into which they can merge, and to look out for threats to themselves. This means that drivers may fail to notice a cyclist crossing ahead, even if he or she has the right of way. At exit slip roads, the problems are usually less, as at least drivers leaving the through road keep their attention straight ahead.

Having recognised the problems, it is usually not too difficult for cyclists to minimise problems at slip roads, although it can mean ceding your priority and manoeuvring in a way contrary to the indications of the road markings. This is unfortunate, but the risks at these locations are otherwise too great. Junctions on this type of road are usually far apart, so you will lose little time overall.

Approaching an entry slip road (Figure 9.8a), direct your attention to the traffic on it. Your aim is to cross the

Figure 9.8 *Crossing a slip road on a high-speed road*

a *Entry slip road*
b *Exit slip road*

slip road as close as possible to where it meets the main carriageway, and you should seek a gap in traffic sufficiently great to enable you to do this. Don't forget to allow adequately for speeds. If traffic flow is not too great, you should be able to pace your riding in such a way that you can manoeuvre as you cycle across the hatch markings, with little disturbance to your journey. Cross the slip road as quickly as possible, at an angle of about 45° to your direction of travel. There is no need to signal.

Where the slip road is busier, you may have to slow down more, or even stop before crossing the slip road. Unless traffic speeds are unusually low, you should not ride along the main carriageway beyond the hatch markings, even if there's no traffic coming yet.

At some entry slip roads, formal cycle crossings are marked which follow the same principles, although they often require a sharper turn by the cyclist to cross the slip road at 90°. If traffic flows are high, it may be best to use these, but otherwise the procedure suggested will give similar protection without so much loss of momentum.

Although fewer collisions happen at exit slip roads (Figure 9.8b), they are still hazardous places, and it can be difficult to judge the intentions of following drivers. Unless there is no traffic which could arrive in the time it would take you to ride at least 50 metres (about 160 feet) across the mouth, you should join the slip road, riding about 1 metre (3 feet) from the edge, and looking back frequently to observe conditions. Try to pace your riding so that there will be a suitable gap in traffic when you are about 20 metres (60 feet or so) from the junction nose, where you should first signal right clearly and then move back to the main carriageway as directly as possible. If there is a continuous stream of traffic leaving the main road, or if you find rearward observation difficult, you should stop until a suitable gap arrives.

Free-flow lanes and merges

Like slip roads, free-flow lanes and merges are designed to keep traffic moving at junctions. Although traffic speeds may not be as high as on slip roads, they can still be uncomfortably so for a cyclist.

The commonest places for free-flow lanes are where there is a heavy left-turning movement at a roundabout and at the entry into a one-way street. Merges exist where two main roads converge, one sometimes being a motorway. The idea is that traffic from the left keeps left and that from the right keeps right, without either having to give way to the other at the junction. Weaving movements to sort out subsequent destinations take place further on. The hazard for a cyclist coming from the right lies in becoming trapped between the two lanes of traffic and being vulnerable to each (Figure 9.9).

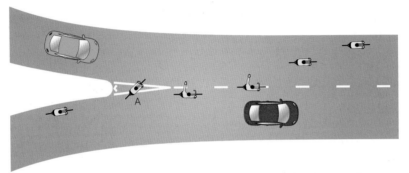

Figure 9.9 *Free-flow lanes and merges*

If you need to stop, adopt the position of cyclist A.

Unless you want to turn right again soon, you should move to the left side of the road as early as possible, ignoring any 'keep to lane' signs. You must do this carefully, for drivers will not necessarily be prepared for your movement, although many will recognise the need for a cyclist to make it. At most traffic speeds, you can negotiate with drivers to let you in, but where speeds are high (e.g. where a motorway joins a main road), the situation is more difficult and you may have to stop until conditions are favourable.

Diverges

Diverges exist where a main road splits into two, sometimes where a motorway begins. A difficult manoeuvre is when a cyclist wants to take the right-hand road, for it is first necessary to cross the left lane(s), in which traffic may be moving fast.

At this diverge off a busy road, care is needed against drivers cutting across the cyclist's path to go left. Moving towards the primary riding position can deter this unsafe behaviour but needs to be initiated in good time.

Where possible, start manoeuvring well in advance; a good place is at the end of the zone where other drivers are making similar lane changes. On the other hand, don't manoeuvre too early. During weaving movements, motorists devote a lot of their attention to their rear-view mirrors and may not notice you in their path.

Use the negotiation technique to cross each lane in turn, as if making a right turn, ending up at least 1.5 metres (5 feet) inside the first right-road lane (Figure 9.10). Do not stay too close to the lane edge, or you might not be seen by a driver who is turning left but who has left it late.

Under difficult circumstances, you may not be able to cross the left-road lane(s), and you will then have to stop and wait for a suitable gap in traffic before proceeding.

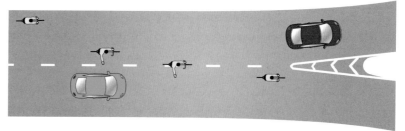

Figure 9.10 *Diverges*

Deceleration lanes

These are similar in appearance to exit slip roads, but are provided at junctions on ordinary main roads to allow left-turning vehicles to slow down without impeding the progress of other traffic (Figure 9.11). Although turning vehicles will usually be slowing down, in the presence of a cyclist going ahead, some drivers accelerate first to overtake and then cut in sharply to turn left, braking at the same time. This can result in insufficient clearance and increased risk for the cyclist.

Some deceleration lanes taper gradually from the main road and are relatively short (Figure 9.11a). These are the ones that give the greatest difficulty. Occupy the primary riding position before the lane commences, and stay there until the lane is passed. This will minimise the possibility of drivers overtaking unsafely.

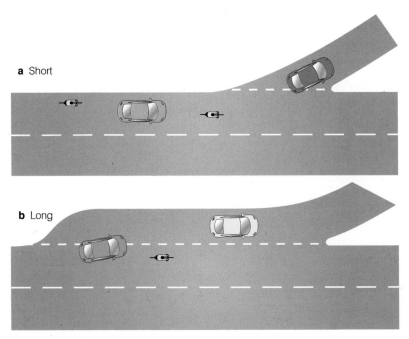

a Short

b Long

Figure 9.11 *Deceleration lanes*

Other deceleration lanes widen into a full-width lane quickly (Figure 9.11b), with the result that drivers can pass a cyclist sooner on the left and do not therefore feel the need to overtake in their haste. As long as you have sufficient confidence to accept vehicles passing on your left, this type of deceleration lane is usually less of a problem.

Check your understanding:

☐ Describe how to apply the standard system of cycle control to the left and right turn manoeuvres discussed in Chapter 8.

☐ What are the principal stages involved in negotiation?

☐ Where do motorists look when using a roundabout and what are the consequences of this for where a cyclist should ride?

☐ What is the safest way to cross a slip road onto or off a high-speed road?

Chapter 10
Non-traffic hazards

This chapter, along with practice in cycling, should help you to:

- → minimise risk and discomfort when passing over bad surfaces
- → recognise the special hazards introduced by railway and tramway tracks
- → share space safely with pedestrians, other cyclists and animals
- → recognise how tiredness and state of mind can affect your cycling.

From what you've read so far, it would be easy to think that motor traffic is the only – or at least the greatest – problem for cyclists using the roads. However, as this chapter will show, there are many other hazards of which to be aware, and they can be less predictable than motorists.

Bad surfaces

At best, bad surfaces result in an uncomfortable ride for a cyclist; at worst, they can lead to loss of control, a spill into the path of following traffic, and serious injury. In general, poor road surfaces probably result in more injuries to cyclists and damage to their bikes than any other cause. Bad surfaces include potholes, bumps, cracks and trenches in the road. All can be difficult to see in advance, especially when riding fast amidst heavy traffic or when the road is wet.

As you ride along, continually scan the surface as far ahead as you can see. Defects are frequently detectable by a change in the colour or texture of the surface. Look out for these, and assume a problem until you are convinced otherwise. Defects are often concentrated along relatively short stretches of road, where the surface is old or where pipes or other services have been renewed; once you encounter one problem, expect others. Road junctions are common places for defects, due to the wear caused by turning vehicles, while sometimes there is also a build-up of loose debris. It can be difficult dividing your attention between the surface and traffic at busy junctions, but both can be a hazard. Develop the habit of scanning the surface as your eyes move from traffic in one direction to traffic in another direction.

If you have sufficient warning of a defect, you can usually avoid it without too much trouble. Alter your course early, being sure to signal clearly to following traffic if you need to move across its path. You cannot rely upon motorists to notice surface defects, as they are seldom affected by them. If you need to keep far out for more than a few metres, perhaps because of a long trench, pointing to the problem can help to inform a driver of the reason. As far as possible, you should not let pressure from impatient drivers force you onto an uncomfortable or hazardous surface.

To avoid a defect, don't look directly at it but to one side. You will as a matter of course go where you look.

Even with very little warning, potholes and other small defects can often be avoided by using the technique described in Chapter 5 for avoiding obstacles. However, there will be times when you will have no choice other than to continue straight on. This will always be the case if you have to cross a transverse trench. It is also preferable to go across a pothole or bump using the correct technique than to turn sharply to try to miss one, which could put you into the path of another vehicle.

To cross a pothole, trench or bump with minimum risk to yourself and your bike, you should:

- Steer as straight as possible and meet the defect square-on (you will be less likely to be deflected or lose control).
- Take your weight off the saddle (to reduce discomfort).
- Release the brakes if applied (to reduce the force on the front forks).
- As you reach the hole or bump, pull up on the handlebar, grasping it firmly.

The last action should result in the bike jumping over the obstacle. When your front wheel has landed on the far side, transfer your weight forward to give the rear wheel a gentler crossing. The whole procedure takes just a second or two to carry out, but needs practice.

Ridges are another hazard. If you must, you can usually mount a 2.5 cm (1 inch) ridge square-on at riding speed, suffering only discomfort, but even a 5 mm (0.2 inch) one will topple you if crossed at too shallow an angle. Ridges are often placed at lay-bys, bus stops and junctions with cycle paths, with little thought of the risk to cyclists. It is useful to learn the effect of different surfaces and edges on your cycle so that you are not caught unawares.

Cobbles and many types of blockwork surfacing are uncomfortable on a cycle, even when newly laid. Vibration can make steering more difficult, while bevelled edges or grooves lead to a 'tram-line' effect. They are particularly hazardous when wet or icy. Similar hazards occur where a road is planed prior to resurfacing. It you have to cycle on such a surface, go slowly and grip the handlebar firmly.

Other bad surfaces cause discomfort and fatigue. General road wear and crumbling are examples, but so is a road recently resurfaced with stone chippings. To minimise discomfort and to protect your bike, slow down, reduce your arm and hand pressure on the handlebar, and freewheel from time to time, lifting your weight off the saddle.

Drains and manholes

Drain covers that can trap a cycle wheel are encountered less frequently today than was once the case, but are still to be found occasionally. Don't cross any drain cover with slots parallel to your direction of travel.

More commonly, drain and manhole covers are sunk (or occasionally raised) relative to the general level of a road. In some cases, the difference in level can be considerable. These are all reasons for keeping at least 0.5 metre (1.5 feet) from the edge of a road and staying alert.

Level crossings

Crossing railway tracks can be hazardous, especially on a cycle with narrow tyres. The smoothness of the rails is in marked contrast to that of a road and this can cause a spill, while the road over a crossing is often uneven.

It is most important to cross railway tracks slowly at 90°. Approach a crossing in the primary riding position to deter overtaking, and then look out for the smoothest place to cross. If the rails are oblique to the road, either move further out and then turn left to cross at 90°, or move left just before the crossing and then turn right to cross, depending on the direction of the rails (Figure 10.1). Signal your intentions clearly, but return your hands to the handlebar before you cross.

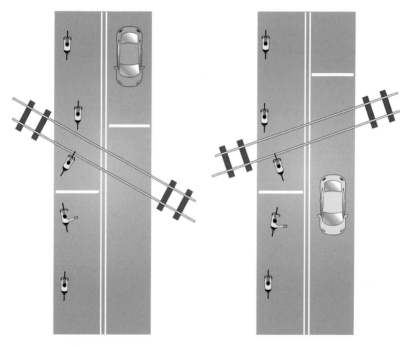

Figure 10.1 *Crossing diagonal railway or tramway tracks*

Tramways

Tram tracks can pose even greater risks of injury to cyclists than railway crossings. In addition to the possibility of slipping on a rail, there is the serious hazard of a cycle wheel falling into a rail groove. A wheel trapped in this way will very quickly throw the rider, it being almost impossible to recover the situation.

When you are riding close to tram tracks, keep alert for any change in direction of the rails towards where you are riding. Places where trams turn are a particular hazard as the rails may cross the carriageway at a very shallow angle. You should also look out for rails moving towards the side of the road near tram stops. Never cross tram rails at an angle of less than 45°; wherever possible cross at 90°, especially if the surface is wet. Use a procedure similar to that previously described for level crossings when you need to change your direction for a safer crossing.

Rails that turn like this are extremely hazardous and need to be avoided. If traffic conditions do not permit a safer crossing, stop and inch your way forward.

Take care, too, that you do not drift sideways into a tram rail groove. If vehicles ahead start to pull out in front of you or block your way, don't cross an adjacent tram track without first making all the right preparations.

If you find yourself about to cross a rail without sufficient notice, pull up on the handlebar to 'jump' the bike across.

Camber

Camber is the arched contour of a road surface from one side to the other. The slope on either side is usually less than 5% and poses no problem to a cyclist, but occasionally steeper cambers will be found, particularly close to the kerb. Reverse cambers, where one edge of the road is higher than the centre, may sometimes be encountered, and some newer roads are superelevated on curves, which means that the road slopes steadily from the outside of the curve to the inside.

For a cyclist, steep camber is mainly a problem on bends, requiring you to lean more when curving right, or less when curving left. If unforeseen, this can result in under- or oversteering, to which the response should be to slow down until the cycle is again under proper control.

When stopping, a steep camber can make it more difficult to set a foot down, potentially leading to a fall. If the camber appears steep, do not ride or stop too close to the road edge, and get off the saddle as you come to a halt.

Slippery surfaces

Surface coverings can reduce grip between wheel and road. Examples include water, mud, oil, ice, leaves and loose gravel. All are worse if the surface is wet, when oil can be difficult to see. Special care is needed on the first wet day after a dry spell. Studs, manhole covers, carriageway markings and zebra crossings may also be slippery when wet.

Whenever slippery surfaces are likely, reduce speed and take extra care when turning or braking. Keep your weight low and both hands on the handlebar. If you see a definite hazard, cross it keeping straight and upright, with the brakes off. Changing to a lower gear can help. Going downhill, you may be more stable by pedalling with the brakes applied.

Pedestrians

All pedestrians are vulnerable, even to a cycle, while the elderly and infirm may be unable to move quickly. You should show caution, consideration and courtesy towards pedestrians.

However, this can give rise to problems for cyclists. For example, all drivers turning at a road junction should give way to pedestrians crossing. Unfortunately, many drivers do not and a cyclist who tries to set an example can be at risk from those less patient. Therefore, the advice must be to give way as far as possible in such situations, but do not do so if it seems likely that a following driver will not.

Approach a zebra or signalled pedestrian crossing in the primary riding position, and be prepared to stop. If you are the first to give way, a slowing-down signal can let following drivers know your intentions so that they slow down too. Don't restart while anyone is crossing; this only causes unnecessary aggravation. At times a pedestrian who is crossing a road will aim to interweave with a cyclist on the far side without expecting the cyclist to give way. Cooperate if you can, so that no one is inconvenienced.

All walkers can change direction suddenly and may step out in front of you, but children are particularly unpredictable. Their traffic sense is underdeveloped, while a cycle can be difficult for anyone to see or hear. Children may emerge unseen from between parked cars. Wherever there are children beside the road, move towards the primary riding position and keep your fingers on the brakes. Look out for tell-tale signs of children's presence such as a ball or bicycle nearby, and take extra care near schools, playgrounds and ice-cream vans.

In places where cyclists and pedestrians are permitted to share space, do not expect to ride as quickly as you might on a road. Put as much distance as you can between you and people walking and ensure that your presence is noticed before you pass. Be prepared to give way or stop.

> It is illegal to cycle on a footway (or pavement) alongside a road (unless specifically signed for sharing by cyclists) and you should not do so. Footways are not designed for cycling speeds, and riding on them is almost always much less safe than cycling on the carriageway.

Sometimes cycling is permitted in confined spaces busy with pedestrians, such as at this bridge. Always ride slowly, showing patience and courtesy. If there's not sufficient space to pass, wait behind or dismount.

Other cyclists

Unfortunately, many cyclists do not ride well and some are a hazard to others as well as to themselves. Look out for other cyclists, especially at junctions, where many will put themselves into unsafe positions. If you are turning left from the primary riding position, take care that another cyclist has not come up on your left, intending to go straight on. When overtaking, allow plenty of room, and don't get led into a race by someone who is determined to show how fast they can go. It is better to slow down or stop until the person has gone. Cycle paths are another place for caution: too many cyclists fail to keep left and are not readily seen at night.

Dogs

Dogs can be a great hazard to cyclists. Whether just playful or not, dogs on the loose are as likely to cause serious injury to a cyclist as a collision with a car. A fall is likely when a dog runs in front of a cycle, or tries to grab a cyclist's ankles. Dogs seem hypnotically fascinated by revolving legs!

Always be cautious when you see a dog off the lead and no less so if a dog is on one side of a path and a pedestrian on the other – there may well be a long lead between the two. In the country, expect to find dogs near farms and houses. Don't just listen out for barking animals; quiet dogs can be just as much of a problem and may appear suddenly. If you have warning, get your hands over the brakes and your feet ready to accelerate; it is hard to tell in advance which might be the best action if a dog proves troublesome. Keep going at a steady pace, moving across the road away from the animal if it's safe to do so. Pretend that you're ignoring it – but don't!

If you're chased, you must decide quickly whether you can outpace the animal, or whether it would be better to slow down or stop. All else being equal, it's better to slow down if the dog's ahead of you; otherwise accelerate. To try to placate a dog, ease off pedalling, and speak to it soothingly or shout firmly; either method will work about as often as the other. If the dog is persistent, stop and repeat the technique, edging your bike on. Most dogs submit very quickly and they will rarely chase you beyond their home territory.

If you are bitten by a dog or any other animal, see a doctor quickly. In countries where rabies is present, urgent medical attention is essential.

Horses

Horses are frightened easily by cycles, and a frightened horse is a hazard to everyone. Ensure that a rider has seen you before you overtake, and if possible exchange a few words of greeting as this can help reassure the horse. Allow time for the rider to take firm control of the animal and to turn it to face you if thought necessary. Always follow a rider's instruction.

Give a horse plenty of room when you pass, even if motorists before you do not. If possible, cross right over to the opposite side of the road before overtaking, signalling clearly first right and then left if other vehicles are following. Pass slowly. It is better to wait for oncoming traffic to pass than to be forced close to a horse.

Give horses as much space as you can and only pass when the rider has consented

Insects

Although they are such small creatures, insects of one kind or another can create problems for cyclists. They may enter a cyclist's eye, causing loss of sight of the way ahead. If this happens, keep steering the way you were, and brake quickly. Re-open at least one eye as soon as possible, if only briefly, to get to the side of the road. It helps if you've practised riding blind. Swarms of insects can be a problem at dusk on summer evenings. Wearing spectacles, sunglasses, a visor or a peaked cap helps to protect the eyes.

Biting insects are a nuisance in some areas, although the draught made by the movement of a bicycle offers some protection. If you find insects a problem, buy an insect repellent.

Fumes

Many people worry about cycling in traffic for fear of the fumes inhaled. Although motor fumes are by no means pleasant, doctors consider that the benefits of the exercise obtained by cycling far outweigh the harmful effect of fumes. You are almost certainly better off than a person sitting motionless in a car. However, riding for a long time in dense traffic can lead to drowsiness, and that means you will be less alert than you should be. You must take this into account when manoeuvring.

It is sensible not to breathe in more gases than you must. Don't stay close to the exhaust pipe of a vehicle in front in queues, and ventilate your lungs well during gaps in traffic. If making a long cross-town journey, use low-trafficked roads where you can. If you find fumes a problem, you might consider wearing a face mask.

Tiredness

Like fumes, tiredness affects attentiveness: you will be that much slower to recognise and respond to traffic hazards. Cycling in the fresh air counteracts tiredness to some extent, but not as much as some people suppose. If you feel tired and you've far to go, you should do something about it.

If your tiredness is mainly the result of physical exhaustion, stopping for a while can help your muscles to renew their strength. Wrapping up warm is also important. Eating a bar of high-energy food is a quick way of topping up your energy reserves.

Mental fatigue is the most unsafe form of tiredness, and is satisfied only by sleep; frequent stops may make you even more tired. Try to find somewhere for an hour's snooze. Alternatively, it may be possible to complete your journey with the assistance of some other mode of transport.

Alcohol and drugs

Apart from the Breathalyser regulations, all the laws about driving under the influence of alcohol or drugs apply as much to cyclists as to motorists, and the limits are the same. But the legal limits are to a large extent arbitrary. Any amount of alcohol impairs a cyclist's ability to assess traffic hazards and increases risk, and it is a mistake to think that a drunk cyclist is a liability to no one else.

Many common medicines also affect the ability to react quickly, in a way that can make you more vulnerable. Do not cycle if any of these make you drowsy. Only fools mix drinking or drugs with their cycling.

State of mind

The effect on safety when one's mind has been disturbed by some recent event is little appreciated. Examples include an argument or bad news, or, indeed, when elated by good news. Make a special effort at these times to forget everything else and to keep your mind on the road.

If you have been aggravated by the actions of another road user, look for the earliest opportunity to have a good interaction with someone else, such as by ceding way to a pedestrian or thanking a driver who is helpful to you.

Check your understanding:

- ☐ What is the best way to cross a bad surface that you can't avoid?
- ☐ What are the principal hazards when crossing a tram track?
- ☐ Under what circumstances may it be best not to give way to pedestrians?
- ☐ What influences on you can make it more difficult to recognise and respond to hazards?

Chapter 11

Cycling in town

This chapter, along with practice in cycling, should help you to:

- ➔ recognise a variety of hazards present in towns and understand how to deal with them
- ➔ ride in busy streets and handle one-way systems
- ➔ filter safely through traffic
- ➔ understand how traffic calming can impact upon cyclists.

Towns provide a concentration of problems for cyclists, with large flows of traffic and pedestrians, and hazards at frequent intervals. Nevertheless, cycling in town is a very practical way of getting about, and it is often quickest, too.

Most of the techniques described so far apply to cycling in town, but there are also some special considerations.

Choosing routes

The choice of route in a town can make a big difference to how agreeable your journey is. In many instances there may be no real choice, or time will dictate that the most direct route must be used, but where there are realistic alternatives, bear the following in mind.

The most obvious places to avoid are large roundabouts and gyratories. Ring roads are also a problem, both because they are circuitous and because fast-weaving movements by motor traffic are common at junctions. Where main roads must be crossed, try to use crossings with traffic signals.

Contrary to popular opinion, back-street routes are not always safer than main roads. Routes where you frequently have to give way to others destroy momentum, tax your brakes and increase the chances of you suffering from someone's error – perhaps your own. Keep with the priority of other traffic wherever possible.

Narrow roads lined by parked cars should be considered a hazard, as should shopping streets. On the other hand, main roads with bus lanes which cyclists can use are often good routes, while dual carriageways where parking is prohibited can be easier for cycling than many people imagine, although this depends very much upon the design of junctions.

③ Traffic-jamming and filtering

'Traffic-jamming' (negotiating traffic jams) is an advanced technique, the basis of which is the fact that cycles are more manoeuvrable than motor vehicles and that cycles can often proceed in congested streets when other vehicles cannot. Traffic-jamming recognises the different characteristics of cycles and motor vehicles and takes advantage of these to enhance a cyclist's progress and safety. It does not condone illegal or anti-social practices. Skilled traffic-jamming is safe as well as useful, acknowledging the responsibilities of cyclists and inconveniencing no one.

The underlying principle of traffic-jamming is to conserve momentum by stopping as infrequently as possible. Although peak speeds of cars are higher than those of cycles, traffic in town tends to rush from one jam to another, and overall speeds are low. By maintaining a more constant velocity, cyclists can often achieve a higher average speed than others.

There are three components to successful traffic-jamming:

- ▶ correct positioning in moving traffic in order to maintain progress and to maximise safety
- ▶ looking ahead to avoid unnecessary stops
- ▶ filtering through stationary traffic.

Where your average speed is similar to that of other traffic, correct positioning means adopting the primary riding position. Although you should not unreasonably impede others, don't move to the secondary riding position, even if safe to do so, if this would merely lead to leap-frogging.

To accelerate from stops quickly and keep up with the flow, a high cadence and frequent gear changes are advantages. Use a low gear for quick starts, and then a higher gear to maintain position. Good brakes are essential, as traffic often stops abruptly or cuts in front. You must have absolute confidence in the reliability of your cycle. When stopping in traffic, brake hard if conditions permit, in order to give yourself time to change down in gear.

In order to stop as infrequently as possible, keep looking ahead, anticipating the movement of traffic and the changing of traffic lights and other controls. Modify your speed so as to arrive at restrictions when conditions are in your favour, but be careful that slowing down does not encourage someone else to cut in.

Filtering

It is unreasonable to expect cyclists to wait in long queues of traffic when there is room for them to pass, but filtering through traffic requires great care. Advantages in saving time must be balanced against your increased vulnerability while filtering. Normally, overtaking should only take place on the right, and this should be your preference. But on congested roads where there is insufficient clearance from oncoming vehicles, or where there is more than one lane in your direction, this may be impractical, and it is acceptable to pass to the left – a process sometimes referred to as 'undertaking', and not without reason!

The obvious risks are that you will be squeezed if drivers move left, that a door will be opened into your path, or that you will hit pedestrians crossing when they expect no one to be moving. You are also vulnerable to vehicles turning at junctions, including those that a driver in the queue ahead allows to turn right across your path.

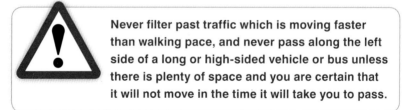

Never filter past traffic which is moving faster than walking pace, and never pass along the left side of a long or high-sided vehicle or bus unless there is plenty of space and you are certain that it will not move in the time it will take you to pass.

On multi-lane roads it can be safer to pass between lanes, riding the lane line. Wherever you ride, move slowly in a low gear, ready for an emergency stop should someone cross your path.

As you filter, keep your eyes open for 'stepping stones' between vehicles, gaps where you can pull back into the flow of traffic if it speeds up, or if you are faced with oncoming traffic from which you need to take refuge. By looking ahead and filtering from stepping stone to stepping stone, the risk in filtering can be much reduced.

Where possible filter to the right of traffic where you are more easily seen by other drivers. Look ahead for the next space into which you can divert when traffic moves off or there is an approaching vehicle.

Filtering by cyclists is legal, so long as you do not cross any continuous white lines and you obey all regulatory signs (such as the keep left signs on traffic islands) and signals. Ride with care when you filter; injudicious filtering can complicate the traffic situation for everyone.

At junctions, it is better to stop behind the first vehicle in a queue, rather than to rush past to the front. Allow that driver to concentrate on choosing a safe moment to move. If possible, adopt the primary riding position whenever you stop in traffic, but in any event ensure that the following driver has seen you (by establishing eye contact) and will allow you priority. If you are first in a queue, always ride in the primary riding position, and if you are only one or two vehicles back, it is often better to wait there in this position too.

At some junctions, advanced stop lines enable cyclists to go ahead of other vehicles. These were described in Chapter 8.

One-way streets

These vary in width and purpose. In narrow streets, typical of older town centres, the usual rules for cycling apply. Where there is only a single moving traffic lane, normally you should ride in the centre of that lane, well away from parked vehicles, their opening doors and any pedestrians who may step out between them. Retain this position to turn left or right.

Wider one-way streets often form the arteries of an area-wide traffic management scheme intended to speed traffic movement by simplifying junctions and reducing conflicting movements. Here problems can arise for cyclists who need to cross from one side to the other of the street, to turn to or from the right, or to go ahead where the main flow turns left. Negotiation can be used, but it is often simpler to use the gaps in traffic, when they occur, to change sides in advance of where you wish to turn, and to ride on the right side of the road in the interim. Likewise, it can be easier and quicker to turn right onto the right side of the road, only crossing to the left when it is clear to do so.

Gaining confidence in riding on the right is a useful skill for towns – and for your holidays abroad! There are still primary and secondary riding positions, but they are mirror images of the left-side positions. Do not ride further right than it is safe to do so. If you understand the underlying principles, you should have little difficulty. It is necessary to be able to look over your left shoulder at traffic behind and you need to have practised riding with only the right hand on the handlebar while doing so.

Something to watch for when riding on the right side of one-way streets is drivers who use the right lane for overtaking fast. This is most likely where there is a long distance between right turns and where a one-way system resembles a gyratory. You must be guided by local conditions, but prominent positioning will always maximise your safety.

Try to avoid weaving across one-way streets unnecessarily. For instance, if making consecutive right turns, stay on the right in between.

Shopping streets

Streets crowded with shoppers are always hazardous places for pedestrians and traffic alike. It is not simply that there are a lot of people around, but that their movements are erratic and in all directions, including across the road. The greatest hazard is from pedestrians stepping onto the road without warning, but drivers will also have their attention distracted. In any crowded street, keep well out from the pavement, with your fingers over the brake levers, poised for immediate action. Do your best to ignore the shops and their wares, and keep your eyes scanning constantly from left to ahead to right and back again. Never creep along the kerb where there is little space, even in stationary traffic, for pedestrians will be mainly looking for larger vehicles and may not notice you. Car doors may also be opened to drop or pick up passengers. Drivers who are concentrating on pedestrians and traffic ahead may restart without noticing a cyclist alongside.

If, despite all your vigilance, someone does dart in front of you without warning, brake hard if you can, but keep steering straight. It might sound harsh, but you are better off colliding with a pedestrian than turning under the wheels of a car.

In busy streets, keep well out from parked cars where you can more easily see and be seen. Cooperate with pedestrians crossing the road.

③ Bus lanes

Bus lanes can be very useful for cyclists, who may use nearly all with-flow and many contraflow lanes. Cyclists may also use some bus-only streets. Local signs will indicate where cycles are permitted, as well as detailing hours of operation.

By using a bus lane you gain some separation from general traffic, sharing space with professional drivers, and you may have a clearer passage through a congested street. With contraflow lanes you may save a considerable distance by avoiding a circuitous detour. In fact, you should think of all bus lanes mainly as a time or distance saver; the safety benefits in practice are usually minimal. Sometimes access to and from bus lanes requires special care if you need to make what for traffic as a whole is an unusual, and therefore less expected, manoeuvre. Use positioning and signalling to make it quite clear where you are going.

Bus lanes are useful in affording separation from most traffic in towns. Take advantage of the space by riding in the centre unless it is safe for another authorised user to pass.

When riding in a bus lane, keep to its centre, unless there is another authorised user behind you and it is safe to be passed. Taxis and motorcycles may use some bus lanes. Buses and taxis should normally overtake a cyclist by straddling the lane line, but motorcyclists may not. Take particular care where bus lanes cross side roads, in case drivers cut across you to turn left. Look out, too, for the illegal use of bus lanes by unauthorised vehicles trying to jump a queue of traffic; they may be in too much of a hurry to look out for a cyclist.

Traffic calming

In many towns, traffic-calming measures and vehicle-restricted areas are being introduced to mitigate the impact of traffic and in particular to reduce vehicle speeds. By reducing the speed, dominance and possibly volume of motor vehicles, these schemes should benefit cyclists. In practice, however, the situation is not so simple, for some of the measures introduce new hazards which can partly or completely negate any advantage.

The following sections describe some of the more common traffic-calming techniques and the implications for cyclists.

Width restrictions

Traffic throttles, centre islands and chicanes are typical forms of width restriction which are intended to slow traffic, or provide easier crossing places for pedestrians, or both.

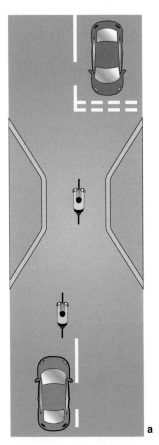 

a   b

Figure 11.1 *Width restrictions*

a Traffic throttle. Always use the primary riding position.
b Centre islands. Be aware that drivers may cut in.

In practice, the effect on vehicle speeds can be minimal unless combined with some form of vertical deflection. The effect on cyclists, though, may be significant. Above all else, cyclists need space – for manoeuvring and comfort, to give warning of the actions of others, and in which to take avoiding action should this be necessary. Width restrictions reduce the amount of space available and may significantly increase risk for a cyclist if a motorist tries to overtake in the limited room remaining.

At traffic throttles (Figure 11.1a), a cyclist can usually take protective action quite easily by adopting the primary riding position at the approach to the restriction. This will mean the cyclist moving close to the centre of the road, and other drivers will then usually stay behind. Signal clearly as you change position, obey the priority signs and keep to the centre of the throttle so that oncoming traffic gives way. Never be tempted yourself to squeeze through a width restriction when traffic is coming towards you.

Centre islands, or refuges, (Figure 11.1b) can be much more difficult, and those with narrow lanes are some of the most intimidating and hazardous places for cyclists on the roads today. Here, too, you should adopt the primary riding position at the approach, but be ready for the driver who overtakes regardless and then pulls in sharply left in front of you. Signalling right can sometimes assert your right of way, but you must always be prepared to move left quickly and hold on.

Try not to be squeezed at refuges. Adopt the primary riding position as you approach.

A chicane is similar to a throttle or centre island, depending upon whether the entry is situated centrally on the road or to one side. Speeds may be lower due to the zigzag path that vehicles must take.

Some width restrictions include cycle bypass lanes, the use of which by cyclists is optional. Use these if they would give you an easier passage, but take care that they don't introduce hazards of their own. Narrow widths, poor surfaces and drainage covers are typical problems. You may also lose your priority in the traffic stream.

Road humps and cushions

Because the inherent suspension system of a cycle is much less effective than that of a car, a cyclist crossing a road hump experiences more discomfort than a motorist at the same speed. There are hazards, too, if there is a vertical step or upstand to mount, or where the surface has become worn or is slippery. Crossing any upstand accelerates cycle headset wear. On private roads, some very abrupt humps are to be found, which require great care.

Road humps should always be approached in the primary riding position to deter overtaking by another driver. Lift your weight off the saddle at each transition to minimise bike shock and discomfort.

Speed cushions (Figure 11.2) are a variant of a road hump, designed to affect cars but not wider vehicles, such as buses. Instead of extending from kerb to kerb, the raised area is of limited width, the normal road surface being retained on either side. As well as benefiting buses, speed cushions overcome many of the problems of road humps for cyclists, who may ride between the cushions.

Approach speed cushions in the primary riding position, moving to one side or the other as you reach each cushion and then returning to the best riding position immediately afterwards. If traffic conditions permit, you may have a straighter and easier ride if you use a gap between cushions rather than at the edge of the road. If you need to maintain your position on the road in order to deter overtaking and the cushion edges are not too abrupt, consider riding across the cushions. Lift your weight off the saddle as for a road hump.

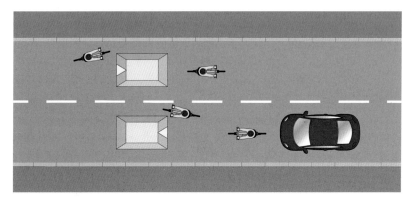

Figure 11.2 *Speed cushions*

Take the centre gap only if there is no oncoming traffic.

Surface treatments

Non-tarmacadam surfaces are often used in traffic-calming schemes to delimit carriageway space, to encourage low speeds or simply for visual appeal. Although some of these treatments have no special effect on cycles, others lead to discomfort and can affect cycle control. Cobbles and some kinds of blockwork are examples. In all cases, lift your weight off the saddle to minimise discomfort and hold the handlebar firmly. Take extra care when it is wet or icy.

Rumble strips of coarse chippings, setts or thermoplastic material, laid transversely across the road, also affect cycle control, sometimes markedly. They can increase risk if crossed at speed. Sometimes it will be possible to pass by the side; if this is not possible, hold tight, proceed slowly and use the primary riding position to deter overtaking.

Environmental areas

In some localities, whole areas have been 'traffic calmed' or closed to through motor traffic by road closures and other measures.

As long as reasonably direct through routes for cyclists remain – such as by the provision of cycle exemption gaps at road closures – environmental areas can be useful for cycling, with the usual caveats that any route should have good surfaces and be reasonably free from dense parking and junctions at which you must give way. On the other hand, if through routes are circuitous, there is no reason – and usually little safety benefit – why cyclists should prefer these to more direct roads.

However effective restrictions may be in reducing speeds at particular places, one result is that drivers spend more of their time accelerating and braking while driving along these roads. One consequence of this is that even good drivers may have their attention distracted from the road, while some drivers react in such a way as to minimise the effect of the restrictions on their progress. To a cyclist, the fierce acceleration and braking of modern cars can be more of a problem than absolute speed. For this reason alone, many experienced cyclists prefer free-flowing main roads to the 'dodgems' problems of some environmental areas. The use by cyclists of roads such as these for through journeys is generally only preferable where the lengths are short and it enables major hazards to be avoided or quiet routes to be linked.

Check your understanding:

☐ What are the risks involved in filtering through traffic and how can you minimise these?

☐ Where and how should you ride through busy shopping streets?

☐ Which consequences of traffic calming should you particularly look out for and how should you respond?

Chapter 12
Cycling in the country

This chapter, along with practice in cycling, should help you to:

❯ climb and descend hills

❯ recognise features of the countryside to which you will need to give particular attention

❯ traverse off-road routes

❯ undertake longer rides.

In the countryside, cycling becomes a real pleasure and you can enjoy the peace and tranquillity of your surroundings in a way that no other driver can. But even in the heart of the country there are new skills to acquire, and although crashes are less frequent on country roads than in town, when they do occur they tend to be more severe as speeds are often higher.

Choosing routes

Roads in the countryside tend to divide between two extremes. The majority of roads offer peaceful riding over considerable distances. Seek particularly the unclassified roads, which are coloured yellow on Ordnance Survey 1:50,000 maps. There are few parts of the UK where these roads cannot be joined together to form very satisfactory routes for the cycle tourist; for the most peaceful routes, keep clear of large towns and industrial areas and give preference to the narrower lanes.

Main roads, on the other hand, and particularly trunk routes (coloured green on maps), can be very busy, with large numbers of heavy lorries. Speeds are often fast, and drivers may not expect to meet cyclists. Busy roads which are narrow can be especially unpleasant. If you are riding in the country simply to get from place to place as quickly as possible, you might have to use these roads, as indeed you might in order to enter a town where there is no alternative route. Wherever possible, however, try to avoid them. As in towns, dual-carriageway trunk roads are usually better for cycling than single carriageways, as drivers will have more room to give you the clearance they should when overtaking.

One consideration in choosing country routes is often the hilliness of the terrain. Don't be misled by the folklore that cycling is easiest on the flat: you pedal for longer where there are no descents to freewheel and fatigue is experienced sooner. Gently undulating roads are much the least tiring overall, as well as being more interesting. In windy weather, it is often better to seek the shelter of hills or a winding, narrow lane than to use a flatter or more direct, open road, even if this means taking a slightly longer route.

Narrow lanes

The width of a road often reflects the amount of traffic using it, so it is not surprising that cyclists cherish riding along narrow country lanes. They are also the place where a cycle is more clearly the equal of other vehicles, for it is not so easy to pass or ignore.

Narrow lanes are ones which can be travelled by four-wheeled vehicles in only one direction at a time, and passing places, often informal, are to be found every so often. Sometimes there is sufficient room in between for a car to overtake a cyclist safely, but if not, you shouldn't hesitate to keep to the centre of the road until a passing place is reached. In the case of a car coming towards you, keep in the centre until the driver has slowed right down, and then pass as best you can to the left side. If you meet a lorry or farm vehicle coming the other way, even a cycle may not be able to pass, and you may have to retrace your path.

The centre of the road should be your preferred riding position along narrow country lanes, but in practice the surface will often be unsuitable and you will need to keep to one side or the other. A factor in choosing which side will be the condition of the road surface, while approaching a left-hand bend, riding on the right side will maximise visibility. All the time keep listening for other vehicles, and be sure to return to the left side of the road at widenings and junctions.

Bends on country roads

Many country roads twist and turn around sharp bends, with restricted visibility. Drivers familiar with the roads sometimes travel much faster than they should and if cycling is not common in the locality, they may not be at all prepared to expect a cyclist. Whenever you ride through bends on roads of this type and it would not be safe for you to be overtaken, prefer the primary riding position.

Moving out on left-hand bends makes it easier for you to see ahead and discourages others from passing you unsafely. Notice how close the Limit Point of Vision (see later in this chapter) is here, which indicates that the turn is severe.

Hill climbing

Climbing hills need not be hard work, but for many cyclists the use of inadequate gears or the wrong technique can make it so. Tackled properly, almost any hill can be climbed more easily by riding than by dismounting and pushing.

As you approach a hill, change to a lower gear as soon as you feel that your cadence is beginning to decrease. By far the commonest fault amongst cyclists in hill climbing is changing gear too late, by which time they are more exhausted than is necessary. With practice you should be able to change before your cadence decreases, in order to anticipate the loss of momentum which inevitably occurs during a gear change. Learn just how much momentum you do lose under differing circumstances and detect the increase in pedalling effort which precedes a reduction in pedalling speed; this is the correct time to change gear. Your aim should be to keep the pedals turning at the cadence which matches your maximum efficiency, at least until you have reached bottom gear and can change down no further.

If a hill is gradual, you should change down one gear at a time following the procedure explained above. As the gradient slackens, change back to higher gears as soon as you can, to increase speed and maintain cadence. However, if a hill is steep, you will waste much less momentum if you change down several gears at a time. When the need to use a smaller chainring seems likely, be sure to change to this in good time; on a derailleur-geared bike, it is more difficult to move the front changer under pressure than the rear. On sudden, severe hills, it is often best to go straight for a very low gear and then to change up slowly if you find that you have gone too far. If that is the case, pedal a bit faster while changing back up; to maintain the same cadence in this instance might reduce control and make balancing more difficult.

As you near the top of a steep hill, change back up again, although you may first find it more refreshing to pedal a short while in what would otherwise be too low a gear. This is particularly beneficial during a series of steep ups and downs, giving the leg muscles some chance to recuperate.

Once you reach bottom gear, it will no longer be possible to maintain normal cadence, and your pedalling will slow down. At first you may feel that this is the point to get off and walk, but don't! Part of the skill in riding up steep hills is having the patience to ride up slowly. Although it may seem dreadfully slow compared with a preceding descent, it will still be faster than walking. It is at this time, if you are on a quiet road with little traffic, that you can look at your surroundings, which will take your mind off your speed. Before you realise it, you will be at the top.

There are two limiting factors which determine how steep a hill you can climb. The first is your ability to maintain balance, and the second is the tendency of the front wheel to lift off the ground on really steep climbs. Given suitable gears, the strength of the rider is less important, although regular hill climbing strengthens the calf muscles and makes the activity easier. At low speeds on steep gradients it is almost impossible to steer a straight line. Climbing can be made easier if you reduce the mean gradient by zigzagging across the road. Obviously, this can only be done if there is no traffic and you are sure that the way ahead is clear. With traffic, take care not to put yourself at risk by riding too irregular a course, although too great an effort to keep straight might mean that a following driver will not appreciate your difficulties and will give you too little clearance. To stop the front wheel lifting, throw your weight towards the front of the bicycle by crouching and keeping your head low, but only do this as much as is necessary, since steering will become more difficult.

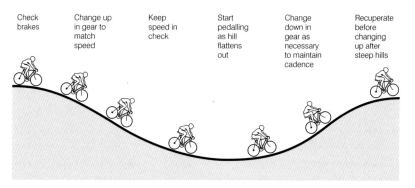

| Check brakes | Change up in gear to match speed | Keep speed in check | Start pedalling as hill flattens out | Change down in gear as necessary to maintain cadence | Recuperate before changing up after steep hills |

Figure 12.1 *Descending and climbing hills*

If you are approaching an uphill after a descent where you were able to freewheel, make the most of the energy gained from going down to help you on the way back up (Figure 12.1). On the way down, select a high gear and start pedalling when the hill flattens out as soon as your freewheeling speed decreases to that matched by the selected gear. Then continue to pedal at your normal cadence while changing down again as necessary. This may seem like a lot of gear changing, but it is the most efficient way of riding. Too many cyclists wait until they have reached the very bottom of a descent before starting to pedal again, even braking when they should be pedalling, with the result that they need to supply much more energy for the new climb. Nearing the bottom of a hill you should not normally brake to a speed less than that at which you can pedal, assuming that visibility and traffic conditions are favourable.

Nowhere in the advice given so far has there been any mention of standing on the pedals to climb a hill. There is a good reason for this. Standing causes the cycle to lurch from side to side to counter the imbalance of the body. Although standing can enable you to transmit more power to the cycle, it is a much less efficient means of pedalling than the correct 'ankling' technique (see Figure 5.2), as the force to turn the pedals is applied through a smaller angle of pedal movement and to only one side at a time. Selecting a lower gear, remaining seated and ankling the pedals is a much less tiring and more elegant way of riding.

There is, however, one circumstance when standing on the pedals can be useful. This is when you have to surmount a very short rise either when travelling fast on an otherwise level road (e.g. over a bridge), where a double gear change in a very short period of time would otherwise be necessary, or if you accidentally failed to change down sufficiently in advance and a further change would make you lose too much momentum.

Should you have to stop on a steep hill, restarting can be difficult even if you are in a low gear. Often you will not be able to gain your balance at the first attempt, but by pushing off again as soon as a foot lands back on the ground, you will have a little more momentum than before and you may then succeed. On really sharp slopes, a multiple push start might be necessary. In all cases, if you are using toe clips or clipless pedals, try to engage them as you mount. You will probably not be able to stop your pedalling sufficiently in order to do this afterwards, and hill climbing is more strenuous without these aids.

Descending hills

Going downhill is the time for a cyclist to rest the legs, but that is the only part of the body that can relax. Although climbing hills requires the most physical energy, it is generally descending a hill that requires the most mental energy and concentration. You will be travelling faster, conditions about you will change more quickly, and the consequences of any fall will be more severe.

The first thing to do at the very beginning of a descent – each and every descent – is to check that your brakes still work! This is the only time that you will be able to stop without brakes with reasonable safety. If the descent is gradual, you can then release the brakes a little, but keep your fingers over the levers, pulling upon them so that the brake blocks are only just clear of the rims. The speed to which you can safely allow yourself to accelerate depends very much upon the nature of the road – its straightness, visibility, surface quality, the number of side roads and entrances, and the presence of other vehicles, moving or parked.

 **At no time should you ride faster than a speed from which you can safely and easily stop within the distance you can see to be clear.**

To ensure this, curb your speed when necessary by applying the brakes continuously once the limiting speed has been reached.

Knowledge of how fast you can go under different circumstances is only gained through experience, and you should practise braking on different types of hill until you are confident about your bike's capabilities. Never assume that you can always brake a bit harder when you need to; the risk is that a brake cable will snap. In fact, to minimise cable wear as well as to have something in reserve for genuine emergencies, you should always apply the brakes gradually, not suddenly.

If a hill is steep, keep your speed right down from the start so that it is well below that which might be safe on a gradual hill, or you may not be able to stop sufficiently quickly if you need to. On very steep hills, this can mean descending at a speed not much faster than that at which you would cycle up, and the braking force required may make your hands hurt. Take care not to weaken your hands by applying this sort of effort for too long.

If the road curves sharply, you need to take care that you can negotiate the bends without being thrown into a verge or the path of other traffic. The Limit Point of Vision is the furthest point you can see ahead where you have a clear view of the road surface. This determines how fast you can safely enter a bend. The closer the Limit Point, the less time and distance you have in which to react, and therefore the slower you must go.

As you approach a bend, watch the Limit Point. If it becomes closer than the distance in which you can stop, slow down. If the Limit Point continues to get closer, the bend is tightening and you will need to slow down more. On the other hand, when the Limit Point starts to move away, you may safely regain speed.

On long, steep hills the wheel rims can get very hot and, in extreme cases, there is a risk of this causing an explosion of an inner tube. Care should be taken not to heat up the rims too much. One way to reduce the heat a little is to apply the brakes with a 'pumping' on-and-off action; another, where there is no traffic, is to zigzag slowly downwards in order to reduce the mean gradient. On the worst hills, stopping is advisable every so often to cool the rims, and to rest your hands. These considerations are particularly important with heavily laden cycles and tandems, as weight is an important factor (which is why tandems are best fitted with an additional hub or disc brake).

Checking your speed is not the only important aspect of keeping your bike under control when descending hills. You should be able to take over control with the pedals if necessary, for example, to outpace a dog or a car coming suddenly into your path. Many motorists considerably underestimate the speed of cycles on hills. To be able to resume pedalling quickly, you need to be in a gear which gives a pedalling speed closest to that at which you freewheel. You should therefore normally change up to a suitable gear at the start of a descent. Don't do this, however, if you are riding through a series of short, sharp hills, when excessive gear changing could be a nuisance.

Long hills

In the country, hills are frequently a mile or more long, and in mountainous areas they may be considerably longer. The physical skills of hill climbing were discussed above, but if you are going to spend a long time climbing a hill it is also necessary to be prepared psychologically. From this point of view, the hardest part of a hill is the beginning, while you strive to find the gear best suited to the gradient. You need to find the pace that best suits you; having found that, you can relax more, admire the scenery and forget the pedalling, which soon becomes automatic! Long uphills can be strenuous, but the exhilaration of reaching the summit entirely by your own power cannot be matched by any other form of travel and makes it all worthwhile.

The technique of zigzagging up or down a hill when there is no other traffic has been mentioned. At the approach to mountain passes, very often the road itself will zigzag, with sharp hairpin bends at the changes of direction. The insides of these bends are sometimes very steep indeed and the camber may be unfavourable. Always adopt the primary riding position approaching a hairpin bend, signalling clearly if you intend to take the bend wide (Figure 12.2). Be alert to traffic from the opposite direction cutting the corner. If there is no other traffic and visibility is good, it can be advantageous to cross to the outside of a steep bend.

Figure 12.2
Hairpin bends

When negotiating hairpin bends on mountainous roads – whether going up or down – take the bend wide.

One of the great joys of cycling is descending a long hill. It is in many ways the just reward for the effort of the last climb up, while part of that joy is undoubtedly the thrill of freewheeling at speed. In many places in the country this experience can be enjoyed quite harmlessly, but it must always be borne in mind that speed increases risk, and you should pay full attention to the cautions about descending hills.

Farms

Farms are the livelihood of the countryside, and fascinating places to observe. Many of the lanes preferred by cyclists pass right by farmyards, which provide a close insight into farm life. However, farms present hazards, too: slow down when approaching one, and keep alert.

Mud on the road is a characteristic of farmyards and field entrances away from the principal traffic routes, as is dung from farm animals. At best this can make a mess of your bike; at worst it can cause a fall under less than pleasant circumstances. Frequently, road surfaces past farms are damaged, with mud hiding potholes and ruts.

Always look out for animals near farms. Larger ones such as cows and sheep are usually no great problem, although not to be argued with! If they are being herded along the road, don't try to pass to the side as you may be crushed. It's better to wait if they're going in your direction, or to retreat if they're coming towards you. Follow the directions of farmers herding cattle.

Smaller creatures such as chickens, geese and ducks can be more of a problem. These will usually try to get out of your way (although geese may be more aggressive), but in doing so they might take the most direct route past your front wheel.

Dogs are frequently to be found in farmyards, and the usual cautions apply (see Chapter 10).

Vegetation

Trees and hedges by the roadside contribute much to the country scene, and can also have important advantages in reducing the effect of wind on a cyclist. However, some vegetation can cause problems. Close hedges reduce forward visibility, not only for yourself but also for anyone coming towards you. On roads of this kind you must be particularly attentive at bends and near junctions of any kind. Sensible positioning and keen listening are important.

Another hazard is caused by twigs or thin branches lying on the road. These can be picked up by a wheel of a cycle and then become stuck at a fork or mudguard stay. In extreme cases, this may cause the mudguard to collapse into the wheel, but in any event there is the possibility of the wheel stopping abruptly. Take great care to avoid debris of this kind on the road, and slow down as necessary.

Low, overhanging branches from trees and unchecked growth from hedges can prove a hazard, especially if at head height. Remember that a cyclist's head is higher than the roof of many cars, so clearance is not guaranteed just because other traffic uses a road. Thin branches without leaves can be very hard to see.

Less hazardous, but very much a nuisance, are thorns on the road that lead to punctures. These can occur anywhere, particularly in autumn, but are most often a problem where roadside hedges have been cut recently. Keep your eyes open for signs of trimming and then avoid remnants on the road as best you can. If you have to pass hedge trimming in progress, have patience, move to the opposite side of the road and ride carefully. It can be useful to stop just afterwards to remove any partially embedded thorns from your tyres before they penetrate further.

Cattle grids

These are commonly encountered in farming areas, often replacing gates at field boundaries along unfenced roads. Although a well-designed and maintained cattle grid poses no problems for cyclists, the same is not true of grids where rails are missing or bent, where the spacing is too wide or where the road surface on either side is uneven. Even those grids which are not unsafe differ considerably in the discomfort they inflict on a cyclist, while all grids are hazardous when wet or icy.

There are conflicting requirements for the speed at which a cyclist should approach a cattle grid. Generally, the faster you cross, the less discomfort you will feel. However, if there is something unsafe about the grid, approaching too quickly will not allow you time to take evasive action. Therefore the advice must be to approach cautiously, looking carefully at the surface. As soon as you can see that it is safe, accelerate. Unless you are going uphill, you should freewheel across the grid itself, holding tightly to the handlebar to counter the vibration produced by the rails. At the same time it is important to lift your weight off the saddle in order to minimise the force of the rail and road edges on the wheels.

Never follow close behind another vehicle crossing a cattle grid in case it slows down more than you have anticipated. Use the primary riding position to deter anyone from overtaking. It is usually possible to pass unsafe cattle grids by an adjacent gate.

Fords

Like cattle grids, fords are another form of barrier through which country lanes pass directly. They, too, pose hazards which can cause a spill, but many cyclists find fords fascinating and delight in 'ford bashing' by riding through them whenever possible!

Fords have an appeal for many cyclists, but slippery surfaces can be treacherous

Three factors need to be considered before crossing a ford and it pays to inspect the site first:

▶ The water should not be too deep; 15 cm (6 inches) or so is about the maximum that can be negotiated easily, as the force of water against the wheels can be considerable. If the water is more than about 5 cm (2 inches) deep you will get your feet wet! There is usually a depth post adjacent to a deep ford.

▶ The water should not be flowing too fast. If it is, the cross current can be sufficient to alter your course, particularly where a ford is wide.

▶ Look carefully at the road surface beneath the ford. If it is loose or uneven, you may skid or a wheel may get caught. And if there is any algae (green slime), the surface will be slippery and not at all suitable for wet cycle tyres. Indeed, fords are sometimes slippery without appearing to be so.

If all seems well, select a low gear and ride through the ford ensuring that you keep a straight course, pedalling all the time. Sometimes the road will dip into and out of the water, so be prepared for sudden changes of inclination.

If you decide not to ride through a ford, there will usually be a footbridge close by.

Ferries

Cyclists can use most ferries, whether vehicular or pedestrian. To use the latter you may have to carry your cycle on board and this is easier if you remove the luggage first. You should also remove anything that could easily fall, such as a pump. As most pedestrian ferry journeys are short, it is best to stay with your bike to make sure that it doesn't fall. Holding the brakes on can help to keep both the bike and yourself still. If the crossing is rough and the cycle not under cover, try to protect it as best you can from salt water spray.

Cyclists ride on and off most vehicular ferries, though some operators require bikes to be loaded onto luggage trailers. When riding, select a low gear, even if the loading ramp goes down. There will often be a short, steep hump where the loading ramp meets the ship, for which a low gear may be necessary, and in any case the exit on the far side of the crossing may well rise steeply.

Loading ramps and ship decks are wet and often slippery, and sometimes there is cross-ribbing on the surface which can affect steering control. You should keep a tight hold of the handlebar while entering and leaving a ship. Ride in the centre of the loading ramp, for it would be unsafe for another vehicle to overtake. Keep your eyes open for slots or other hazards, steering as straight a line as you can. If you feel unhappy about riding, walk.

Off-road routes

Ordinary roads are not the only places where cyclists may ride in the countryside. Cyclists also have a legal right to use bridleways (but must give way to horse riders and walkers), and byways. In Scotland, but not elsewhere, cyclists may use cross-country footpaths.

In addition, there are country lanes which have not been metalled but which are, nevertheless, available for anyone to use. These are often referred to as 'white roads', because of their colour on OS maps, although this does not mean that all uncoloured roads shown on a map are public roads. It can be difficult to tell which are which, but it is usually reasonable to assume that a road is public if other defined rights of way, such as footpaths and bridleways, terminate on it.

Further, there are a number of routes in the country which cyclists are permitted to use, but which are not necessarily rights of way and on which, occasionally, a toll may be payable or permit required. Examples include routes through forests and country parks, cycle/walking trails along old railway lines, canal towpaths and private roads.

Although some of these routes may be sealed, in the majority of cases surfaces will be rough and unsuited to fast riding. They may also be subject to considerable variation in condition depending upon recent weather. Many bridleways are difficult to ride at any time (cyclists may use them, but they are only maintained in a condition suitable for horses), and it can be a real challenge to wheel or carry a cycle through a quagmire! The better paths are often those shown on a map as fenced on both sides.

These routes, then, are seldom time savers, but for the cycle tourist with time to explore, they can offer very peaceful and traffic-free penetration into the heart of the countryside. In some parts of the country there are long-distance bridleways and 'rough-stuff' routes, which can take several days to cover by cycle.

Riding rough tracks

Cycling along the easier routes – such as those promoted as cycle trails (see Chapter 13) – will probably require a lower gear than for on-road cycling, and you may have to endure the lesser comfort of a poor surface, but at a leisurely speed there should not be too many difficulties. Loose surfaces, potholes, bumps and mud are likely to be the greatest hazards to look out for.

This off-road track is quite easy to ride, with mud and submerged potholes the main things to watch for. Rougher tracks can be more challenging.

Riding rougher tracks, on the other hand, is a much more skilful business and needs to be treated seriously. The potential for losing control is always high, and it would be no joke to be stranded a mile or more from the nearest road with a buckled wheel or even a broken leg. You must have complete mastery of your machine, good judgement of surfaces, and the ability to react quickly to sudden changes in conditions. You must also be able to recognise the point at which you should get off and walk.

There are two essentials of a bike for rough riding: very low gears, and a front fork rake such that your feet cannot hit the front mudguard. All-terrain bikes have the advantage of being more robust, with wide tyres affording better grip, and there may be no mudguards to clog up.

Always keep firm hold of the handlebar, with your hands over the brake levers, even if climbing a hill. Also keep your feet on the pedals (toe clips and clipless pedals are an asset here). Keeping your body low and weight off the saddle will maximise stability and comfort. Rough riding is hard work mentally as well as physically and demands your continuous attention. If you want to admire the scenery, stop in order to do so.

Because of the need for firm steering control, gear changing is not always easy when riding a rough path. Engage a low gear before the going gets too difficult and then alter your cadence to compensate for changing conditions.

Keep your eyes fixed on the path ahead, concentrating on the zone 1–5 metres (3–15 feet or so) beyond your front wheel. Look out for rocks and holes in the path and other hazards. Plan your course quickly but carefully to the limit of the zone. Especially with narrow tyres, don't try to go over any loose material that's bigger than a cherry; it will probably slip from under you. Be careful, too, on inclined surfaces where you may skid.

Steer the front wheel firmly to miss obstacles, taking particular care not to hit the gear mechanism, cranks, pedals or your ankles on anything hard. Shuffle the pedals and pump the brakes on and off as necessary to achieve this. Continually keep your eyes open for somewhere to put a foot down. Choose your course so that you steer straight after any narrow gap or ridge to ensure that the rear wheel follows. Going downhill, keep the brakes applied and proceed very, very cautiously. Descending rough hills is often more difficult and hazardous than climbing them. Where a path dips into a gulley or hollow, ease the bike down by careful use of the brakes, then quickly accelerate to climb back out. Precise steering control and prudent use of the brakes and pedals are the principal skills of rough riding.

Where there is a choice, ride on firm earth or grass rather than stones, rock or mud. Never try to ride through sand or shingle. Mud and peat can quickly compact if the bike has mudguards, stopping the wheels from turning. On paths which are generally firm, if muddy, puddles are usually shallow and can be ridden through. Paths used by farm vehicles may have puddles in deep ruts which need to be avoided. Fords on tracks with stone surfaces may well topple you; you can sometimes use your cycle as a pivot to vault across narrow streams. Wet rocks should always be treated cautiously; bare chalk in particular becomes very slippery and should be avoided. If there are many large rocks in the path, it may be better to walk.

Always have respect for the countryside across which you ride and do your best not to cause damage or to erode surfaces.

Long rides

In terms of distance, what constitutes a 'long ride' will vary from cyclist to cyclist. Most people of reasonable fitness should be able to cover 80–110 km (50–70 miles) in a day – but not on their first outing! As with any physical activity, cycling gets easier with regular practice. About 160 km (100 miles) in a day is the upper limit for experienced cycle tourists, but more sports-orientated riders might double that.

For the purposes of this section, a 'long ride' means simply a ride which is long for the person making it, whether it is 140 km (about 90 miles) or 50 km (about 30 miles). It also includes shorter rides which need, for some reason, to be made unusually quickly. What is significant in all cases is that you will be riding close to your limits, and you must therefore take care not to overstretch yourself. Think about this carefully when planning such a ride, remembering to make sufficient allowance for the hilliness of the terrain and the possibility of adverse weather, especially a wind not in your favour.

The first thing to remember on a long ride is that you should not exhaust yourself early by riding too quickly. Climbing steep hills may seem deceptively easy at the beginning of a day, but this could be counterbalanced by the earlier onset of fatigue later on. It is best to take things easy and to make good use of low gears.

Common discomforts brought on by riding continuously for a long time are the numbness of bottom and hands. Changing your position on the saddle from time to time will help relieve the former, and it is often refreshing to lift your weight off the saddle when descending hills and when surfaces are rough. Hand and arm fatigue can be reduced with dropped handlebars by changing hand positions from time to time. In the country, away from traffic, you can take advantage of the alternative positions further from the brakes. Wearing gloves or cycling mittens, or using cushioned handlebar coverings, also helps.

On any long ride it is best to stop as infrequently as possible – and try not to make a prolonged stop until you have covered at least half of the total distance. Although short stops from time to time can be useful for regaining energy, each successive stop will replenish you less than the previous one, and you will subsequently tire more quickly.

Whenever you are riding close to your capabilities, make sure that you are carrying some high-energy food and fruit such as bananas. It is best to eat little and often when cycling, and in the country you may be able to do this while riding along. Do not wait until you are too weak or feel cramp before you replenish your energy. You should also drink frequently to avoid dehydration – take plenty of water or an energy drink. During a full day's riding, you should make one or two longer stops to allow you to eat a proper meal and regain your strength. But make sure that you have digested well before restarting, and then be wary of drowsiness impairing your attention. Fortunately for a cyclist in the fresh air, this effect usually passes quickly.

Check your understanding:

- ☐ Describe how to use your gears when riding through undulating country.
- ☐ What are the potential hazards when descending steep hills and what should you look out for?
- ☐ Which features of country roads require special care when it has been raining?
- ☐ How does riding a rough track differ from cycling along a tarmacadam road?

Chapter 13

Cycle paths and other facilities

This chapter, along with practice in cycling, should help you to:

- ➔ appreciate the benefits and limitations of cycle facilities
- ➔ recognise aspects of design that determine how suitable a path is likely to be for cycling
- ➔ understand how other drivers may respond when you ride along a road with cycle lanes
- ➔ exercise discretion in your use of cycle facilities.

Most people believe that the segregation of cyclists from other traffic by the provision of cycle paths and other facilities is the ideal way to improve cycling safety. But in reality experienced cyclists often avoid using cycle paths, even if this means riding along busy roads. The value of cycle facilities varies considerably, as does the quality of what is provided.

It is a mistake to think that cycle facilities are inherently safer than using the general roads.

Most facilities are not safer, particularly for a similar level of mobility, and there is evidence that some facilities are both hazardous in themselves and lead to unsafe cycling practices.

Segregation may increase perceived safety compared with riding in traffic, but perceptions of risk – particularly by those who have little cycling experience – are often incorrect. Cycle facilities are usually compromises rather than optimum solutions, for there is rarely the space or money to implement high-quality designs suitable for a broad cross-section of cyclists. Furthermore, some facilities complicate the traffic situation and require cyclists to ride in a way that is not compatible with good cycling practice. Knowledge about cycling is often limited amongst the providers of cycle facilities in the UK.

Facilities segregated from the carriageway mainly benefit people who fear motor traffic. As long as they are prepared to ride more slowly and submissively, they can have greater control over (and responsibility for) their own safety. But cyclists who take the trouble to learn the skills of integrating with traffic often find conditions on the road much easier to contend with than the less obvious hazards present on many cycle paths. Using cycle paths can result in these cyclists being more at risk. Furthermore, local knowledge is often essential to the safe use of facilities. In an unfamiliar area, it is often easier and more predictable to keep with traffic.

To the skilled cyclist, cycle facilities are more likely to offer advantages in terms of convenience rather than safety. You may find them useful where they would result in a shorter, quicker or more agreeable journey. Always be discriminating and cautious, having regard to local circumstances and the purpose of your journey.

 **Ride within the limits of what you can see to be safe and within your capabilities, never on the assumption that a different route is safer just because it is marked for use by cyclists.**

This chapter is concerned principally with cycle facilities as they exist in the UK. Unlike in some other countries, there is no legal obligation to use any cycle facility. Take advantage of facilities where they help you, but ignore those that don't.

Vehicular design

Cycles are vehicles that travel at significant speed, often close to that of motor vehicles in towns. This has implications in terms of the visibility cyclists require (to see and respond to potential hazards), design speed (so that cyclists can ride at optimum cadence), geometric design (so that cycles can be manoeuvred easily), signing and markings (to forewarn of hazards and to maintain user discipline). In addition, for cycle infrastructure the conservation of momentum is important, so that cycling is not unnecessarily strenuous. Vehicular design – the basis of general road design – has proper regard for all these requirements and results in layouts suitable for the vehicles to be accommodated.

Vehicular design is quite different to pedestrian design, which relies heavily on a pedestrian's ability to turn on the spot, move sideways and stop suddenly, all without losing balance. It is usually more difficult and less safe to cycle on infrastructure designed only for pedestrians moving slowly.

In countries renowned for cycle-friendly infrastructure, such as the Netherlands, vehicular design is the norm and can be used safely and easily by a broad range of people cycling. In the UK, unfortunately, most cycling infrastructure is pedestrian in design and this can have serious consequences for both safety and ease of use at typical cycling speeds.

Always look critically at cycling infrastructure before you use it. Do you ever have to look behind to see traffic that might conflict with you? Are there blind spots at crossings or bends? Are bends sharp? Are there changes in level at road junctions? Are there barriers across the path? If the answer to any of these questions is 'yes', you are probably looking at pedestrian design. You may still decide to use it, but you must then be prepared to deal with the shortcomings you have identified, in particular by riding more slowly.

② Cycle tracks

Cycle tracks and similar paths away from roads

Ideally, a cycle track should be a carriageway identical in all respects to a road, except for its width and a lack of motor vehicles. In practice, it is rare to find cycle tracks that are as well-designed as roads. Most are the result of compromises in fitting a new track into an existing town infrastructure, while some extensive networks built on green-field sites have been designed to very low standards. The result all too often is further hazards with which a cyclist must contend, and frequently an uncomfortable and poorly maintained surface on which to ride.

To use cycle tracks safely requires at least as much skill and concentration as when using the roads, and even the most skilled of cyclists often find themselves having to learn new techniques to deal with the different conditions. Be prepared to ride more slowly than usual, for design speeds of such paths are usually low. Hazards such as bad visibility, sharp bends and steep gradients are more common on cycle tracks than on the roads, while there may also be different hazards to look out for, such as bollards and barriers. Look out, too, for kerbs at road junctions which have not been laid flush. These can be uncomfortable to cross, while bumping up even a centimetre step too often will damage your bike's headset and impair steering.

Good cycle tracks are clearly signed and marked to indicate road crossings and any other hazards. Be very cautious of those that aren't, and of ones of unusual design. Take particular care at road junctions, for there is evidence that collisions at these places are on average more serious than ordinary road crashes. If there are barriers or bollards nearby, be careful that manoeuvring past them does not distract your attention from traffic.

The surfaces of cycle tracks are frequently not as comfortable as those of roads, and the lack of regular flexing by wide-tyred vehicles can lead to premature break-up. Setts and blockwork can be unsuitable for cycling and may be slippery when wet, but both are used on some tracks. Although minor shortcomings might be tolerable on short lengths of track or for low-speed leisure riding, serious defects can pose real problems, while, with time or distance, even minor irritations soon accumulate.

Even well-designed cycle tracks are notorious for broken glass, persistent mud and other nuisances, for they do not benefit from the cleansing action of motor vehicles, whose tyres push debris to one side. If you use a poorly surfaced track, keep your weight off the saddle and ride more slowly.

Positioning is as important a consideration on cycle tracks as on roads, but you must allow for the much greater likelihood of oncoming vehicles being on the wrong side – a common cycle track problem, aggravated by the typical lack of a centre line. User discipline on cycle tracks is usually much poorer than on roads, even though the consequences of two cyclists, each riding at 25 km/h (15 mph), colliding head-on are not much different from a single cyclist colliding with a car. The fatalities which have occurred on cycle tracks illustrate this.

The primary riding position should be just to the left of centre of the track, moving well left when meeting someone coming the other way. Take great care at bends, for it is here that head-on collisions are most likely to occur. It is not advisable to move too far right for a left-hand bend, as you might on a narrow road, as another cyclist may be cutting the corner. It can be easier to see a car coming than a cyclist. Stay left, reduce speed and shout or ring a bell if visibility is bad. Always keep well left on right-hand bends. You will usually have less margin for error on a cycle track than on a road, as there is less distance between vehicles travelling in opposite directions. You must be able to stop within *half* the distance you can see to be clear. It is always safer to give way than to assume that someone else will.

Most cycle tracks are shared with pedestrians, sometimes with segregation – which pedestrians tend not to observe – and sometimes not. With similar numbers, cycles and pedestrians generally mix less well than cycles and cars, as discipline is poorer. All walkers are liable to change direction suddenly, but children are particularly unpredictable and need to be passed very cautiously. A ring of a bell, or just a polite 'excuse me' can be useful before overtaking pedestrians. Dogs can be a considerable hazard on cycle tracks, where they are more likely to be off the lead than when on a road. Keep well clear.

Roadside cycle tracks

When discussing ways of improving safety for cyclists, many people think intuitively about the provision of cycle tracks adjacent to roads. But these have long been the most controversial of cycling facilities amongst cyclists, rarely used by experienced riders. The reasons reflect the often misunderstood differences between perceived and actual risk.

The purpose of a roadside cycle track is to reduce conflict between cyclists and motor traffic by keeping the two apart for as great a distance as possible. However, collisions involving cyclists are not equally likely to happen anywhere along a road. Relatively few occur between junctions, and the one type of collision that roadside tracks reduce, the rear hit, was observed in Chapter 7 to be one of the least common.

Most cyclist crashes occur at junctions and are a result of turning or crossing movements. Roadside cycle tracks usually increase the number of junctions that a cyclist meets, for they are interrupted by every driveway as well as every road. In each case, the cyclist must be prepared to give way to crossing traffic, unlike on the road where the cyclist has the same priority as accompanying vehicles. The result of this is not only a slower and more submissive journey for the cyclist; it also removes much of the burden for taking care from others, and places virtually all the responsibility for avoiding a crash on your shoulders. On the road, not only would you be more likely to receive a clear passage through the junction, but there would be the important safeguard of others being obliged to take care in case you err.

Observing other traffic can be very difficult, too, for it is necessary to look for potential conflict through an angle of up to 270° (Figure 13.1). This requires much movement of the head, which takes time, and the only way to be really sure that it is safe in all directions will often be to stop. On the road, you can use positioning and listening to reduce the angle over which you need to concentrate to less than 90° close to a junction, which is within the compass of eye movement alone and can therefore be carried out much more easily and quickly.

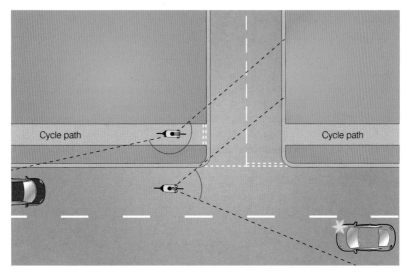

Figure 13.1 *Typical surveillance angles from roadside cycle path and road*

It is particularly difficult from a roadside cycle track to know whether a vehicle on the parallel road will turn into a side road that you are approaching (you must not rely on signalling by drivers), and you cannot use positioning to deter conflicting movements. This difficulty increases with reduced distance between track and road, or if the road junction design permits fast turning. If in doubt you must wait.

A further problem of roadside cycle tracks is that they increase the complexity of every junction, for cyclists and motorists alike. For example, a three-way junction becomes a five-way one when a cycle track is added. Making a junction more complicated invariably increases the likelihood of someone making a mistake.

To use roadside cycle tracks safely requires considerable vigilance, and often considerable tolerance too, for such paths are frequently poorly surfaced and get a lot of debris thrown onto them from the road. They can also be more tiring, for it has been estimated that each time you have to slow down or stop at a road crossing, it is equivalent, in energy terms, to riding 100 metres (330 feet) further.

The risk of conflict is greatest when using a roadside cycle track in the opposite direction to nearside road traffic flow, because drivers will least expect vehicles to be coming towards them on that side of the road. At night you may be dazzled even by dipped headlights coming towards you.

If you cycle abroad, the use of roadside cycle tracks is often compulsory, although some countries have modified their laws in a bid to cut cycling casualties. Otherwise, a track is most likely to be to your advantage to bypass congestion on the parallel road, or where a well-surfaced track has a long distance between junctions of any kind and the adjacent road is narrow and used by heavy goods vehicles. On these occasions you should recognise that the advantages gained will be in terms of speed or peace of mind rather than safety, and that you may need to ride more cautiously and submissively than usual.

Where it is your choice, you should not feel obliged to use a roadside cycle track just because it is there, nor be dissuaded from using a road, if that is your preference, merely because others suggest that you should not.

Shared-use footways

The rush to introduce cycle facilities for minimum cost has led to the shared-use footway, usually little different from a pavement for pedestrians only. These low-quality facilities share all the problems of the roadside cycle track but accentuated due to their closeness to the carriageway. The low quality of shared footways also typically manifests itself with a less comfortable riding surface and conflict with pedestrians.

If you can cycle competently on the road, you should avoid the inherently less safe environment of the shared-use footway.

② Cycle lanes

A cycle lane is a part of the main carriageway that is marked for use by cyclists. Motor vehicles are prohibited from entering mandatory lanes (marked with a continuous white line), and should only enter advisory lanes (marked with a broken white line) if they cannot pass outside, when they must give priority to cyclists in the lane. The term 'mandatory' refers only to the fact that it is illegal for motor vehicles to enter these lanes. In the UK, there is no obligation for cyclists to use a cycle lane of any kind and you should decide whether to do so according to the prevailing circumstances.

With-flow lanes

With-flow cycle lanes overcome some of the problems of roadside cycle tracks, but they do not improve the safety of cycling. These facilities have become increasingly controversial and narrow lanes – those less than 2.0 m (6 feet) in width, which may include a hatched dividing zone – have led to some very difficult conditions for cycling.

The greatest benefit of with-flow lanes is where they result in an increase in the total road space available for manoeuvring. This is most likely where a cycle lane of adequate width has been added to the adjacent general traffic lane (perhaps by reducing the number of such lanes) rather than being taken from it. Widening the left-hand traffic lane, but without marking a cycle lane, has similar advantages without most of the problems.

The principal disadvantage of cycle lanes is that they restrict the movements of cyclists, encouraging the unsafe practice of riding too far to the left where cyclists are less easily seen by drivers behind, to the side and ahead. Some cycle lane markings are placed well to the left of where a cyclist should be riding on an open road; very few allow for correct positioning when approaching a junction.

At the same time, cycle lanes are interpreted by many motorists as defining the space a cyclist needs and, where lanes are too narrow, drivers often overtake closer and faster than without a lane present. If a cyclist feels it necessary in enhancing their safety to ride outside the lane, this can lead to resentment and hostility towards them.

There are additional problems where a cycle lane is obstructed, or where there are potholes or debris. Debris may in any case be more common where there is no motor traffic to clear it out of the way. Without a cycle lane, the cyclist has right of way over following vehicles in the same traffic lane to pass the obstruction. The presence of cycle lane markings removes this priority, creating confusion and requiring you to give way to overtaking traffic.

Cycle lanes this narrow greatly increase risk as you will often get less clearance from overtaking vehicles. The lorry has just passed the cyclist but it would be foolish for her to repass it in the cycle lane, particularly as the lorry is signalling left. Never undertake long vehicles.

Where traffic is congested, a with-flow lane may give a cyclist a freer passage, although, as with any other form of filtering, you must watch out for pedestrians crossing and vehicle doors opening.

When cycling along a road with a with-flow cycle lane, try not to let it affect your judgement as to where it is safest to ride. Position yourself as you would if the lane were not there, but be extra careful when moving outside the lane, because other drivers may not expect you to do this. Treat the movement like that of changing lanes on a multi-lane road, moving right by negotiation well in advance of where you need to be in the new position.

If you find yourself forced to choose between keeping within a lane and compromising safety, and riding outside the lane and incurring the wrath of others, riding the lane line can be a pragmatic, if unsatisfactory, compromise.

At side roads, always leave a cycle lane if there is any possibility that another vehicle might emerge, because cycle lanes direct you to the very places where conflict is most likely. Similarly, at principal junctions, join the general traffic lane appropriate to your direction of travel.

Contraflow lanes

Contraflow cycle lanes in one-way streets can be useful to cyclists where they enable circuitous detours to be avoided. Like other exemptions, their benefit is mainly one of convenience, except if they enable greater hazards to be bypassed, for contraflow lanes retain many of the disadvantages of with-flow lanes. Contraflow bus and cycle lanes are better because they are wider, giving a greater separation from traffic in the opposite direction and allowing you to maintain correct positioning.

Take care when entering and leaving contraflow lanes, when passing intermediate junctions, and if you need to pass an obstruction by moving outside the lane. Assume that others will not see you. Normally, you should not ride outside the lane because of the possibility of conflict with opposing traffic, and special care will be necessary if this requires you to compromise your position on the road. Be watchful, too, for the movements of pedestrians. They can easily overlook the presence of a cycle lane while concentrating their attention on traffic from the opposite direction.

Flank lanes

Sometimes along main roads the white line indicating the edge of the carriageway is some distance from the edge of the road, creating a flank lane. Although not implemented for cyclists – it is intended to minimise road wear by keeping heavy vehicles away from the edge – it may be used as an informal cycle lane.

Flank lanes can be useful in giving a cyclist a little more clearance from traffic on roads which are typically used by heavy traffic at high speed. Because distances between junctions are usually much greater, some of the normal disadvantages of cycle lanes are less serious. Much will depend, however, on the lane width, its cleanliness and whether the dividing line includes studs or transverse ridges (to warn drivers going off course), which can be hazardous for a cyclist to cross.

If you use a flank lane, watch out for it ending abruptly, and be sure to leave it at the approach to junctions.

② Exemptions

Exemptions for cyclists from banned turns, road closures, bus lanes and other controls on general traffic are generally the most useful of all facilities, and were mentioned in Chapter 11. However, even these facilities cannot be considered safe in themselves if a cyclist has to make a movement at variance with other traffic in order to use them, although they can lead to a safer journey overall if they permit greater hazards to be avoided. When using any exemption, always make extra allowance for the fact that others might not expect the movement that you are making.

Other cycle facilities

Advanced stop lines, at traffic signal controlled junctions, were discussed in Chapter 8.

For **slip-road crossings**, at split-level junctions on main roads, see Chapter 9.

---

② Cycle routes

In some towns, special routes for cyclists are signed, often using a combination of minor roads and special facilities. Their usefulness to a skilled cyclist is usually low and related to whether or not they permit a quicker journey or allow really difficult junctions to be avoided. Winding or heavily parked routes, those that add significant extra distance or where you frequently have to cede right of way generally have little to recommend them and may be less safe than a direct main road. A common disadvantage is the use of local place names on signing, which can make the course of a route unclear to a stranger.

② Off-road cycle trails

In many parts of the country, off-road cycle routes, or cycle trails, exist in order to encourage more people to cycle. They may use disused railway lines or other corridors away from motor traffic. Cycle trails sometimes afford pleasant and useful routes, but only occasionally are they speedy ones, for which the surface needs to be smooth, visibility good, the route direct and access convenient. Most paths are much less good but may be acceptable for leisure cycling. In some cases surfaces become very muddy after wet weather and maintenance issues can be a problem.

Cycle trails are not inherently safe routes, nor are they safer than most roads. The paths often demand a degree of skill that is not elementary, yet is rarely appreciated, but people often think that they are safe and therefore take less care. Common hazards are uneven and loose surfaces, bad visibility (particularly near bends), the behaviour of other cyclists (who often do not keep left) and dogs. Road crossings always require special care.

To enjoy these trails to the full you need to recognise their limitations, but to expect others not to do likewise.

Some trails have barriers or other physical restrictions which effectively put them out of bounds to tandems, trikes, trailers and other large machines.

② Road crossings

Various forms of special crossing exist to enable cyclists to cross busy roads independently of other traffic. Sometimes these crossings are linked to cycle paths on either side; sometimes they are isolated facilities to overcome particular problems.

Purpose-built cycle underpasses and bridges should be the best and safest forms of crossing. Just how good and safe particular examples are depends very much upon the detailed design and access arrangements, and the general comments about cycle paths given earlier in the chapter apply. At underpasses it can be useful to use the speed of descent to reduce the effort needed to climb again, but be very careful about this as there are sometimes blind corners and junctions.

Traffic signals are also a satisfactory form of crossing, although they can result in delay to all concerned at less busy times. At conventional signals the usual rules apply.

Upstands such as this are often to be found where cycle paths cross roads, and can be hazardous as well as uncomfortable. Oblique upstands may deflect a cycle wheel and throw the rider.

The situation is a little different at Toucan crossings, which are shared with pedestrians. There are two types.

Older Toucans have full-size cycle and pedestrian signal heads on the far side of the crossing: a green cycle symbol alongside red and green men. There is no red cycle signal and, as the pedestrian aspects do not apply to cycles, there is no legal requirement for cyclists crossing the road to stop when the green cycle is not lit. This is very confusing, potentially unsafe and certain to be misunderstood by most people. So although you may take advantage of your right to proceed at any time, it is best to do so only when the green cycle is lit, or if the road is clear and your movement is unlikely to confuse or inconvenience anybody.

Later Toucans have the cycle and pedestrian signals on a small panel on the near side of the crossing. In this case there is a red cycle symbol which, when lit, should not be passed. The disadvantage of near side signals is that, with your eyes low, you may not so easily notice other traffic while waiting for the signal to change. Always look to left and right before proceeding.

If you're cycling on the road through a Toucan crossing, you must always obey the red light.

Some cycle crossings are not protected in any way and are similar, from a cyclist's point of view, to a conventional crossroads. However, from the point of view of a driver on the road, it must be assumed that it doesn't exist, for it may not have the appearance of a conventional junction. The onus, therefore, is always on the cyclist to give way, and to ensure a clear passage before proceeding. The presence of advisory crossing markings does not change this.

Crossings are sometimes included where new facilities have been added to existing road junctions, perhaps by adapting former pedestrian routes. These must be treated on their individual merits, but there's no point in taking a longer or less convenient route if you are able to ride confidently with traffic on the road. Most of these facilities are only really suitable for the more nervous and slow rider who is prepared to accept the delay and shortcomings of an indirect route. Be particularly cautious about schemes which direct cyclists to use the pavement in order to avoid a junction, as these frequently introduce more hazards than they remove.

Check your understanding:

- ☐ In the UK, is there any obligation on cyclists to use cycle facilities?
- ☐ What hazards should you be prepared to meet using a roadside cycle track?
- ☐ How should you ride in the presence of narrow cycle lanes?

Chapter 14

Cycling at night and in all weathers

> **This chapter, along with practice in cycling, should help you to:**
> - understand how to use your lights and modify your riding when cycling at night
> - appreciate how weather conditions can affect your cycling.

As an all-purpose means of transport, cycling is not something that stops just because the hour is late or the weather is bad. Cyclists need to travel at all hours of day and night and whatever the weather, but you must modify how you ride to suit the different circumstances when conditions are less favourable.

Cycling at night

This section deals with cycling technique when it is dark. To cycle anywhere at night, good lights are essential, and the requirements for these and other visibility aids were discussed in Chapter 4.

Cycle lights can be used steady or flashing, but not legally in the strobe modes with which many rear lamps are also equipped. A flashing light is great for drawing attention to your presence, but it makes your precise location more difficult to determine. If you're riding where it is particularly important that your position is judged accurately (along a busy, narrow road, for example, with little space to be overtaken), you will probably be safer using a steady light.

On unlit roads at night, you should always use a steady front light to be able to see where you are going. Use a steady front light, too, on narrow roads and cycle paths even if lit, as a flashing light can startle anyone approaching you. Wherever you ride at night, you must remember that it will be harder for others to see you and it will be harder for everyone – including yourself – to judge conditions. All movements must therefore be made more cautiously, giving time for you to be seen and your intentions understood. Techniques such as negotiation become more difficult when visibility is poor, and it is usually better to use gaps in traffic in order to make complicated manoeuvres. Fortunately, during the hours of darkness, traffic volumes are often lower, although this can be offset to some extent if the drivers who are on the road travel faster.

Seeing where you're going is usually only a problem on unlit country roads, where your lights need to be particularly effective. With a powerful beam aimed at the surface about 5–10 metres (16– 32 feet) ahead, you may be able to proceed at a speed similar to that you could use during the day, but with poorer lights you must be prepared to ride more slowly. The light beam should be angled a little so that you can see the left edge of the road clearly. On a relatively open road this should not be difficult to follow, but where there is dense roadside vegetation, conditions can be very dark and you must look more carefully for where the road goes. The primary riding position will normally keep you away from the worst of the potholes and give you warning if you veer off course.

White lines and cat's eyes along the road edge or in the centre are a considerable aid to navigation at night, as are reflective road signs giving warning of bends and junctions. Edge markers and reflectors help, too. Signs which may seem superfluous by day take on a new significance when it is dark. The lights of other vehicles can also give useful information about the course that a road takes.

The oncoming headlights of other vehicles, however, can be a considerable hazard to cyclists at night. If blinded, the tendency is to ride towards the source of the light. In any event, dazzle by bright lights will make it harder for you to discern the detail of the road surface ahead of you. Drivers should always dip their lights at the approach of another vehicle, but sometimes cyclists are not noticed easily, while some drivers mistakenly think that they're helping to light your way by not dipping!

When you meet a vehicle coming in the opposite direction on an unlit road, don't look straight at it. Although you must keep aware of the vehicle's movements, focus your attention on the road ahead, and ensure that you stay a safe distance from the edge. If you are dazzled, slow down, look just ahead of your front wheel and be prepared to stop. Sometimes a flash of your own front light by deflecting the handlebar can be successful in reminding a driver to dip. A peaked cap can provide a shield against oncoming headlights and enable you to see the road more clearly.

Cycling at night is more tiring than cycling during the day as extra concentration is necessary in order to pick out the information you need to plan your movements. In addition, you may already be tired from the activities of the day, while in the early hours of the morning the body's metabolism runs slower. Be alert to symptoms of fatigue. If necessary, stop and walk or have a drink (non-alcoholic, and preferably warm) in order to revive yourself.

Wind

Most non-cyclists think that rain is the principal weather problem for cycling. In practice, wind is much worse, although, of course, the combination of wind and rain is worst of all.

The only time when wind is a good thing is when it's behind you, and such occasions seem decidedly rare! Even when it is pushing you along, you need to take care that it doesn't encourage you to go too fast, and that you are not vulnerable to a side wind or an eddy current as you turn a bend, pass a building or are overtaken by another vehicle.

In contrast, head winds can make cycling a struggle and increase fatigue. The lower and more streamlined your body, the easier it will be to keep going, so if there's no hazard ahead, now is the time to use the drop position if you have dropped handlebars. Change to a lower gear until you can maintain your normal cadence, and try to steer as straight a course as you can.

When riding slowly into a headwind, the secondary riding position will be appropriate away from junctions and will relieve you of the need to give quite so much attention to what's behind. Wind makes it more difficult to hear other traffic. Take care, however, not to drift too close to the road edge, as accurate steering is always more difficult when it's windy. It may be possible to choose a less direct route which avoids the need to ride head-on into the wind for the greater part of the distance.

Crosswinds are the most hazardous type of wind: the full strength of gale-force crosswinds can move a cycle sideways across a road. If possible, seek the shelter of roads with hedges, but be careful at gateways and other openings where the wind may suddenly gust against you.

When you must battle against a strong crosswind, keep your body low, engage a low gear and keep firm control of the steering. Most of the time you will need to steer towards the wind in order to go straight ahead, but be very cautious about sudden changes in conditions near junctions, buildings and whenever you meet another vehicle.

Windproof jackets, which greatly reduce the discomfort of a cold wind, are readily available.

Rain

So long as you dress appropriately, rain by itself does not have to be unpleasant for cycling. There are many styles of waterproof clothing designed for cycling, often employing breathable fabrics, under-arm vents and a wickable liner to keep you cool and comfortable. Some cyclists prefer to use a cape because this allows sweat and condensation to escape easily and it helps to keep the handlebar, gear and brake levers dry. However, a cape can be difficult to control in wind or traffic and can result in less clear hand signals being given. Rain hats are available for head protection, but don't use a hood in traffic as you may not be able to look behind properly. Overshoes can be useful when riding for a long time in the rain.

The main problem during rain is that your brakes will work less well – possibly much less so. You will need to allow additional time when braking, and to be more cautious approaching possible hazards. Brake with equal force on front and rear brakes.

In heavy rain brake early, as it may be some seconds after you pull the levers before the brakes begin to bite because the blocks must first remove water from the rims. Continue to apply pressure gently; squeezing hard in desperation may result in a wheel locking when rim contact is made. You should become familiar with the time that it takes for your brakes to operate under such conditions. Consider putting your lights on in heavy rain.

In very heavy rain you may be quite unable to stop. Of course, you shouldn't get into such a situation in the first place. Chase water off the rims periodically by applying the brakes while riding along. Stop and wait if the rain becomes a deluge, and don't try to descend a steep hill in such conditions.

Rain after a dry spell can result in slippery roads, as the water mixes with surface oil. Take particular care at bends and near junctions.

Spray from overtaking traffic can be a problem, both in the rain and for some while after; heavy lorries are a particular nuisance in this respect. If you can, try to pace your riding so that you are not overtaken near large puddles on the road, possibly by adopting the primary riding position at such places. Be prepared in case puddles are potholes in disguise.

Unless you wear spectacles, your ability to see should not be greatly impaired by rain, but motorists will find it harder to see through a wet windscreen. In the winter, windscreens can steam up, especially if a vehicle heater is in use. This can considerably reduce a driver's ability to see you, and is another reason for riding with special caution during wet weather. If you do normally wear spectacles, it may be better to remove them when it is raining so long as you can still see sufficiently well to cycle safely. Alternatively, a peaked hat may help.

Thunderstorms

Thunderstorms present two special problems for cyclists. The first is that the rain is likely to be heavy, and all the previous comments about braking in heavy rain apply. Secondly, in exposed areas there is a small, but real, risk of a cyclist being hit by lightning. This is most likely if you are one of the tallest objects around, as might be the case on an open moor. Under such circumstances you should try to seek cover (but not under a tree!) until the storm passes.

Snow, ice and cold weather

It may not be the most pleasant time for cycling when the temperature is below freezing point and the roads are covered by snow or ice, but cycling is nevertheless possible in all but the most severe of conditions. However, do consider first whether your journey is really necessary.

The first requirement is to wrap up well. Warm hands are essential for proper braking, but take care that gloves or mittens do not impede the use of the brake levers. Sheepskin gloves are amongst the warmest. A woolly hat or balaclava will restrict heat loss from the head; it should certainly cover the ears, which feel the cold a lot when cycling. Warm socks and shoes are also important; despite the pedalling, toes remain relatively motionless and in a cold draught they can become numb very quickly. If you're going a long way, take a flask with a hot drink and some additional clothes.

From late autumn until the arrival of spring, always assume there will be ice after a cold night and start out cautiously. Even if all seems clear, there may still be ice hollows where the road dips or turns, or at other places for no apparent reason. Reducing tyre pressure just a little can give better adhesion on slippery surfaces, and is worth doing if there is a lot of snow or ice. Studded snow tyres are available. Make every move gently – starting, cornering and braking. Be as relaxed as possible, but always ready for a tumble. Brake as little as possible, and only when steering straight. Ride slowly, in a lower gear than normal, and regulate your speed as far as possible by changing your cadence. It is important to keep both hands on the handlebar as much as you can. As long as you do not pedal too hard, you are more stable pedalling than freewheeling. Where there's a risk of falling, select a low gear and pedal gently all the time, and with the brakes applied downhill. Never make sharp turns; if necessary stop to check that all is clear, change direction and then ride off again in a straight line. Don't be rushed by traffic or allow yourself to be pushed into the roadside slush, but do try to keep out of others' way where possible.

If you see ice ahead that you can't avoid, keep going in a straight line. As long as you stay relaxed and do not turn, the chances of toppling are not very great. Skidding can be caused by braking, acceleration or changing direction. If your rear wheel skids, this can often be corrected by easing off power and freewheeling a little, steering straight. Front-wheel skids are very difficult to correct, but if you have the presence of mind, try to restore your body and the cycle to an upright position and you may succeed. Alternatively, you may be able to put a foot down quickly to counter a skid.

Fresh, uncompacted snow is usually easy to cycle through as long as it is not too deep. After recent snowfall, it can be best to keep to those parts of a road not yet travelled by other vehicles. On the other hand, the ridges of ice produced by the thawing and re-freezing of snow can present serious difficulties for cycling. When in doubt, get off and walk.

Snowfall itself makes cycling difficult, even if it does not settle. Snowflakes can badly sting the eyes, making it hard to look ahead. Spectacles or other forms of eye protection do not really help, for they are easily obscured by falling flakes. A peaked cap is probably the best solution. At night, snowfall can be hypnotic, distracting attention from the road.

Fog and mist

At times of bad visibility a cyclist is particularly vulnerable. Use your lights as if it were night-time, but allow for the fact that the light from your lamps will penetrate much less far. Flashing front and rear lights may make it easier for you to be seen. High-visibility clothing can be a real benefit at these times.

Keep closer to the road edge than usual, both to allow for the fact that others will have greater difficulty seeing you and so that you can follow the road more easily. In dense fog, keep your speed well down, to give you better warning of potholes and the like. Do not follow another vehicle too closely; it may have to stop suddenly. Fog and mist can seriously impair braking, in a similar way to rain, and you should allow for this.

When seeing is difficult, hearing becomes an even more important sense for the cyclist. Listen carefully for the movements of others. In this way you can change, if you wish, between the position and speed best suited to your progress and those best suited to your protection. Don't hesitate to shout if it might help someone detect your presence.

Fog, mist, fine rain and perspiration transfer salt from the face into the eyes, which can lead to eye irritation and fatigue. In these conditions use a cloth or a glove to wipe at least your forehead from time to time.

Sun

The brightness of a sunny day can be very tiring; sunglasses and a hat are useful accessories. Polarising sunglasses are particularly useful in reducing the glare reflected by road surfaces. Another hazard to heed is the hypnotic effect of a low sun to your side, broken up by a series of closely spaced trees or railings which result in pulses of bright light across your path. Slow down if you meet this, and look low.

In very hot weather, sunstroke or sunburn are potential problems, as is dehydration. Always drink regularly when cycling.

Another very distinct hazard is that either you or another driver may be temporarily blinded. This is most likely to occur when a bright sun is low in the sky and within the field of view of a driver looking ahead. It can happen in the centre of a town as easily as in the middle of the countryside. If you are riding in line with the direction of the sun, make extra allowance for the fact that any driver heading towards it may be blinded and fail to see you. If you are blinded yourself, concentrate on the road immediately ahead, and slow down.

Check your understanding:

☐ What are the main hazards to expect when cycling on an unlit road at night, and how should you respond to them?

☐ What precautions should you take when it is both wet and windy?

☐ How might the sun affect your cycling?

Part III
Wider
horizons

>

Chapter 15
Carrying children and goods

This chapter, along with practice in cycling, should help you to:

➔ understand the options for taking children with you when you cycle

➔ identify the best means of carrying luggage or shopping

➔ ride successfully when towing a trailer.

Like other vehicles, cycles often need to carry more than just their driver. In fact, cycles are very effective as general beasts of burden, as scenes from developing countries of grossly overloaded bicycles, carrying all nature of goods, illustrate well. It is always much less tiring to carry goods on a cycle than as a pedestrian, and there is a wide range of fitments and accessories that can extend the capabilities of cycles as people and goods carriers.

Children

The ability to carry children on their cycles is important to many parents for everyday journeys such as shopping and the trip to school, as well as for leisure trips by bike.

Children can travel by cycle almost from birth. In the earliest weeks, a baby can be carried in a sling strapped to the chest of a parent. This is most easily done riding on the back of a tandem. The parent needs to adopt a near-upright riding position so as not to cramp the child, and some adjustment to the handlebar position or angle may be needed. Babies carried this way are kept warm and secure by the parent and seem to enjoy the rhythm of cycling, which pacifies them and makes sleep easy.

Child trailers

Babies may also be carried in a towed child trailer if there is sufficient space and straps to contain a car-seat baby carrier or a purpose-designed trailer baby carrier.

As infants grow, they can travel seated in a towed child trailer, usually facing forwards so the parent can keep an eye on the child by looking back. Some towed trailers allow two young children to sit side by side. For security, children should wear the harness that is provided. For advice on riding with a trailer, see later in this chapter.

Rare, but valued, are cycle sidecars, which perform a similar function to a towed trailer. However, as the child is always to the side of the parent, it is easier to maintain ongoing contact. Sidecars effectively make bicycles into tricycles, but lop-sided ones. For this reason, riding with a sidecar is more difficult than towing a trailer and needs practice.

Child seats

When children have gained the ability to sit up unsupported (at about 7 months old), they can be carried in a child seat attached to the rear of a parent's cycle. Always buy a child seat that has a full harness to secure the child at both the waist and shoulders. There should be a full back and head rest, and the child's legs and feet must be protected so they can't possibly reach into the rear wheel.

Child seats may be fitted semi-permanently to a cycle or via a detachable bracket that allows the seat to be removed easily and swapped between bikes. Some seats can be fitted on top of an existing rear pannier carrier (to which they attach) and it is then possible to fit small pannier bags at the same time as the child seat. But if your cycle is able to take a front pannier rack, that is a better place to put luggage, where it will counter-balance the weight of the child, helping to stabilise the steering. Take care not to overload front panniers, so if you want to go touring with a young child and someone else cannot carry the luggage, a goods trailer may also be needed.

Putting a child into and out of a child seat, mounting and dismounting the bike, riding and parking it, all require special care when a child seat is in use, as the child may move unpredictably and the bike will be less stable with the added weight high up.

To put a child into or out of a seat, make sure that the bicycle is well supported against a wall higher than the seat itself and lean the bike towards it. From the time you start to sit the child to the time he or she is taken off the bike you should never let go of the machine. Fit and adjust the harness so that the child is held firmly but without discomfort. It is particularly important that the shoulders are held close against the back rest so that when the child falls asleep its back will stay straight. There are then no ill-effects when the head and neck droop.

Getting on and off the bike yourself with a child seated will need some practice, which should be carried out before you add the child. There is no difficulty with a step-through or ladies' frame, but if you normally mount a bike with a top tube by throwing your leg over the saddle, you will need to bend it at the knee to keep clear of the child seat, and a similar movement will be necessary to dismount. However you mount your cycle, always ensure that you are gripping it firmly with both hands at all times so that the front wheel cannot turn and the machine fall.

When riding with a child in a seat, the bicycle will feel more top-heavy than usual and this difference will become more accentuated as the child grows. You will also need to accommodate the unpredictable movements of the child and to allow for the extra weight when starting and stopping (change to a lower gear before you stop). However, you will soon learn to adjust to these factors, and you will find that cycling with a young child in this way can be an enjoyable experience for both of you.

Tandems and trailer-cycles

By four years of age, most children become too heavy for a child seat but they may not be quite ready to ride their own bike. Even if they do, it will still be some years before they acquire the skills and confidence to ride in traffic. There are, however, other means by which they may still accompany their parents on busy roads.

One option is to ride as stoker on a tandem, which children can do from about the age of four. The tandem is fitted with 'kiddy cranks' at the back and the child can help propel the machine while the parent keeps full responsibility for its control. Riding a tandem with a child is discussed in detail in Chapter 16.

Another option is to use a trailer-cycle. This is less efficient, heavier and less stable than a tandem but also much less expensive. It is, in effect, the rear half of a bicycle that attaches, where the front wheel would normally be, to the back of the parent's bike. The trailer has its own handlebar and pedals for the child to use, and may also have its own gears and pannier carrier for luggage. The child can pedal when willing and able, but at other times is towed by the parent. Trailer-cycles come in various designs, some relatively high with a full-size wheel, others lower down with a small wheel. You will need to ensure that the type you select is of a size suitable for your child, with sufficient adjustment for growth. A special bracket or carrier needs to be fitted to the parent's cycle to which the trailer is hitched.

This trailer-cycle clamps securely to a special bike carrier and is one way for children to take part in cycle rides under the protection of a parent. Riding with a trailer requires practice, however, particularly on corners and hills.

Riding with a trailer-cycle is quite different from riding your machine without and less easy than riding a tandem. The relatively high fixing point of the trailer will try to lean your bike more on turns. Don't try turning too sharp a corner – even when wheeling your bike – or the bike/trailer combination may jack-knife. You may also experience a pronounced side-to-side movement or wobble, which can be unpleasant and is potentially hazardous. Keep your speed down until you learn to compensate for this. Going uphill, encourage the child to pedal to reduce the extra effort required. Coming downhill, brake early to keep your speed under control and to ensure there is no wobble.

Trailer-cycles can accommodate children up to about the age of 10, at which age the back of a tandem (this time without kiddy cranks) becomes the only option for them to ride with you. By this age, however, children who have been taught the principles of *Cyclecraft* should be able to ride their own bikes on-road for many journeys.

Dogs and other pets

Like children, dogs are often taken on cycling trips around town or for days out. There are two options for carrying a dog.

If the dog is small, placid and docile, it can be carried in a basket attached to the front of a cycle. The dog must not interfere in any way with the attention you give to traffic. A small dog carried this way should not make a noticeable difference to your control of the bike.

For larger or more excitable dogs, or to carry cats or other pets, a trailer can be used. Purpose-built dog trailers are available which feature all-round visibility, ventilation and leash hooks. They can usually accommodate one large or two medium-size pets. An enclosed towed child trailer can also be used if the absence of the special features is not important to you.

Commuting

The special needs of the commuter or student cyclist are to be able to carry books, documents and other artefacts securely and without damage; perhaps also a change of clothing and a lunch box.

Pannier bags are the best solution to these needs and there are special types available designed to take A4 documents without bending and sometimes a laptop computer too. Some bags include a number of pockets to separate, and thus protect, the different items you carry. For example, one pocket may be used to carry your wet-weather wear without the risk of spoiling anything else.

These bags usually clip on and off a rear pannier carrier in seconds through the use of special hooks. They may have an additional 'briefcase' handle and shoulder strap for carrying off the bike, and in some cases a flap that folds back to hide the carrying hooks and road dirt.

If you need to carry a laptop computer, be aware that it will be vulnerable to road shock. Never carry it strapped directly to the bike or pannier carrier. A padded case in a pannier bag will provide reasonable protection – try to keep it to the middle of the pannier so that it doesn't bounce against the carrier. If it's just electronic documents that you need to transfer between home and work, you should consider using a memory stick instead.

Office clothes are best carried by rolling rather than trying to keep them flat. Pack them in a protective bag and place them on top of other items in your pannier so that nothing will bear down on them – or you could carry them in a separate pannier. If you need to carry shoes, bag these separately and pack them lower down.

Pannier bags are always the best way to carry everyday loads, especially heavier ones, on a bike, for the weight is kept low, it does not move and there is little impact on bike control. By contrast, backpacks and shoulder bags raise your centre of gravity, may swing to the side suddenly and cause the bike to swerve unsafely. You will also sweat more. If you have to wear a backpack, do the straps up tight, but whenever possible use panniers instead.

Shopping

Pannier bags are also the principal choice for carrying shopping. Large shopping panniers are available that, between a pair, can carry most of what will fit into a standard supermarket trolley. Larger purchases, such as cereal boxes, can be strapped with bungee cords on top of the carrier, enclosed in plastic bags, if necessary, for weather protection. Of course, if your needs are more modest, smaller panniers are readily available.

When you load pannier bags, put heavy items in the bottom and more delicate ones at the top. It is important to balance the weight between a pair of panniers as far as possible; not doing so will make cycling harder work, and it will also put asymmetrical forces on the pannier carrier and your rear wheel, which may damage them.

With heavy panniers loaded with shopping, use a lower gear than normal and be aware that your ability to accelerate and brake quickly may be restricted. Allow extra time for all manoeuvres. The hardest job, however, may be to lift the bags off the bike when you get home – you will quickly discover how much more efficient it is to let a bicycle carry the load!

If your shopping purchases are large – either in total volume or in the size of individual items – you may find it useful to acquire a goods trailer. These two-wheeled trailers come in various shapes and sizes, with and without a cover, and the larger ones can carry substantial loads. Some may be detached from the bike and wheeled directly into shops as pedestrian trolleys. For advice on riding with a goods trailer, see later in this chapter.

Another good way to carry shopping is to use a tricycle with a boot. Because these machines are completely stable even when ridden slowly, they are ideal for shopping trips by people with impaired mobility. Tricycles are discussed further in Chapter 16.

Touring

For most touring purposes, rear pannier bags are the most practical way to carry luggage. They keep the weight low, which minimises their impact on bike control, and this will be appreciated all the more as the miles pass. Panniers suitable for touring are available in a wide range of sizes and most clip on and off a pannier carrier easily. Pockets are useful for packing tools, a spare inner tube and a puncture kit. Bags should be held securely at the

Pannier bags are the best way to carry shopping or luggage on a bike

bottom so that they do not sway from side to side on rough roads, and a strap around the base of the carrier is one way of doing this – keep it tight. Distribute weight evenly between the pair of panniers and put the heaviest items at the bottom.

An alternative to panniers for day trips, and a possible addition for longer trips, is a saddlebag. This is suspended from saddle loops or an attachment to the seat tube. Because the weight is higher up, a saddlebag shouldn't be used for anything heavy, but it can be convenient for clothing, wet-weather wear, maps and the like.

If you're undertaking a long tour, you may want further luggage capacity. Front panniers can be purchased that fit to a front carrier or to 'low-rider' brackets mounted either side of the front wheel. Don't put anything too heavy at the front and, again, ensure that weight is balanced or it will affect steering.

Very useful for items that you need to access during a journey is a handlebar bag. Maps, purse or wallet and camera are some of the items suitable for carrying here as well as any documents that are valuable. For security, a handlebar bag can be detached very quickly and carried with you when you stop. Because a handlebar bag is suspended from the handlebar, it is a good place to carry anything that is fragile.

If there is insufficient space on your cycle for what you need to carry, perhaps because you have a child seat fitted, are riding a tandem or want to take camping gear (or even all three!), a goods trailer is another option. For touring use, single-wheel trailers are a suitable choice. These are more limited in capacity than two-wheel trailers, but are easier to tow over rough roads and long distances. They must be loaded symmetrically to keep the trailer upright.

Whenever you go touring, make a list of everything you take. When you come back, strike off the list anything you have not used (apart from tools and other special items) and don't take it again! If you do this repeatedly, you will soon refine what you take to what is really needed, your load will become lighter and easier to manage, and your cycling will be more enjoyable.

This touring trailer has as much capacity as should be needed for a holiday. It should be loaded symmetrically.

Specialist equipment

The range of goods you can carry with you on a bike, or tow behind it, is remarkable. With suitable trailers, people have carried refrigerators and moved house! In many cases custom equipment has been necessary to carry these items, but some specialist equipment is available commercially, although it may be hard to find.

Tennis racquet holders have been available on and off over many years. They enable a tennis racquet or other similar equipment to be secured to the bicycle frame without impeding the rider. Golf trailers are available that double as a caddy on the course. They're also sold for carrying trombones! Canoe and kayak trailers enable small boats up to 6.5 metres (21 feet) or more to be towed. In turn, canoes can be adapted to carry a bicycle!

Riding with a trailer

One-wheel trailers are easy to tow as they follow and lean with the bicycle. With two-wheel trailers (for children or goods) you must take more care, as one wheel will lift if you try to turn a corner too fast and then the trailer may roll over. Two-wheel trailers are also more vulnerable to bad surfaces, for a bike and two-wheel-trailer combination is a three-track vehicle, like a tricycle. You need to avoid, or travel slowly over, defects in three places on the road at the same time. If a trailer wheel sinks into a pothole (or is thrown by a raised manhole), at best it will give the child or your load a rough ride; at worst it could topple the trailer.

Towing a loaded trailer should not affect your riding very much on a good, level surface, although to ensure that a two-wheel trailer keeps away from drain covers, steep cambers and the like you may need to keep the bicycle further out from the road edge than normal. Climbing hills is more difficult; even gentle inclines will require a noticeable increase in effort. Coming downhill, it is essential to limit your speed a lot more than you might when riding a bicycle alone, as the trailer's weight will try to push you down the hill and may also exert a sideways force. Until you get a feel for the extra care you need to take, ride cautiously.

Parking a bike with a trailer also requires some care. The width of a two-wheel trailer will make it more difficult to lean the bicycle against a wall, but the bike must be parked securely. If it falls, the trailer coupling or the bicycle frame may bend and be difficult to repair. Likewise, when the trailer is loaded or unloaded, the bicycle should not be able to move. It may be better to hitch the trailer after loading and unhitch before unloading.

Trailer fittings and lighting

Both child and goods trailers are attached via a detachable coupling to the rear of a bicycle either at or near the rear axle or higher up on the seat post. It is always better for a trailer to be attached at axle level as this makes for a lower centre of gravity and easier bike handling.

Cycle trailers need their own rear light and reflector if they are to be used after dark. Two-wheel trailers are sometimes fitted with one light on either side. Sidecars require their own front light too.

Delivering newspapers

Teenagers often earn pocket money by delivering newspapers, and the bicycle is a good way to cover the round efficiently. Newspapers, however, can be a heavy load and one that isn't stable if the papers and magazines can slide across one another. The shoulder bags that are often used for carrying papers are not a good choice for cycle deliveries because the bag and its contents can move too easily. This will at best affect the balance of the cyclist – it may cause him or her to overbalance and be thrown. The uneven surfaces that are often encountered entering and leaving driveways aggravate the problems.

The safest way to carry newspapers is in pannier bags where the weight is kept low and they will not interfere with riding the bike. Two bags should be used and they should be evenly loaded in such a way that there will remain a close balance of weight between them throughout the delivery. Another possibility – but only practical if the news agency has its own bicycle fleet – is to use special delivery bicycles or trailers.

Youngsters doing newspaper deliveries should be made aware of the
hazards when entering and leaving the carriageway and of the no less
significant hazards if they ride on the pavement. These are all places where
teenage casualties peak, often because the cyclist has not taken sufficient
care.

It is important that bikes are checked regularly for roadworthiness, as the
frequent carrying of heavy loads under arduous conditions will take its
toll. When deliveries take place during the hours of darkness, parents and
newsagents must accept joint responsibility for ensuring that lights are used
(both front and back), and that these are bright and not obscured in any
way by the delivery bag or clothing. The clothes worn should also be light in
colour, or supplemented with high-visibility garments.

Check your understanding:

- [ ] How do the options for taking children with you when you cycle
  change as they grow older?
- [ ] Considering the journeys you make, what are the best ways for you
  to carry goods?
- [ ] How is cycle control affected when you tow a trailer?

Chapter 16

Tandems, tricycles and recumbents

> **This chapter, along with practice in cycling, should help you to:**
> - ➔ ride a tandem, whether as pilot or stoker
> - ➔ understand the special considerations when you share a tandem with a child or visually impaired person
> - ➔ realise the important differences between riding a bicycle and riding a tricycle
> - ➔ consider whether a recumbent cycle might be suitable for you.

Tandems

Cycling gives enormous pleasure on any kind of machine, but for most people who try it, riding a tandem is the ultimate cycling experience. The two riders share every aspect of their journey, acting as a team, helping each other along and enjoying the ability to converse sociably with ease as they go. Tandeming is twice the fun of riding a solo cycle.

A tandem is a remarkably effective machine at promoting equity. Strong and weak riders can ride together at all times, each contributing to the effort required as they are able. Riding a tandem can also bring the joy of cycling to people who could never cycle alone. Blind and partially sighted people can ride as 'stokers' – playing as full a part in propelling the machine as a person with normal sight – as can people who find it difficult to balance on their own. Young children can be tandem partners, contributing their effort to covering quite substantial distances without having to cope by themselves with difficult traffic conditions.

Riding together

Tandem partners need to perform as one, so it is essential for there to be an excellent personal relationship between them. The 'pilot' is 'in charge' and the 'stoker' needs to respond promptly to changes in pedalling demand and to requests for signals and reports on the traffic situation. At the same time the stoker must have complete confidence in the pilot with regard to all decisions made in traffic. Unlike a passenger in a car, the stoker has direct influence on the motion of the vehicle, but must cede to the pilot the principal decisions as to when to exert that influence.

Although most people are able to enjoy tandeming after only a little practice, there are, alas, some people for whom the psychological demands are just too great.

The roles of pilot and stoker

The **pilot** – also known sometimes as the 'helmsman' or 'captain' – is responsible for steering, braking, changing gear and manoeuvring on the road. The **stoker**, who is at the back (except on some recumbent tandems), cooperates in supplying pedalling effort as required and usually undertakes signalling and map-reading. The stoker may also operate an auxiliary brake on steep descents.

To a large extent, the demands on the pilot are the same as those when riding a solo bicycle. Indeed, it is possible for a pilot to ride a tandem solo. (If toe clips are fitted, use bungee cords to connect together the front and rear pedals so that the clips do not drag along the ground on corners). When the pilot decides to pedal, he or she does so; when the pilot wants to stop pedalling, he or she stops. The pilot controls the tandem in almost all the ways that are necessary in order to match the requirements of traffic, terrain and direction.

The stoker soon learns to follow the pedalling actions of the pilot, which are transmitted directly through the linking chain, and to continue pedalling for as long as the pedals are turning. The pilot must take care not to spin the pedals too quickly, or the stoker's feet may be thrown off.

Where traffic conditions do not dictate the riding style, each rider needs to be sensitive to the other rider's wishes to vary pace or to freewheel from time to time. The stronger rider of a pair should take special care not to force the pace.

When changing gear, the stoker should learn to detect automatically the slight relaxation in pressure on the chain in order to allow a smooth transition, and to follow suit. Until this skill is perfected, it is helpful for the pilot to warn his or her partner that a gear change is to take place.

Verbal communication between pilot and stoker is important to respond properly to traffic conditions. If rapid acceleration is required, the stoker must be asked to assist, while the stoker has an important job keeping track of the movements of following vehicles – perhaps as a prerequisite to turning – and reporting this to the pilot. Although the pilot retains overall responsibility for the tandem, with a good stoker to assist, manoeuvring in traffic can be easier than when riding solo. Also, other road users generally show more courtesy to tandems, in part because they are uncommon and provide a conversation point.

Tandems enable riders of differing ability to ride together and are great sociable machines

The pilot should give a verbal warning to his or her partner at the approach to bumps and dips in the road (including speed humps) and other surface irregularities. In response, the stoker should hold on firmly and lift his or her weight off the saddle to ensure a safer and more comfortable ride for everyone.

Giving responsibility for signalling to the stoker (this cannot be done with young children) is particularly useful in assisting progress through traffic. A stoker may signal continuously, irrespective of traffic conditions, and engage eye-to-eye contact with following drivers in a way that is not otherwise possible. Although the act of signalling is usually carried out by the stoker, this is done in response to requests from the pilot, who should warn the stoker as early as possible of manoeuvres. The stoker must be ready to respond to requests immediately.

Because of their weight, tandems should be equipped with a third brake, usually in the form of a hub or disc brake acting on the rear wheel. It can be useful to give control of this brake to the stoker, both in order to spread the hand effort required to apply the brakes, and to have an emergency brake under independent control in an emergency. It is essential, however, that the stoker is disciplined about the use of the extra brake, which must only be applied in response to a request by the pilot. If the stoker were to apply the brake at a time when the pilot had decided to accelerate to avoid a conflict, the consequences could be serious. It is imperative that all decisions about the motion of a tandem rest with the pilot.

An auxiliary role for the stoker which has many benefits is as navigator and map-reader. On a solo bicycle it is hazardous to read a map while going along, but the stoker on a tandem can do this easily. The stoker should practise riding with no hands on the handlebar (toe clips or clipless pedals are essential), which enables a map to be held and unfolded as required. However, the stoker should grasp the handlebar at the approach of any hazard.

Gaining proficiency

When you first ride a tandem it can be like learning to cycle all over again, especially if neither pilot nor stoker has ridden such a machine before.

Although you will soon get used to it, an important difference between riding a solo and a tandem is that on the former you compensate only for your own movements, while on a tandem you must adjust to the movements of your partner as well, and these are less predictable. It is not unusual on a first tandem ride to wobble from side to side in quite an unnerving manner, and practice will be necessary for you both to learn the new balancing skills. Keep relaxed and use a low gear.

There are two alternative ways to move off on a tandem. In the first option, the stoker is seated and puts both feet onto the pedals while the pilot, astride the crossbar, holds the tandem steady. When the stoker is settled, the pilot pushes off in a similar manner as to start a solo bicycle, and the stoker adds power to achieve speed and balance. This is usually the best – and may be the only – option when the stoker is much shorter or lighter than the pilot, or with a child stoker using kiddy cranks. The stoker must have confidence in the pilot's ability to hold the tandem steady, and the pilot must fulfil that confidence.

The other way to start a tandem is for both riders to push off as if they are on separate solos. Each rider, seated, puts one foot on a pedal and then they push off together with the other foot. This method requires greater synchronisation and is best suited to partners of similar weight and build, but it can result in quicker starts, which are an advantage in traffic.

Differences in riding technique

Although most of the skills acquired for a solo cycle apply equally to a tandem, there are some differences in technique on account of a tandem being heavier and longer.

One is that a tandem is slower and more sluggish to accelerate than a solo. This is felt particularly in town traffic, where a tandem is less able to get away quickly from traffic signals and other stops. This will have consequences for your ability to keep up with traffic, and you may find that progress is therefore slower.

Similarly, tandems stop more slowly than solos when the brakes are applied, and more hand pressure is required on the brake levers for a given stopping distance. This is also a particular disadvantage in towns, where the stop-go nature of traffic can be very wearing for both a tandem and its riders. Tandems are not well suited to use in circumstances where car drivers overtake fast and then hit the brakes sharply to stop.

It is important to agree the technique to be used when a stop and restart are necessary, such as at junctions. The pilot alone or both riders may put a foot down when stopping. The pilot will then reposition the pedals for restarting, and the stoker should accommodate this. A quick word from the pilot is useful as the tandem moves off to confirm to the stoker that now is the time to add power.

Where riders are well matched, hill climbing on a tandem is only marginally more difficult than on solos, but with the more usual combination of unmatched riders, climbing hills is more strenuous. It is more important than ever to change down in gear in good time and for both riders to develop a smooth rhythm to their pedalling. Aligning the cranks of one rider at 90° to those of the other can result in a more efficient pedalling technique, but this practice can make synchronisation difficult at other times and is probably of little overall benefit.

Going downhill a tandem can travel significantly faster than a solo, although whether or not it is wise to take advantage of this will depend upon the circumstances. The benefits of a third brake on a tandem have already been mentioned for use on steep or long descents. If this brake is applied through a ratchet-operated gear-type lever (often inset into one end of the handlebar), efficient braking can be achieved without continuous hand pressure. However, hub and disc brakes are not suitable for rapid deceleration, so do make sure that your speed never exceeds that from which you can stop within the distance you can see to be clear.

The greater length of a tandem means that, given good enough brakes, it can stop in a shorter distance than a solo bicycle without any risk of toppling forwards. On the other hand, this also means that it is possible to skid the front wheel of a tandem on ordinary road surfaces that are wet. As mentioned previously (Chapter 5), a front-wheel skid usually results in loss of control of a bicycle. Fortunately, the rear wheel is less likely to skid, so the rear brake(s) can play a greater role in stopping a tandem than a solo, but the front brake must still do most of the work when stopping quickly.

A considerable benefit of tandems is the fact that the vehicle has twice the pedal-power for only one-and-a-half times the wind resistance of a solo bicycle. This means that progress against a headwind is easier, the stoker in particular being less affected by it. Sidewinds, too, are less troublesome as a tandem's additional weight makes it more stable.

Riding with a visually impaired stoker

Tandeming with a blind or visually impaired stoker can be an enjoyable experience for both partners, and most of the general advice on riding a tandem applies. The main difference when riding with a visually impaired rather than a sighted stoker is that the stoker is less able to predict changes of circumstances. The pilot must therefore give attention to keeping the stoker fully informed of events that might affect progress while riding. Frequent oral communication is very important.

A good cyclist will always try to anticipate road conditions to avoid sudden movements, whether on account of traffic or surface hazards. With a blind stoker this is all the more important, so that the stoker is not taken by surprise. Try not to stop suddenly, in case the stoker is thrown forward in a frightening way. Always give a succinct explanation if unusual movements are required.

At junctions, describe the traffic situation and road layout to your partner, and express aloud your thought process in deciding how best to manoeuvre.

Always forewarn the stoker of approaching hills, whether they are going up or down, the approximate length and severity. Some tandemists use a scale of 1 to 10 to assess gradient in a way that enables the stoker to make meaningful comparisons.

Give warning of bends, so that the stoker will not be worried when the tandem starts to lean. The stoker should be told in advance whether the bend is to left or right and how severe it is likely to be. It is also important to announce when the bend actually begins. Similarly, when turning at road junctions, give both advance warning and a further warning as you start to turn. The stoker may do the signalling, but will need to be told when to stop as well as when to start.

You should also learn the other situations that can cause discomfort that is unpredictable to someone who cannot see. For example, when you enter a wood there can be a sudden change of temperature; a long bridge or tunnel over the road brings a change in the ambient sound. By describing the surroundings at regular intervals you keep the stoker aware, as well as adding interest to the journey.

Communication with a blind stoker is not a one-way process. Visually impaired people often have a more acute sense of hearing than a sighted person, and you should take advantage of this to detect traffic movements and other hazards earlier.

Finally, don't forget your partner when you reach the destination! You will need to be extra careful getting on and off the tandem in order not to strike the stoker, who will also need to be escorted from the bike to a place of safety.

Tandems with children

Tandems afford families with young children the ability to cover significant distances by cycle, while the children themselves enjoy the experience of riding a 'full-size' bike at such an early age. For families with two or more young children, triplets can be purchased.

The simplest way for young children to ride tandem is by the fitting of 'kiddy cranks' – a separate bottom bracket, chainset and pedals fitted to the rear seat tube at a height which the child, sitting on the rear saddle, can reach. The normal rear cranks are bypassed or removed and the link chain re-routed to the kiddy cranks' chainwheel. It is also necessary to extend the rear handlebar so that it can be reached easily by the child. Kiddy cranks can be used by children from about the age of four, as soon as they have the ability to remain seated still. The use of toe clips is desirable so that the child's feet do not slip, and is all that is usually required to keep the child secure.

A machine for four! The child in the middle is using kiddy cranks while his sister pedals directly from a low seat. The child seat can accommodate a younger sibling. Note the low-rider pannier mounts at the front.

Cycling with a child on a tandem becomes progressively harder work for the pilot until such time as the child is able to contribute meaningfully to the pedalling (around nine years of age), and control of the machine is also more difficult. This needs to be taken into account when manoeuvring in traffic. Nonetheless, young children can contribute usefully to the power required over relatively short distances, such as when climbing hills, and this should be encouraged. The rest of the time the child's legs will spin as the pilot pedals. Using kiddy cranks, the child's legs will rotate much faster than the pilot's, but the child soon becomes used to this and there are no untoward consequences.

Although responsibility for signalling should not be given to young children and the pilot should always ensure that clear hand signals are given, it is good to teach children to signal as soon as possible. This has the advantage of developing good signalling technique, which will then be copied when the child rides his or her own bike. Tandeming is in general a very good way for children to acquire traffic skills.

Tricycles

Tricycles have distinct qualities as a form of human-powered vehicle that gain them many advocates. But they are more than just enthusiast machines, for they have unique advantages which can benefit a wider public. This section concentrates on the more usual type of tricycle with one wheel at the front and two behind. There are also models with the two wheels at the front, and recumbent variants of each.

The stability of a tricycle is a great asset. On icy roads a trike may skid, but it is very unlikely to fall over. In high winds, a trike is less susceptible to being blown across the road than a two-wheeler. People who find it difficult to balance on a bicycle are often able to ride a trike.

A tricycle handles very well when heavily loaded: an advantage when shopping or for taking camping gear on holiday. The same applies for carrying children – a solo trike can be fitted with one or two child seats, or a tandem trike can have a child stoker. It is simple for a parent to lift a child on and off a trike, as there is no need to hold the trike upright.

In towns, tricycles are less manoeuvrable in congested streets and are often forced to follow the queue of traffic. Some cycle facilities are also too narrow to be used with ease. On the other hand, a tricyclist has a good view over cars by sitting up in the saddle, and where changes of direction are required, a trike can turn around almost on the spot. It is also easy to restart a tricycle in traffic, for there is no initial wobble.

A great convenience of a trike is that it can be parked anywhere, as support is not required. However, a parking brake is essential if the vehicle is to stay where it is placed.

Learning to ride a tricycle

If you have never ridden a bicycle, then riding a trike is easy. Just get on and go! It is rather more difficult for a bicyclist to adapt to a tricycle. The reason has more to do with the peculiarities of bicycle riding than with anything special about a tricycle.

Riding a bicycle is a balancing act. The machine is inherently unstable, and subtle movements of the body counteract the bicycle's tendency to tilt first in one direction and then the other. A tricycle, on the other hand, is perfectly stable. It is not necessary to compensate for oscillations from side to side, as there are none. Yet a bicycle rider will intuitively seek to do this.

The difference in riding technique is most noticeable when turning a bend. As was pointed out in Chapter 5, a bicycle is rarely steered around a bend, but moves in the required direction by the bicyclist leaning slightly into the curve. Leaning will not make a tricycle turn, however – it needs to be steered! A bicyclist riding a trike must therefore learn to steer when turning.

Find a large flat area, such as a quiet car park, for some practice. Pedal slowly – very low speeds and stopping are no problem on a trike – and apply the brakes if the machine does not go where you want it to. Then try again. Closing your eyes can help to counter your instinctive bicycling balance. With a little practice you will soon succeed.

Although leaning on a trike will not initiate a turn, leaning is nonetheless necessary in addition to steering when cornering sharply or at speed in order to keep both rear wheels on the ground. If there is not enough lean, the wheel on the inside of the turn will lift up. You therefore lean in the direction to which you wish to turn. The amount of lean required is more pronounced than when riding a bicycle, and to facilitate this be sure to push the pedal down on the side to which you lean. Do not try cornering fast until you have perfected this technique.

Tricycles with a rigid rear axle are the most difficult to handle on corners due to drag, while machines with single-wheel drive suffer from slippage. Two-wheel drive, through coupled freewheels or a differential transmission system, is an asset.

Tricycles are much more affected by the camber of the road than are bicycles, and this has a marked effect on steering. When the camber slopes down to the left it is necessary to steer right to compensate, and vice versa. Some British tricycles are built with the rear axle offset slightly about the line of the front wheel in order to assist handling on typical cambers. However, such machines are all the more difficult to ride in countries that drive on the right!

A tricycle is a three-track vehicle – each wheel follows its own path – compared with the single track of a bicycle, where one wheel generally follows the other. This means that tricyclists need to be much more adept at avoiding potholes and other bad surfaces. Although a trike is unlikely to be overturned, potholes can still damage wheels and cause discomfort.

A tricycle has more drag than a bicycle on account of the extra wheel and long axle. This can make hill climbing more strenuous. On the other hand, you can use very low gears more easily as effort is not wasted in maintaining balance, and you can also stop to have a rest and then restart with comparative ease.

On many trikes, both brakes act on the front wheel (because it is difficult to fit brakes to the rear wheels), and on these machines in particular, going downhill requires care. It has already been mentioned that cornering at speed requires special skill, and in general, tricycles are less well suited to fast descents than bicycles. Care is always needed when braking on a curve, as this has a marked effect on the handling of the tricycle.

Recumbent cycles

The differences between conventional cycles are to a large degree due to subtle changes of geometry, gearing and wheels. Recumbents, on the other hand, come in a much wider range of shapes and sizes, and have greatly increased the variety of cycles from which to choose. Recumbent tandems and tricycles are available, as well as recumbent solo bicycles.

Common advantages of recumbent cycles are greater efficiency and comfort. Recumbent cycling means an end to saddle-soreness, neck ache and pressure on the hands; some people with back and neck problems especially can benefit.

From a safety point of view, weight is more evenly distributed on a recumbent, and this means that more braking force can be obtained from the front brake until ultimately the front wheel skids. You are less likely to be pitched over the front wheel, and in a frontal impact it is the rider's feet which make contact first, rather than the upper body. A frequent concern about recumbents is that in some (but by no means all) models the rider is lower than on an ordinary cycle, and recumbents can be difficult to see over a car. This is probably more of a perceived problem than a real one, for recumbents certainly attract a lot of attention. If you wish, an upright flag on a lightweight pole can be added. Recumbents with colourful fairings are often imposing vehicles, making it easy to command a place on the road.

Riding a recumbent

Recumbent bicycles and recumbent tricycles are fundamentally different. Recumbent tricycles are inherently stable and in this case the lower the seat the better for manoeuvring. With bicycles, however, the higher the seat, the easier the machine is to balance. This is because it will tilt more slowly, which gives more time for the rider to compensate for its movement. On the other hand, higher pedals may make it less easy to put a foot down when stopping, so practice is needed to gain confidence. Being relaxed is the main requirement to ride a recumbent bicycle successfully.

Handlebars on a recumbent may be either above or below the legs. The low bar position is not the optimum aerodynamically, but otherwise affords very relaxed control of the machine, requiring only a light touch. Compared with a conventional bicycle, it is less easy to move your body weight when turning, and more movement of the handlebar is required.

Recumbents have a reputation for being difficult when climbing hills but this is not justified. Indeed, they make more effective use of the power of the rider.

Forward visibility from a recumbent is excellent, but side views over hedges tend to be lost. It is also more difficult to turn your body to see behind, so a rear-view mirror can be useful. Emerging from side roads, too, is less easy than on a conventional cycle, as the rider is further back and can see less of the intersecting road. These situations require you to act as if you are in a car – stop at the junction and lean forward to obtain the best view. In general, recumbents are not best suited for riding in heavy traffic.

Most recumbents have the rider's arm height below that of car roofs. This means that hand signals need some care. Always keep sufficiently far from other vehicles so that clear signals may be given, retracting your arm briefly if someone drives too close.

Other occasions which require special care are when meeting animals. The coloured fairings of some recumbents can be more frightening to a horse than a conventional cycle, and if a dog attacks, the cyclist is within easier reach.

Check your understanding:

☐ When and how do tandem riders need to cooperate when riding along?

☐ What differences are there between having an adult and a child stoker on a tandem?

☐ What new skills does a bicycle rider need to acquire to ride a tricycle?

☐ What are the pros and cons of recumbent compared with conventional cycles?

Chapter 17
Cycling more often, more widely

This chapter, along with practice in cycling, should help you to:

> ● understand the additional factors to consider when you ride with other cyclists
> ● assist and safeguard children riding in a group
> ● be informed about other types of cycling and the organisations that support cyclists.

Cycling with others

Cycling is a very sociable activity and many people derive great pleasure from going out with others for a few hours, a day or a holiday. Cycling with a group can be a very enjoyable way of seeing an area and getting healthy exercise.

You may have family or friends with whom to cycle, but if you'd like to meet others on a regular basis, contact a local cycling group or club. For details of groups near where you live, ask at the local library.

All cycling groups are different. Some are concerned mainly with cycle sport, some specialise in touring or off-road riding, others arrange short rides about town. Within any one group there may be different types of ride – some easy, some harder. Although most groups ride at weekends, some organise rides during the week. There are also dedicated rides for retired people and women. Seek out a group that has rides to suit your style and pace.

Riding with friends or a local club adds a sociable dimension to cycling, which can give a great deal of pleasure and enjoyment

Riding in a group

When you ride close to others, everyone is vulnerable to mistakes made by anyone else. Whatever your group size, riding in a group requires discipline and an agreement to follow a few rules.

How close?

Club cyclists will often ride with less than 30 cm (1 foot) between riders. This is a very efficient way to ride because of the slipstream effect, whereby air resistance is greatly reduced for everyone except the lead riders, who are changed from time to time. Keeping close together in this way can enhance the group's safety in traffic as it becomes a more dominant unit of which other road users take more notice. To ride in this way requires the ability to ride as fast and responsively as everyone else and a good deal of practice. Match your cadence to that of the other riders by using a similar gear and copy what they do. Keep your eyes on everyone in front of you as well as the traffic, and don't change your speed or direction suddenly in a way that might create difficulties for anyone behind you.

Most people will prefer to ride further apart, and here the important factors are the amount of other traffic and your impact upon it. The longer the riding group, the more difficult it will be for other vehicles to overtake and the more likely they will be to cut in between riders. For these reasons, groups should divide, as necessary, into sub-groups about five riders long, with a gap of at least 20 metres (65 feet) between sub-groups. This allows traffic to overtake one sub-group at a time. On narrow roads with a lot of oncoming traffic, all cyclists should space out more.

You should always have a full rear mudguard on your bike when riding in a group, otherwise water spray, or fine gravel thrown up from a loose surface, can be a nuisance to the person behind.

Riding along

When riding with a group, always look over your shoulder before starting and whenever you need to change your position on the road. If you need to stop for any reason, call out 'stopping' before you start to slow down and give time for people behind to respond.

Except where a road is narrow or busy (a matter for judgement), cyclists may ride two, but never more, abreast. This is the most sociable way to ride as you are able to converse more readily with one another, and it also enables you to be seen more easily by traffic. Unfortunately, some motorists do not appreciate that the law permits cyclists to ride in this way – they seem to forget that two cyclists side by side take up less road space than a lone car driver – and from time to time you may meet some who, from their gestures, clearly feel that you are acting wrongly.

Of course, if you do seem to be causing a real problem to people behind, having regard to the traffic flow, and it is safe to do so, it is sensible to move back to single file. It is particularly helpful to do this for lorries and buses, which need more room to pass. To move to single file, the cyclist nearest the centre of the road should initiate the action by accelerating or easing off, while the inside rider cooperates by doing the opposite. Normally the inside rider moves forward and the outside rider slips in behind. When riding in a group, everyone should merge in the same way, and the whole group must space out quickly, perhaps to twice its former length, for the merge to be possible. People riding at the back should therefore be prepared to slow down if necessary to accomplish this.

If the road situation is such that it would be unsafe for traffic to pass cyclists riding in single file, then riding two abreast can help to dissuade following drivers from doing so. Conversely, if you are approaching a blind bend, it may be safer to single out.

As you ride, each cyclist should assume responsibility for the progress of the person behind. If someone is no longer following, they may have taken a wrong turning, suffered a puncture or just be tired. Stop. If everyone does this, news of a problem will pass to the front of the group very quickly. After waiting a short time, you should ride back to offer assistance if needed. If anyone needs to leave the group, it is important that they inform those ahead (and preferably the leader) first.

If you need to pass through a busy junction, it is likely that the group will become fragmented. Riders at the front should stop afterwards as soon as it is safe to do so for everyone to arrive. Do not, at this or any other time, stop too close to a junction, on the inside of a bend or near other potential hazards. If there is a need to check a signpost at a junction before proceeding, let one rider go ahead to do this alone.

Road and traffic hazards

Bad road surfaces present problems for all cyclists but all the more so for people riding in a group. If one cyclist is brought down by a pothole, those following will probably fall too. Similarly, if someone swerves to avoid a hazard, others may be vulnerable. It is therefore vitally important that the lead riders in a group take responsibility for warning those behind as early as possible of any potential hazard ahead, and that each subsequent rider echoes this warning back to the end of the group.

Groups often have their own codes to warn of hazards – get to know what they are. Typically a rider will call out 'pothole' or 'bump' to succinctly describe a hazard, and then point to it as it gets closer with a down-stretched arm on the side that is to be avoided. If there is a need to slow down, call out 'slowing' and reduce speed as smoothly as possible. If the surface is generally poor, it may be best to 'space out' and increase the distance between riders.

Riders must also be informed about passing traffic unless the stream of vehicles is continuous and therefore more predictable. Here the responsibility is shared between the front and back riders who call out 'car down' or 'car up', respectively, to warn of a car coming from ahead or behind. Again, the message must be propagated along the group. More specific messages should be used to warn of larger vehicles.

Riding with a group of children

There is every reason why children, too, should benefit from group rides either as activities in their own right or as a way of travelling between places for other purposes. Group rides with children require at least two adults to control the group; if there are more than 10 children, more adults are needed.

The method used to ride with a group of children is sometimes known as a snake or bike train. Before you set off, select the order in which the children should ride. Put a more capable child at the back, who is less likely to be intimidated by traffic, and weaker riders at the front. All of the children must be told to keep to the order and not to overtake one another.

The aim is for the whole snake to keep together and to behave as a single road user. For safety, the group needs to be prominent in the traffic in which it rides, and this may mean everyone keeping to the primary riding position for much of the time.

One adult leads off and will stay at the front of the group. The leader's role is to ensure that the group does not travel any faster than the slowest rider, looking back frequently to be sure of what's happening behind. The leader should ride on the road exactly where the children should follow.

The other adult has a more versatile role and will be referred to as the marshaller. When riding along the road, the marshaller will usually stay at the back of the group, but comes forward along the outside of the group to assist or correct the riding of any child as required. If road space is tight, the marshaller should ride a little outside of the line of children in order to encourage traffic to overtake more widely.

Manoeuvring and junctions

If the marshaller sees the leader move to the right on the road ahead (in preparation to overtake or to turn right), the marshaller also moves right as soon as possible, in order to reserve the road space for the children to move into. The two adults then instruct the children to move out as a group between them. Whenever possible, the marshaller should foresee when the leader might move right and move out first in order to afford the greatest protection to the group (Figure 17.1). This requires the marshaller to know the route well or to respond to an agreed signal from the leader. At all times the marshaller needs to plan ahead.

At junctions where you may need to give way, the marshaller should leave the back of the group and ride quickly past the children to join the leader at the front. When it is safe, the leader proceeds and the children follow, but the marshaller stays put until the last child passes. If it is necessary for the group to split, perhaps because traffic signals have changed to red, the marshaller is responsible for stopping the remaining children and keeping charge of them until it is again safe to proceed. If the snake does split, the leader should pull in and wait at the first safe place for all the children and the marshaller to catch up.

It is always best for the children to keep together, and at a give-way junction the marshaller, and sometimes the leader too, may position themselves within the junction as a request to traffic to allow the group to continue when the right of way is not theirs. You have no right to stop traffic in this way and must be ready to halt the children if someone with right of way decides to continue, but in practice most drivers willingly cede priority to a group of children.

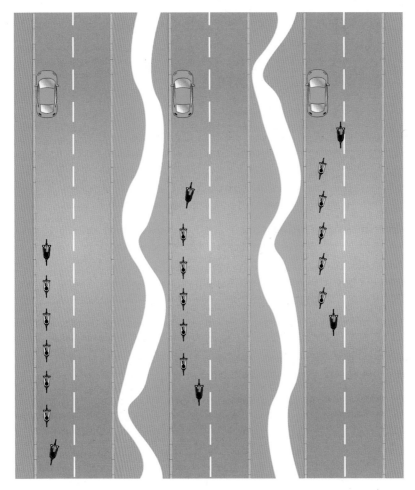

Figure 17.1 *Moving across the road with a group of children*

First the marshaller moves out to reserve space, followed by the leader. Then the children move out en-masse between the adults. By planning ahead, there is no need to stop.

If more than two adults accompany the children, they can assist the marshaller but must not undermine the marshaller's authority. Alternatively, the group can be split into sub-groups riding some distance apart, each with its own leader and marshaller, and this is preferable on busy roads.

Cycling for sport, fun and adventure

If you're interested in more competitive cycling, there are plenty of activities to choose from.

For each activity, training or coaching courses are available, usually organised by the associated governing body. If in doubt, contact British Cycling (see 'Further information' below).

In **time trials**, riders set off at intervals, usually one minute. Although the fastest rider wins, during the event riders are competing against the clock rather than directly against each other. For this reason, time trials are allowed on public roads and usually take place early in the morning.

Road and circuit racing is a test of speed, endurance and tactics in races where riders set off in a group together, on closed circuits or roads. Road racing is a strenuous sport, sometimes taking place in stages that last several weeks over arduous terrain. The Tour de France is a well-known example of a road race.

Track racing takes place in specially built velodromes with banked tracks or on grass tracks marked out on sports fields. There are many race formats, including some where the fastest time is important, and others where the aim is to catch and overtake your competitors.

Cyclocross races involve repeated laps of short courses that include grass, woodland trails, steep hills and obstacles that riders pass by dismounting and carrying their bike. It is a winter sport, with the emphasis on endurance and bike-handling skills.

BMX racing is for youngsters and takes place on purpose-built dirt tracks made up of various jumps, banked and flat corners.

Mountain bike racing is sometimes a competition of speed, sometimes only of skill. There are downhill and cross-country events. **Mountain bike riding** over rough ground is a popular pastime in itself without the competitive element.

Audax and **cyclo sportif** are long-distance, organised rides which challenge you to ride a set distance (e.g. 100 km) within a certain time period. Riders take part for the sense of achievement rather than to compete. Some shorter events are run for charities.

Triathlons involve the three activities of swimming, cycling and running, and some events are run for community participation.

Polaris is a blend of cycling and orienteering involving off-road riding in the country and camping. Points are awarded at check places, but people take part mainly for the fun of it.

Check your understanding:

☐ In which particular ways do you need to consider other riders when you cycle in a group?

☐ Describe the sequence for turning right when riding with a group of children.

Further information

The national cycling organisations

In the UK, the following are the principal organisations that promote cycling. They may be able to provide information or services to assist you.

CTC

Parklands, Railton Road, Guildford, Surrey, GU2 9JX.
www.ctc.org.uk
Everyday cycling, commuting, touring, off-road, political lobbying, insurance, legal assistance

British Cycling

National Cycling Centre, Stuart Street, Manchester, M11 4DQ.
www.britishcycling.org.uk
Cycle sport, insurance, legal assistance

Cyclenation

www.cyclenation.org.uk
Federation of local cycling groups concerned with cycling as a mode of transport

Tandem Club

www.tandem-club.org.uk
Tandem rides and events

Tricycle Association

tricycleassociation.org.uk
Tricycle touring, racing and events

Sustrans

2 Cathedral Square, College Green, Bristol, BS1 5DD.
www.sustrans.org.uk
Coordinators of the National Cycle Network

Audax UK
www.aukweb.net
Long-distance cycling

British Triathlon
www.britishtriathlon.org
Triathlon events and coaching

Also:

European Cyclists' Federation
www.ecf.com
Pan-European organisation with links to national cycling groups throughout Europe and beyond

Cycle training resources

Cyclecraft
www.cyclecraft.co.uk

Cycling Instructor's Manual
www.cycletraining.co.uk
How to teach and organise cycle training to the national standard, written by Cycle Training UK

List of accredited National Cycle Training Standard instructors
www.ctc-maps.org.uk/training

CTC cycle training website
www.ctc.org.uk/courses-and-training

Bikeability, the National Cycle Training Standard
bikeability.dft.gov.uk

The Association of Bikeability Schemes (TABS)
www.tabs-uk.org.uk
Trade association for organisations delivering Bikeability

Index